DATE DUE

Everyday Bible
INSIGHTS

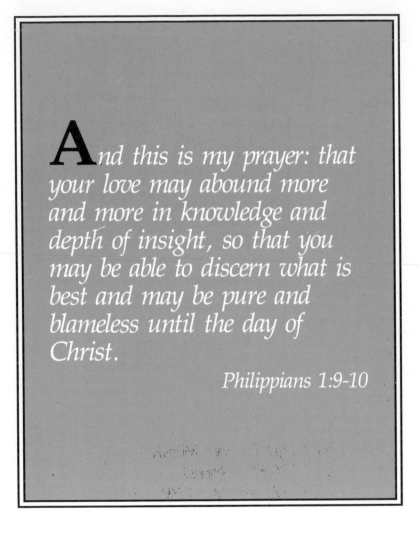

And this is my prayer: that your love may abound more and more in knowledge and depth of insight, so that you may be able to discern what is best and may be pure and blameless until the day of Christ.

Philippians 1:9-10

Everyday Bible
INSIGHTS

LAWRENCE RICHARDS

WORD PUBLISHING
Dallas · London · Sydney · Singapore

*E*veryday Bible
INSIGHTS

Unless otherwise indicated, Scripture quotations are from *The Everyday Bible, New Century Version* (EB), copyright 1987, 1988 by Word Publishing, Dallas, Texas 75039. Other quotations, including the quotation on page 2, are from the *Holy Bible, New International Version (NIV)*, copyright 1973, 1978, 1984 International Bible Society. Used by permission of Zondervan Bible Publishers.

Editors: Mary Hollingsworth / Carol Bartley
Assistant Editors: Lyn Rose, Stephanie
   and Dessain Terry
Consulting Editor: Dr. Lynn McMillon

Illustrations: Chris Garborg, Steve Kilborn

Maps: Myron Netterlund

Photographs: Ed Arness; V. Gilbert Beers; The Bettmann Archive; DRK Photo; Ewing Galloway; Eye-O-Graphic Holy Land Exhibit; The Genesis Project; Israel Museum, Jerusalem; Koechel/Peterson Design; KSTP Weather Services; Dick Lederhaus; Larry Lundstrom; John McRay; Zev Radovan; Terry White; Wide World Photos. Photographs from *The New Media Bible* were used by permission of The Genesis Project, 630 Fifth Avenue, New York, NY 10020.

Graphic Design: *Exterior:* Koechel/Peterson Design; *Interior:* Advertising, Graphics & Marketing, Inc.

ISBN: 0-8499-0707-1

Library of Congress #88-50488

Printed in the United States of America
980123DP987654321

Special insights for every day

Everyday Bible Insights provides a narrative overview of the Bible, God's living and vital word. Whether you've long enjoyed reading the Bible, or have just begun reading it, you'll find this book a simple but indispensible help.

Here are some of the features that will enrich your reading of God's word with special insights for following Christ every day.

Units. *Everyday Bible Insights* divides the Bible into 36 historical units. Each unit helps you understand the setting of the Old and New Testament books or passages written in that time period.

Overview. Each unit contains a paragraph which puts the significance of that time period in clear perspective.

Mastery Keys. Each unit identifies keys that tell you what you need to understand or to learn to have a mastery of the important truths taught in that unit's Scripture passages.

Summaries. Each unit provides brief, clear comments on key passages and events.

Insights. Many comments on a Bible passage or event include an Insight, which summarizes the meaning of that passage or event, provides special background information on the Bible or helps you apply Bible truths to your own life.

Color photographs. *Everyday Bible Insights* contains dozens of beautiful, color photographs that have been chosen to provide visual insights into life in Bible times. Included in the photographs are ancient artifacts, historical and biblical places, modern-day cities that have survived since ancient times, Bible clothing, coinage and other significant articles.

Charts. Throughout the book are summary charts that help organize like topics into quick reference pages, such as the "Stories Jesus told" on page 145 or "Paul's Missionary Journeys" on page 180.

Diagrams. Illustrative diagrams help identify important biblical objects, such as the diagram of the Tabernacle on page 51, or clarify specific information, such as the diagram on page 33.

Illustrations. Fine-line, pen-and-ink drawings of biblical objects, people or places give visual understanding of obscure information, such as the drawings of the many gods of Egypt on pages 44-45 or the musical instruments on pages 84-85.

Timeline. Unit 2 of *Everyday Bible Insights* draws together important events from biblical history and secular history into a unique timeline to help you coordinate Bible events with concurrent secular events.

Color maps. Throughout the book are accurate maps of Bible lands and times to aid your understanding of Bible geography and to put a peg on your mental map where Bible events happened.

These features all combine to make *Everyday Bible Insights* a unique aid to studying and teaching God's word. Its simple, non-technical language and its focus on major Bible themes will help you to a personal mastery of the Bible that you never dreamed was possible. And its insight into the spiritually significant will help you deepen your personal relationship with God.

Table of Contents

NEW TESTAMENT

1 How to find Bible insights for your life

The exciting adventure of studying the Bible is a lifelong journey into the heart of God. The Bible is a book of history; that's true. But more importantly, it's a love letter from God to you, personally. It's God's loving guidance to help you come to know him and to develop a close relationship with him and his children.

Where do I start?

The place to begin is by choosing a Bible that's right for you. If you choose a Bible that's too difficult for you to read and understand for yourself, you start with one strike against you.

Translation or paraphrase? A *translation* of the Bible is the most reliable and accurate type of Bible. It is a word-by-word or phrase-by-phrase restatement of the original biblical language in the equivalent meanings of another language—English, for instance.

A *paraphrased* version of the Bible, on the other hand, does not claim to be a literal word-by-word equivalent to the original languages. Instead, the purpose of a paraphrased Bible is to help explain what the original text meant.

While a good translation is more reliable than a paraphrased Bible, a paraphrased text can be very helpful in shedding light on the meaning of the text. Both have their places. If you can choose only one Bible, however, choose a translation.

Fortunately, there are now some excellent Bible *translations* available that are easy to read and understand. For instance, *The Everyday Bible, New Century Version* (Word, 1987), which we have chosen as the basis for *Everyday Bible Insights,* is an accurate translation prepared by 21 prominent Bible scholars. Readability tests show that it is the most readable and understandable translation available today.

There are, of course, other excellent new versions of the Scriptures available, such as the *New International Version (NIV),* the *New American Standard Bible (NASB)* and others.

Approaching the study

When you have chosen the Bible version you prefer, you can approach Bible study on several different levels.

First, you can read the Bible purely for historical information. On this basis, you might read the account of the Israelites taking Canaan just to learn about the events. Even though historians have doubted the authenticity of the Bible at times, every archaeological discovery has served only to reinforce the Bible's historical accuracy.

Second, you can read the Bible as an account of God's actions on the earth. What kind of person is he? What has he done? By reading accounts of God's work in the creation, flood, and the plagues, you can begin to understand God and his purposes better.

Third, you can read the Bible on a biographical level and see God's interaction with mankind. How does God feel about his children? What kind of relationship does he want with them? In

A Bible student during the days of Christ would have read Bible scrolls much like this portion of the book of *Isaiah* found in 1947 in caves by the Dead Sea.

seeing God's work with people in the past, you can better understand God's relationship with you.

Fourth, you can read the Bible as a revelation of true information on the nature and causes of the human condition in general. What are God's plans and purposes for his people?

Fifth, you can read the Bible personally. On this level you read to learn what God communicates of himself and to develop a personal relationship with God. At this stage you begin to know God, how to keep his commandments and how you can respond to him. This is the ultimate level when you begin to shift from just an intellectual *knowledge* of the Scriptures to developing an *insight* into it that brings about life-changing responses in you.

Methods of study

There are two basic methods of learning, each of which can be applied on any of these five levels of study. One method is called *deductive*; the other is *inductive*. What is the difference?

Deductive reasoning begins with a premise, and all information is interpreted from that perspective so as to maintain that premise. This process is sometimes called "proof-texting" and is often used for persuasion.

Inductive reasoning is the opposite of deductive. Inductive begins with specific facts and information from various sources, combines those bits of data, and finally draws a conclusion based on that data. It is much like putting together the pieces of a jigsaw puzzle until you can see the whole picture. As more information becomes available, the conclusion may be altered. Sometimes we call this method "discovery learning."

Let's compare these two methods by using the account of Jesus and the rich young man in Matthew 19. The passage focuses on the young man's question to Jesus: "What can I do to inherit eternal life?" Jesus answers: "Go and sell everything you have and come follow me."

The deductive approach would generalize that in order to inherit eternal life you must sell everything you have and follow Jesus. And in looking for support of that premise, the deductive student might find specific incidences in the Bible where people sold their possessions for the work of the Lord, such as Acts 4:32–5:11. The Poor Men of Lyon, for instance, took this passage literally, sold all their goods, kept only a single cloak and spent the rest of their lives as poverty-committed preachers, calling for total abandonment of the world.

The inductive approach would begin by questioning the passage for specifics. What does it say specifically? What does it mean? To whom was Jesus speaking? Why did Jesus answer this specific man in this specific way? What does this passage mean to me? How should I apply this to my life today?

This approach would reveal that Jesus was not speaking to his disciples as a whole, but to this particular rich man about his specific problem—riches vs. God. These facts, then, might lead an inductive student to determine that this was not a universal commandment from Christ but that Christ was addressing an individual's need. He may, then, conclude that it is important to allow Christ to help him overcome his specific areas of weakness.

Both deductive and inductive reasoning have value. The inductive method is preferable for personal Bible study on a continuing basis. This chapter offers some practical inductive ways to help you gain insights into God's word.

The five *W*s

One good way to study sections of the Bible is to pretend you are a newspaper reporter writing a story about the passage you are studying. In newswriting style, you must answer five important questions that begin with *w* to be sure you have obtained the most important facts. These questions will help you understand the context in which the pas-

sage occurs—an important thing to know. Apply these five *W*s to each new passage you study:

Who? Who wrote this passage? And, to whom was it written? For instance, was it written by Paul to Christians, or was it written by Luke to unbelievers? Was it written to Jews or Gentiles?

What? What does it actually say to the original readers? What is the message?

Where? Where was it written? Where were its readers? For example, where was Paul when he wrote the joyful letter to the Philippians?

When? When was this passage or book written? Was it written, for instance, before Christ died on the cross or after? Was it written when Christians were being persecuted or when they were living in peace?

Why? Why was this particular passage written? What is its purpose in the Bible? Why did Paul write a letter to his old friend Philemon? Why is the book of Esther, which does not even mention God's name, in the Bible?

Questions to ask

The golden thread that ties a Scripture into a neat, understandable passage is not always easy to find. Understanding the organization of a passage will often help clarify its message. Asking questions can help uncover that organization. Here are some questions to ask yourself when struggling with a more difficult passage:

Does the passage reveal any contrasts? Is there a list of causes and effects, problems and solutions, benefits and losses, or advantages and disadvantages?

Is there a thought progression in the passage? The progression of sin is vivid in James 1:14-15: "It is the evil that a person wants that tempts him. His own evil desire leads him away and holds him. This desire causes sin. Then the sin grows and brings death." Another example of progressive thought is seen in 1 Timothy 6:3-19 where Paul discusses the problems of wealth.

Does the passage use an analogy to clarify its teaching? James 3:1-8 uses a series of analogies to describe the small, but powerful, nature of the tongue: It's compared to the small bit that turns a large horse (vs. 3); a small rudder that steers a huge ship (vs. 4) and a tiny spark that sets a great forest on fire (vss. 5-6).

Does the passage list reasons to support its point or lesson? In 1 Corinthians 4:1-5 Paul gives three reasons for not judging your fellow Christian: We are not competent even to judge ourselves (vss. 3-4); judgment belongs only to God, not fellow Christians (vss. 4-5) and any judgment before the Lord comes again is premature (vs. 5).

Absorbing the message

It's one thing to study the Bible. It's quite another to really *absorb* the message of the Bible and to remember it effectively. Here are three tips on how to better absorb the Bible's message.

Good learners vocalize, reread and acti-vate. Here's how to apply these techniques to your Bible study:

- *Vocalize.* Read the Bible passage aloud so that you actually hear, as well as see, the message. The more senses you can involve in your learning, the better you will retain the material.
- *Reread.* Ask yourself questions periodically to find out if you are really comprehending the passage. For instance, ask yourself, "Now, what did that say to me?" Then restate in your own words what you have read. Finally, reread the passage for confirmation.
- *Activate.* Get involved with the material. Use a notebook to take notes on the passage, or develop study questions to research at a later time. Probe into the background of the passage by using your other Bible study aids, such as Bible dictionaries, Bible handbooks, commentaries and maps.

Applying God's word to your life

The most important aspect of Bible study is to apply God's principles to your own life.

LANDS OF THE BIBLE

Here's how:

1. *Read to find out how you can please God.* What does God want you to do? How does he want you to relate to him? How does he want you to relate to other people? When you find something that pleases God, put it into practice in your life. Pray and ask God for opportunities to please him.

2. *Read to find answers to personal problems.* As you have a personal need or concern, look for guidance in the Bible. Try to find Bible characters that suffered from the same problem you have and discover how they handled the problem with God's help. Ask God to help you find the answers you need.

3. *Read to find examples you can follow.* This is a biographical study. The experiences of Bible people provide excellent examples to follow. Look for people who exhibited great faith. Look for people with leadership qualities. Study how people used their specific talents and abilities in God's service. Find out which people God blessed and why, and try to follow their examples. He will bless you, too. Look for mistakes that people in the Bible made, and try to avoid making those same mistakes in your life.

4. *Read to claim promises.* God has made some incredible promises to you as his child. You have to claim those promises to be richly blessed by him. Read to discover the wonderful gifts he offers to you, such as his saving grace and the "peace that passes understanding." When you discover one of his promises, thank him for what he will surely do for you. Then study to learn what you must do to claim that promise.

A final word

The Bible should be studied as you would read and reread a letter from a loved one. Read it with love; read it with passion; read it with an open heart; read it with expectation and read it often. It's from your faithful Father, your best friend—the God of life, who loves you so much he was willing to die for you.

2 The Bible in history

The Bible contains the story of how God has revealed himself to humankind. Gradually, over the centuries, God unveiled his plans and his purposes—and himself.

As time passed, God unveiled his plan through the history of the nation Israel and through the prophets who spoke not only to that people but who speak also to us. Ultimately, God stepped into history in the person of his Son, Jesus Christ. The meaning of Jesus' birth, life, death and resurrection are foretold in the Old Testament and explained fully in the Gospels and the letters of the New Testament.

The timeline in this unit will help you visualize major events, both biblical and secular, beginning about 7000 B.C. and continuing through about 485 B.C. This is the exciting historical background for God's people and his word.

While not all dates can be exact, each approximate date given fits both the Bible's own story and the research of conservative Bible scholars.

7000 Jericho protected by high wall and a moat
4236 First date on Egyptian calendar
3500 Insurance used in Babylon; oldest long-distance road built in Mesopotamia; tin first used as alloy with copper to make bronze

3372 First date on Mayan calendar

3100 First Egyptian dynasty established; hieroglyphic writing used on Egyptian monuments; wheeled vehicles came into use in Mesopotamia

7000 BC

3000 BC

3000 Oldest papyrus (paper) book produced in Egypt; bricks used in Egypt and Mesopotamia

2900 Earliest known dam built across the Nile at Kosherh; Egyptian reed warships appeared on the Nile; first Egyptian physician, Imhotep, designed the first (step) pyramid
2750 Paved streets with drains built in India

2735 In China, Shen Nung wrote book on medicinal plants and herbs
2697 First Emperor established dynasty in China

2697 First formula for ink developed
2600 Egyptian queen Hetepherea slept in gold, canopy bed

3000 BC

2500 BC

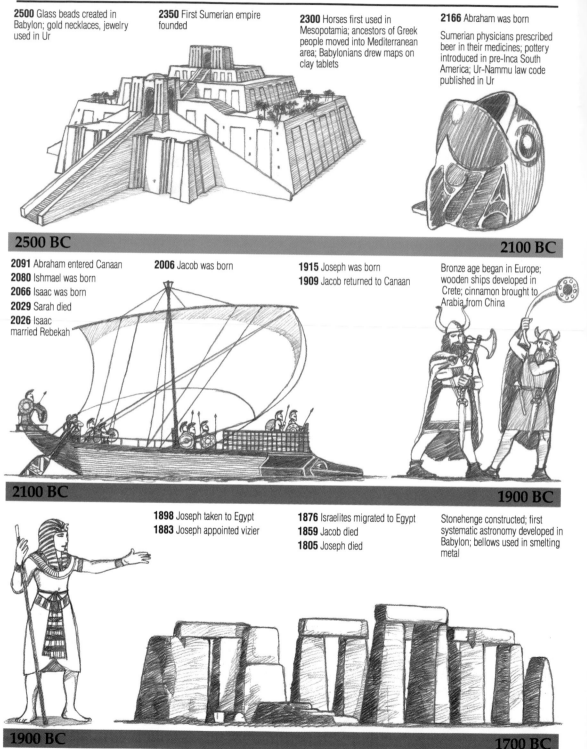

2500 Glass beads created in Babylon; gold necklaces, jewelry used in Ur

2350 First Sumerian empire founded

2300 Horses first used in Mesopotamia; ancestors of Greek people moved into Mediterranean area; Babylonians drew maps on clay tablets

2166 Abraham was born

Sumerian physicians prescribed beer in their medicines; pottery introduced in pre-Inca South America; Ur-Nammu law code published in Ur

2500 BC   **2100 BC**

2091 Abraham entered Canaan
2080 Ishmael was born
2066 Isaac was born
2029 Sarah died
2026 Isaac married Rebekah

2006 Jacob was born

1915 Joseph was born
1909 Jacob returned to Canaan

Bronze age began in Europe; wooden ships developed in Crete; cinnamon brought to Arabia from China

2100 BC   **1900 BC**

1898 Joseph taken to Egypt
1883 Joseph appointed vizier

1876 Israelites migrated to Egypt
1859 Jacob died
1805 Joseph died

Stonehenge constructed; first systematic astronomy developed in Babylon; bellows used in smelting metal

1900 BC   **1700 BC**

1700 Silk trade well established in China; Law Code of Hammurabi published in Babylon; Hyksos entered Egypt

1600 First all-glass vessel used; rise of Hittite Empire

1527 Moses was born
First log roads built in Europe

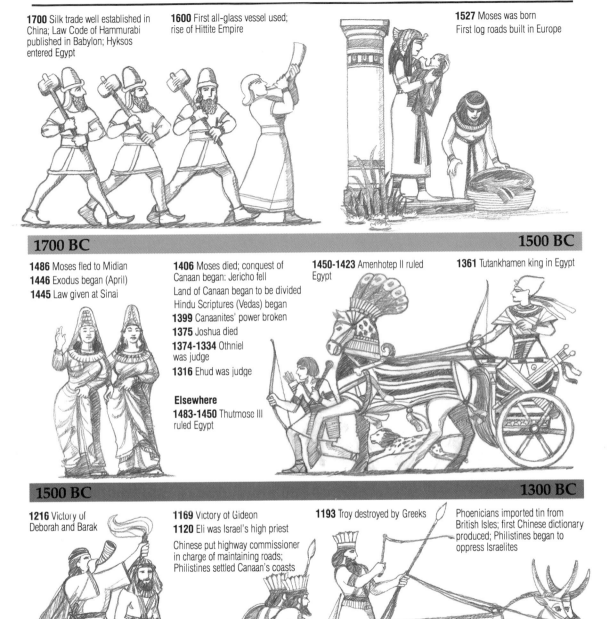

1700 BC

1500 BC

1486 Moses fled to Midian
1446 Exodus began (April)
1445 Law given at Sinai

1406 Moses died; conquest of Canaan began: Jericho fell
Land of Canaan began to be divided
Hindu Scriptures (Vedas) began
1399 Canaanites' power broken
1375 Joshua died
1374-1334 Othniel was judge
1316 Ehud was judge

Elsewhere
1483-1450 Thutmose III ruled Egypt

1450-1423 Amenhotep II ruled Egypt

1361 Tutankhamen king in Egypt

1500 BC

1300 BC

1216 Victory of Deborah and Barak

1169 Victory of Gideon
1120 Eli was Israel's high priest

Chinese put highway commissioner in charge of maintaining roads; Philistines settled Canaan's coasts

1193 Troy destroyed by Greeks

Phoenicians imported tin from British Isles; first Chinese dictionary produced; Philistines began to oppress Israelites

1300 BC

1100 BC

1085 Jepthah's victory over Ammonites
1095-1075 Samson's career against Philistines
1080 Battle of Shiloh
1063 Samuel in office
1043 Saul became king

1040 David was born

1010 Death of Saul and Jonathan; David made king of Judah
1003 David crowned king of all Israel

China developed postal relay system; Duke of Zhou ruled 1800 small feudal states

1100 BC

1000 BC

996 David captured Jerusalem
970 Death of David; Solomon became king
966 Temple building began
959 Temple was dedicated
930 Solomon died; kingdom divided

In Judah
931-913 Rehoboam
913-910 Abijah
910-869 Asa

In Israel
930-910 Jeroboam I
910-909 Nadab
909-886 Baasha

1000 BC

900 BC

In Judah
872-848 Jehoshaphat
848-841 Jehoram
841 Azariah
841-835 Athaliah
835-796 Joash

In Israel
886-885 Elah
885 Zimri
885-874 Omri
874-853 Ahab
853-852 Azariah
852-841 Jehoram
841-814 Jehu
814-798 Jehoahaz

Elsewhere
Homer composed *Iliad, Odyssey*; Carthage founded; beginning of Etruscan culture
885-859 Ashurnasirpal II, king of Assyria, rebuilt Nimrud

900 BC

800 BC

In Judah
796-767 Amaziah
790-739 Azariah/Uzziah
751-736 Jotham

In Israel
798-782 Jehoash
793-753 Jeroboam II
753-752 Zechariah
752 Shallum
752-742 Menahem

Elsewhere
776 First Olympic Games held in Greece
753 Traditional founding of Rome

800 BC   **750 BC**

In Judah
742-728 Ahaz
728-697 Hezekiah

In Israel
752-732 Pekah
742-740 Pekahiah
732-723 Hoshea
722 Samaria fell to Assyria

Elsewhere
744-727 Tiglath Pileser III ruled Assyria
727-722 Shalmaneser V king in Assyria

722-705 Sargon II ruled Assyria

750 BC   **700 BC**

In Judah
697-642 Manasseh, king at age 12, pays tribute to Assyria

Elsewhere
689 Chaldean-ruled Babylon fell to Sennacherib; city destroyed
Sennacherib built 50-mile canal to supply water to Nineveh

671 Egypt ruled by Assyrian Esarhaddon after fall of Memphis

663-633 Ashurbanipal ruled Assyria

700 BC   **650 BC**

In Judah
642-640 Amon
640-606 Josiah
609-608 Jehoahaz
608-597 Jehoiakim

605-652 Nebuchadnezzar
Elsewhere
616 Babylon has become a city of a million people

612 Assyrian capital of Nineveh fell to Median King Cyaxares
609 Nebuchadnezzar defeated Egypt at Carchemish

Phoenecians made and sold soap; quill pens were invented

650 BC

600 BC

In Judah
597-587 Zedekiah
Judah fell to Babylon; Temple destroyed; last Jews sent into exile

In Babylonian Empire
562-555 Awil-Marduk king, murdered by Neriglissar who succeeds to throne

555-539 Reign of Nabonidus

563 Buddah was born
551 Confucius was born

600 BC

550 BC

550-539 Belshazzar viceroy in Babylon
539-538 Babylon taken by Cyrus and Persian Empire; Darius the Mede viceroy; Cyrus crowned king

538 Jews returned under Zerubbabel
536 Temple foundations laid
516 Temple finished and dedicated

529-523 Chambyses ruled, incorporated Egypt into Persian Empire

522-485 Darius the Great reigned

Pythagorus invented geometry; book publishing began in Greece; Tarquinius last Etruscan king of Rome

550 BC

500 BC

Progressive revelation

Our look at the historical framework of the Bible came to us over a long period of time. In each chapter of this book we will see, gradually, how God has unveiled more and more about himself and his purposes. History itself becomes exciting and a fresh way of understanding the Bible. The covenant promises given Abraham reveal that God has a plan and purpose that will be worked out in history. The Exodus reveals God's faithfulness to his covenant and his willingness to use his power to keep his promises. The law shows that God is holy and that he expects his worshipers to live a holy life. The experiences of Old Testament generations show that God rewards righteousness and punishes sin. And then, in Jesus, God fully reveals his love and his willingness to forgive. In Jesus, God unveils the certainty of resurrection and the promise of an eternity to be spent in God's presence. In the New Testament we have the ultimate revelation, an unveiling of the full meaning of our faith.

Insight: You can master Bible history either by knowing about a few key people or a few key events. The key people? Adam, Abraham, Moses, David, Jeremiah, Nehemiah, Jesus, Peter and Paul. The key events? creation, giving the covenant, giving the law, unifying the kingdom, going into captivity, returning to the land, Jesus' birth, death and resurrection, and the church.

BOOKS OF THE BIBLE
THE OLD TESTAMENT

Books of Law	2 Samuel	Proverbs	Amos
Genesis	1 Kings	Ecclesiastes	Obadiah
Exodus	2 Kings	Song of Solomon	Jonah
Leviticus	1 Chronicles	*Books of the Prophets*	Micah
Numbers	2 Chronicles	Isaiah	Nahum
Deuteronomy	Ezra	Jeremiah	Habakkuk
Books of History	Nehemiah	Lamentations	Zephaniah
Joshua	Esther	Ezekiel	Haggai
Judges	*Books of Poetry*	Daniel	Zechariah
Ruth	Job	Hosea	Malachi
1 Samuel	Psalms	Joel	

THE NEW TESTAMENT

The Gospels	*Letters to Christians*	1 Thessalonians	1 Peter
Matthew	Romans	2 Thessalonians	2 Peter
Mark	1 Corinthians	1 Timothy	1 John
Luke	2 Corinthians	2 Timothy	2 John
John	Galatians	Titus	3 John
Church History	Ephesians	Philemon	Jude
Acts	Philippians	Hebrews	*Book of Prophecy*
	Colossians	James	Revelation

3 Creation and the Creator

Genesis 1

There are only two possible explanations for the origin of life. Either the universe, our earth and life itself happened by chance, or all was created. The Bible teaches that all was created and reports that event in Genesis 1.

Does it make any real difference whether God or chance is the source of our universe? Yes, a vital difference. Either the universe was created and is personal in nature, or the universe is a cold, empty, impersonal and purposeless place.

MASTERY KEYS to creation:

- What does creation itself reveal about God?
- What special role do humans have in the creation order?
- How have Christians understood the "seven days" of creation?

There was a beginning

The Bible says nothing about when God created the universe. The Bible teaches that once there was nothing but God. Then God spoke, and the universe sprang into existence (Genesis 1:1; John 1:1-3). Psalm 148:5 says of the heavens, ". . . they were created by his command." Thus the Bible's explanation of our universe is clear and straightforward. God is, and God is the Creator and Cause of everything.

In contrast, there is no "scientific" explanation for the origin of the universe. Most

God created the skies and the earth as a place for his ultimate creation—man.

scientists believe the universe began in a titanic explosion some five to ten billion years ago that has been nicknamed the "Big Bang." But no one can determine what might have caused such an event. Even scientists who do not believe in God are now sure that our universe had a beginning!

Creation's witness to God

Throughout the Bible, creation is seen as a powerful witness to the existence of God. The Bible teaches that creation was *ex nihilo*, a Latin phrase that means "from nothing." Hebrews 11:3 says that it is "by faith we understand that the universe was formed at God's command, so that what is seen was not made out of what was visible" (NIV).

Creation was also by God's word. This has a double meaning. Psalm 33:9 relates, "He [God] spoke, and it happened. He commanded, and it appeared." But Jesus is also called the "Word" of God. John 1:3 says that "all things were made through him" (see John 1:1-14). Jesus is the second person of the Trinity, the one who died to save us is the Creator of our life.

While the Bible tells us about creation, what God created tells us much about him.

First, creation is evidence that God exists. No one finding a watch lying on the ground supposes that its intricate parts fell together by chance. It must have been made by an intelligent being. Just so, the intricate balance of the planets and of nature reveals the existence of a Designer.

Second, creation provides evidence of what God is like. We can deduce truths about God's nature by observing characteristics of the created universe. Among them are the following:

Differentiation. The Bible says God "divided the light from the darkness" (Genesis 1:4). The Hebrew word means to "make a distinction." By making distinctions between light and dark, earth and sea, day and night, God established stable patterns within his universe. God is not a God of chaos, but of order, and did not leave his universe "formless and empty" (Genesis 1:2, NIV).

Dependability. When we look closely at the patterns God has designed, we find consistency. Day follows night; season follows season. The regularity shows us that God is a consistent, dependable Being.

Design. Our world is filled with a complex variety that demonstrates the creativity of God. When the Lord spoke to Job (Job 37–41), God emphasized the wisdom and the power that these traits of creation demonstrate. Such a God knows all and can do all.

Yet despite the complexity of creation, each person, each animal and even each snowflake is unique. Clearly, God has a deep concern for the individual.

There is much that we could not know about God without the Bible. But God's existence, his stability, his wisdom, power, creativity and concern with the individual are all revealed in the things God has made.

Insight: Christians have often debated the question: Are the heathen without knowledge of God? The answer is no. Creation proclaims God to all people everywhere (Psalm 19:1-4).

Our response to creation

There are two ways a person can respond to God's revelation of himself in creation. The Bible describes one of these responses in Romans 1:18. Some human beings "suppress the truth by their wickedness." The Bible says "there are things about God that people cannot see—his eternal power and all the things that make him God. But since the beginning of the world those things have been easy to understand. They are made clear by what God has made. So people have no excuse for the evil things they do. They knew God. But they did not give glory to God, and they did not thank him " (Romans 1:20-21, NIV).

The passage goes on to describe the results of failing to acknowledge God. Human beings began to worship idols (Romans 1:21-25) and to engage in wicked practices (Romans 1:26-32).

But the passage also suggests a different response. As we see God in the things he has made, we can acknowledge him and worship him! The book of Psalms contains many poems praising God as Creator. These psalms, such as Psalm 148, can guide us in giving our Creator the thanks his goodness deserves.

God's self-revelation in nature is incomplete. But the evidence for God is compelling. Anyone who searches for God will discover his hand in the things he has made.

Humanity's place in creation

Several things in Genesis 1 teach us that human beings are special to God. (1) The whole earth was carefully prepared and was populated with life before God made human beings. (2) Genesis 1:26 tells us that God chose to "make human beings in our image, and likeness." In all creation only human beings are to be compared with God. How different this perspective is from the modern notion that mankind's roots must be sought in animal evolution! (3) In the same verse God chooses to "let them rule" over all living creatures. The Hebrew word "rule" (*radah*) does not indicate raw power but rather responsibility. To rule is to "be responsible for" or "to take care of"! We are God's deputies, guardians of all living things.

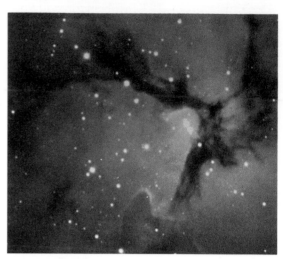

Out of chaos God created order.

So three things in Genesis 1 introduce the theme of human significance. God designed earth as a home for humanity. He made us in his own image. And he granted us the privilege of caring for what he has made.

The process of creation

Biblical scholars have noted that the first three days of creation described in Genesis involved preparation of the material universe. God flooded the universe with light, shaped earth's waters and sky and filled the land with plants.

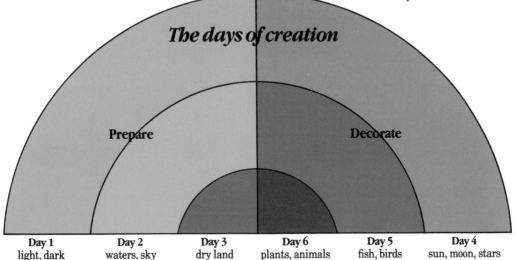

The days of creation

Prepare   **Decorate**

Day 1	Day 2	Day 3	Day 6	Day 5	Day 4
light, dark	waters, sky	dry land	plants, animals	fish, birds	sun, moon, stars

The next three days involved a decoration of the universe, particularly with living things. On the fourth day God filled space with stars and made our sun and moon. On the fifth day he populated earth with fish and birds. On the sixth day he made animal life. Only when our world had been prepared, did God create human beings.

The "seven days" of creation

Many Christians throughout the centuries have understood Genesis 1 as a literal account of creation. However, the author of Genesis does not tell how much time came between "the beginning" and the "first day." In 1650-1654, Archbishop James Ussher of the Church of England published a study of the Old Testament in which he concluded that God created the heavens and the earth in 4004 B.C. His conclusions were published in the margin of some editions of the *King James Version*. Some readers have concluded falsely that these marginal dates were part of the original text. The truth is, they are one man's opinions, which have now been disproved. Since the Bible does not state how long the earth was without form and void, any geological estimate of the age of the earth is compatible with what is explicitly stated in Genesis 1. Also, there have been different views of the seven days. These views reflect the struggle of Christians to understand how the Bible fits with current theories about the age of our earth. The following five theories have been suggested by believers who accept Scripture as the word of God.

1. The *gap theory* holds that the earth was created (Genesis 1:1), but then shattered when Satan sinned. A great time gap passed before the next verses (Genesis 1:2f) which describe how God redesigned the ruin in seven 24-hour days.

2. The *indefinite-age theory* sees the "days" of Genesis 1 as figurative rather than as literal 24-hour periods. Those who hold this theory think that the creative activity described may have required geologic eras.

3. The *creation in situ theory* holds that the creation took place in seven 24-hour days just a few thousand years ago. Coal and other fossils were created in place, as if they had been preserved in the far distant past. This gives the earth an appearance of great age, but it is only an appearance.

4. The *revelatory day theory* suggests that the seven days of Genesis are days in which God showed Moses what he had done. The seven days were days in Moses' life, not days of creation.

5. The *revelatory device theory* argues that the writer simply used "days" to organize his description. The facts are true, in that God did create, but not the seven-day framework.

Many books and articles argue over these theories. Genesis 1 does mention an "evening and morning" for six of the days. This supports the 24-hour day theories. But no evening and morning are indicated for the seventh day (Genesis 2:1-3). The Jewish rabbis understood the lack of an evening for the seventh day to mean that God is still at rest: the seventh day has no end. Yet if one of the "days" is an extended time, why not the others? (Also see 2 Peter 3:8.)

Why hasn't God provided answers to the questions about how he created and when? Perhaps these questions are not all that important. What God wants us to grasp is simply that he did create all things. And he wants us to realize, as we read the Genesis account, that he shaped the world to be a home for man. We may not be able to answer all the questions that have been raised about "how," but we have a clear answer for questions about "who" [God] and "why" [to be a home for mankind].

Insight: Did you know that the Bible makes statements that contradict ancient ideas about the universe? Earth is a "circle" (Isaiah 40:22) that is "suspended over nothing" (Job 26:7). Astronomers reached these conclusions at least 2,000 years after the Bible affirmed them!

Mirror Image
Genesis 2–11

These chapters of Genesis have been called "the Gospel in a nutshell." They provide an essential introduction to the entire Bible and answer some crucial questions necessary to understand the importance of the call of Abram in chapter 11. Chapter 1 answers the question "Where did the world come from?" Chapter 2 answers "Where did man and woman come from?" Chapter 3 answers "Where did sin and evil come from?" Chapter 4 answers "How did murder begin?" Chapter 6 answers "How did the world become so evil?" Chapters 6-10 answer "How did God save his people through Noah?" Chapter 11 answers "How did the world get many languages?"

MASTERY KEYS to mankind's creation and fall:

- How is the "image and likeness" of God reflected in human beings?
- What effects of the Fall are demonstrated in these chapters?
- What passages in early Genesis reveal how God views and deals with sin?

God's image
Genesis 2:4-20

Human beings are unique in all God's creation. Only we were created by God "in his own image" (1:27). Only we were formed by God from earth's dust (giving us a physical nature) and were given by him the breath of life (giving us a spiritual nature).

This passage helps us see how we are like God. God is a person, who enjoys beauty and who found satisfaction in his creative work, calling it "good." God shaped Eden, where Adam was placed, to meet the needs of persons like himself. Adam was given trees "pleasing to the eye and good for food" (2:9, NIV). He was assigned meaningful work (2:15) and invited to exercise his own creativity by naming the animals (2:19-20). Even the tree God planted in Eden, which led to Adam's downfall, must be seen as a good gift (2:13-14). God is a moral being, who chooses good rather than evil. To be truly like God, human beings, too, must have the opportunity to choose between good and evil.

God's "image" in us in Genesis is not sinlessness, for even after the fall the image persists (see Genesis 9:6; James 3:9).

What the Bible teaches is that in all creation only human beings have been made in the image of God and bear his likeness. Only human beings are persons as God is a person. Because of this, each individual has great worth and value to God.

Adam and Eve
Genesis 2:20-25

The story of Eve's creation teaches important truths. One is that human beings need intimate relationships with others (2:18). Another is that women are by nature in no way inferior to men.

God formed Eve from Adam's rib, not the dust, to affirm the common identity of men and women. Adam recognized this when he saw Eve and said, "Now, this is someone whose bones came from my bones. Her body came from my body" (2:23). Women have as full a share in human nature and in the image of God as do men (see Genesis 1:27).

The Jewish rabbis commented on God's choice of a rib. He did not take a bone from Adam's foot, lest men lord it over women, or from his head, lest women look down on men. God chose a rib so that men and women might live in this world and before God side by side, arm in arm.

Insight: "Adam" is the Hebrew word for "man." "Eve" is from a Hebrew word that means "life" or "life-giving." Paul points out in 1 Corinthians 11:11-12 that while Adam

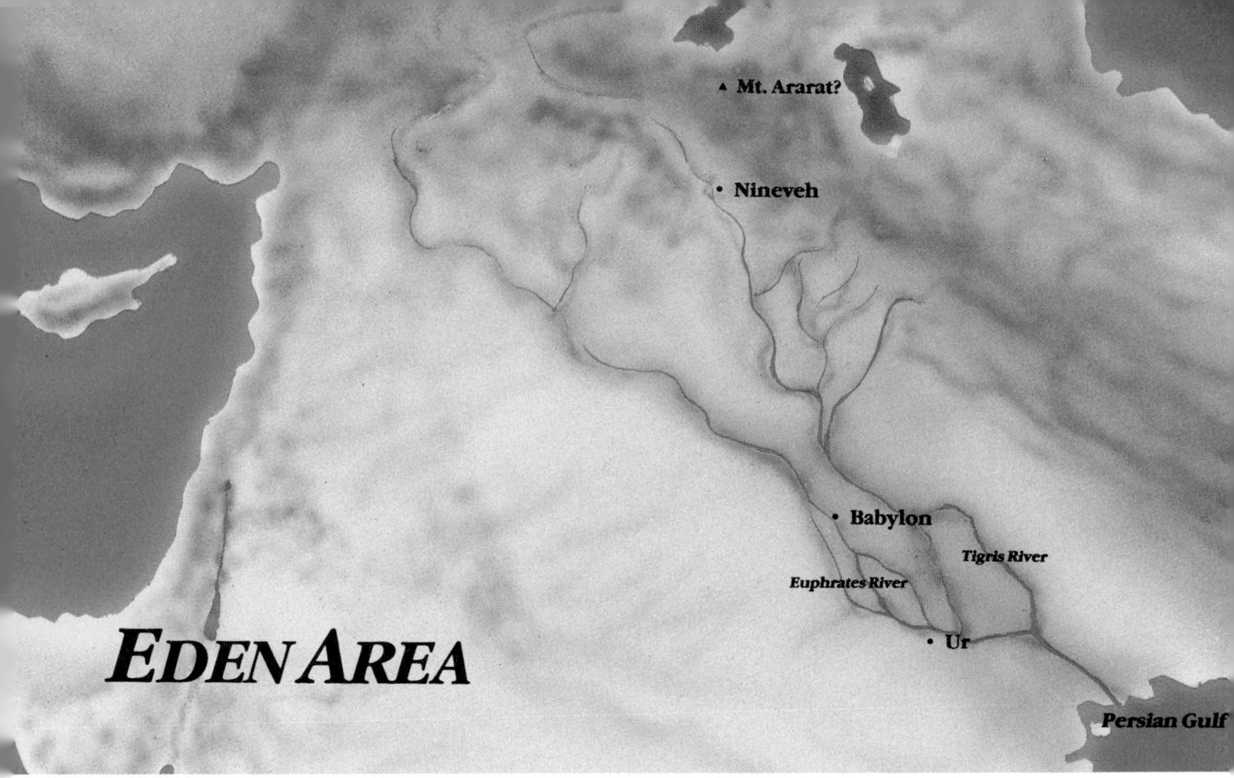

EDEN AREA

Mt. Ararat?

Nineveh

Babylon

Tigris River

Euphrates River

Ur

Persian Gulf

was created first and Eve came from him, men and women are interdependent, for "so also man is born from woman."

Eden

Genesis 2 places Eden at the source of four rivers. Two are known: the Tigris (Hebrew *hiddekel*) and the Euphrates (*prath*). These can be located on the "Eden Area" map. While most agree on the general area where Eden lay, no one knows the exact location. Many believe that the Genesis Flood caused major topographical changes on earth, so that the other two rivers mentioned in Scripture no longer exist.

If God had created human beings without the freedom to choose between good and evil, he would have had puppets. But God wanted persons who would be like him, moral beings.

In this light, the tree of knowledge was not placed in Eden as a temptation or a trap. It was placed there to give Adam and Eve the opportunity to choose what is good. God made his will clear and carefully explained to Adam the consequences of disobedience.

Adam's decision to disobey was tragically wrong. But if Adam were to be a responsible moral agent, he had to be given a chance to make a real choice between good and evil.

Insight: Jesus taught us to pray, "lead us not into temptation" (Matthew 6:13). We are not to seek tests of our faithfulness to God. But when temptations come, we do not *have* to follow Adam's example. We can choose what is good and so become stronger Christians.

The first sin
Genesis 3:1-7

Though Genesis does not specifically identify the serpent with Satan, it certainly appears to represent him, and Revelation 12:9 and 20:2 call Satan "that old snake." Satan's approach to Eve illustrates his strategy for temptation. First, there was questioning of God's word: "Did God really say . . . ?" Second, there was flat denial of God's word: "You will not die." Third, there was questioning of God's motives: "God knows that if you eat the fruit from that tree, you will learn about good and evil. Then you will be like God."

The result was that Eve decided to abandon God as the measure of right and wrong and to rely on her own wisdom. She was vulnerable both to her physical passions (she "saw that the tree was beautiful. She saw that its fruit was good to eat . . .") and to her lack of understanding (she decided "it would make her wise"). When we abandon God's word as the standard by which to evaluate right and wrong, we become as vulnerable to deception as Eve proved to be.

In 1 Timothy 2:14 Paul comments that Eve was tricked, but Adam was not. Thus Adam and Eve illustrate two aspects of "sin" as the concept is developed in Hebrew and Greek terms for wrongdoing. In one aspect "sin" is "falling short of the mark." We sin because we are human and imperfect. In another aspect "sin" is "willful rebellion." We also sin because we knowingly choose to do wrong. Eve was tricked; her sin illustrates human limitations. Adam sinned knowingly.

The interpersonal results of sin
Genesis 3:7-13

The first evidence of the Fall is seen in the relationship of Adam and Eve and in their shared relationship with God.

First, they experienced shame and tried to cover their nakedness with leaves. Second, wrongdoing made them fear the God who loved and had created them. They hid from God instead of seeking him. Third, Adam tried to blame his wife ("She gave me fruit from the tree") and even God ("You gave me this woman") rather than accept responsibility for his actions. And Eve tried to shift responsibility to the serpent. Today, too, awareness that we have done wrong creates a shame and guilt which drive us away from God and which creates barriers between us and those we love.

Insight: If we are to deal with our sin, we must accept responsibility for our choices and turn to God for forgiveness. We must not hide from God as Adam and Eve did.

God's "curse"
Genesis 3:14-20

Here, as in other passages, "curse" is a solemn warning, stating the consequences to each participant of the Fall. Adam's sin changed his own character and had an impact on nature itself (see Romans 8:20-21).

The serpent was to crawl in the dust from that time forward. Some believe the serpent was a willing host to Satan. Many scholars feel that verse 15 is addressed to Satan, not the serpent. The woman's offspring is Christ, who will one day destroy Satan. Eve's curse (3:16) was twofold. Multiplied pain in childbearing may indicate introduction of a monthly menstrual cycle. Many animals ovulate only once or twice a year. Or it may refer to the pain that would be caused as Eve saw the consequences of sin expressed in her own children's lives. Reference to the husband's rule reminds us that before sin entered, Adam and Eve lived in harmony because each was responsive to God. With sin, hierarchy and human government were introduced. The first pair's spontaneous freedom was replaced by the need to repress and control sinful tendencies in human relationships.

Adam's curse (3:17-19) reflects sin's impact on creation. The original vitality and fertility of the land was lost. Death and decay were introduced (see Romans 8:18-21). In the future, work would be drudgery and survival a chore. And, ultimately, Adam's physical body would return to the dust from which it was originally formed.

Sin infects every relationship in life, from relationship with God to relationship with other persons and to relationship with the world in which we live.

Garments of skin
Genesis 3:21-24

Insight: Adam and Eve tried to clothe themselves in leaves. But God himself made them coverings of animal skins. This is the Bible's first shedding of blood and introduces the theme of sacrifice. Blood must be shed to cover the guilt of the sinner. Later this principle is clearly stated (see Leviticus 17:11; Hebrews 10).

Thus from the very first incident of sin, God began to instruct human beings about sin's remedy. Every Old Testament sacrifice pictures Christ as the remedy for sin. For only through his blood, shed for us on Calvary, can we find forgiveness and be restored to relationship with God.

Adam and Eve used fig leaves to cover themselves. The fig is an important food in Bible lands, and its leaves are very broad. So Adam and Eve tried to use something good as a covering. It's important to learn that doing good things cannot cover or make up for sins.

Death and sin
Genesis 2–4

God warned Adam that "If you ever eat fruit from that tree, you will die!" (Genesis 2:17). "Death" in Scripture includes biological death, but involves more. "Death" includes our insensitivity to God and others and our responsiveness to the sinful desires and cravings that lead us to do wrong (see Romans 6:16; Ephesians 2:1-4; 1 John 3:14).

Spiritual death is demonstrated in chapter 3 by Adam's flight from God and by his blaming Eve for his decision to eat the forbidden fruit. In Genesis 4 Cain's anger and his murder of his brother Abel, reveal how terrible spiritual death is. The story of Lamech provides further evidence when he took a second wife, and he tried to justify killing a youth who injured him.

Our newspapers provide even more conclusive evidence of the impact of spiritual death on our race. Daily stories of crime, injustice, murder and rape all testify to the truth of Scripture's teaching that humanity is fallen and in the grip of sin.

Cain's sacrifice
Genesis 4:1-7

Why was Abel's sacrifice acceptable to God, but Cain's was not? Many people have concluded that the difference lay in the type of sacrifice that the two men brought to God—Abel brought an animal (or blood) sacrifice; Cain brought grain and vegetables.

The contrast, however, is probably not between an offering of plant life and an offering of animal life. Rather, the difference God observed was between Cain's careless, thoughtless offering and Abel's choice, generous offering (see Leviticus 3:16). The important consideration here is motivation and heart attitude. God looked with kindness on Abel and his offering because of Abel's faith (Hebrews 11:4).

Instead of responding to God's disfavor with repentence and obedience, Cain became angry with his brother and murdered him.

Insight: Attitude of heart is still God's top priority for his children today. Sacrifice is meaningless without a pure heart.

Long life before the Flood
Genesis 5

In excavating the palaces of Assyrian and Babylonian kings, archaeologists have found many ancient documents inscribed on clay cylinders. One such document, the Summerian King List, which dates from 2250 to 2000 B.C., speaks of kings who are supposed to have ruled before "the Flood swept over the earth." Their reigns are said to have lasted from 18,600 to 43,200 years.

The Bible's report is conservative in comparison: the longest lifespan listed in Genesis is Methuselah who lived some 969 years. The King List shows the tendency of ancient documents to exaggerate numbers. But it also shows that traditions about long life and a great Flood are found outside Scripture.

How could people have lived so long then? One suggestion is that heavy cloud cover before the Flood blocked out cosmic rays that are associated with aging. Another theory holds that just as a spring is purer close to its source, so generations close to Adam were physically healthier.

But we need not explain how Scripture happened. We know that it did.

The "sons of God"
Genesis 6:1-5

Some argue that these were fallen angels who fathered Nephilim ("giants," KJV). Others see the passage as a description of intermarriage of the godly line of Seth (Genesis 5) with the line of Cain. But what this obscure reference does is illustrate that wickedness increased on earth until "their thoughts were only about evil all the time," and the righteous were corrupted by the unrighteous.

God's attitude toward sin
Genesis 6–8

Early Genesis does not leave us in doubt about God's attitude toward sin. The story of the Genesis Flood introduces the theme of divine judgment. God is revealed as the moral ruler of his universe. God may delay judgment, but judgment will surely come. Peter warns those who scoff about future judgment, saying "they do not want to remember" that the world was once flooded and destroyed in an act of divine judgment (2 Peter 3:5-6).

The extent of the flood
Genesis 7–8

Both rain and subterranean waters were unleashed during the Flood. The text says that "even the highest mountains under the sky" were covered to a depth of over 20 feet (7:17-20). Also, when the ark came to rest, it was "on the mountains of Ararat" (8:4). Lake Van, center of the Ararat district, is 6,000 feet above sea level, with the mountains around it towering up to nearly 17,000 feet! Surely the Bible describes a flood of cataclysmic extent.

Some have argued that there is not enough water on our planet to cover the mountains. Others believe the Earth was flatter then, and the Flood lifted up mountains and deepened the sea basins. But whatever its extent, the Flood accomplished God's purpose: "All living things that moved on the earth died" (7:21).

God's grace
Genesis 6

The story of the Genesis Flood reveals God's judgment on sin. But it also reveals God's grace and love. God did not totally abandon humankind. In grace God delivered Noah, a man who "walked with God." The phrase means to live in harmony with God's will. Grace was also shown during the 120 years it could have taken to build the ark (6:3). The great boat, built so far from any sea, must have provoked endless questions from onlookers. Noah's report that God was about to judge the world provided onlookers with an opportunity to repent.

Mount Ararat and the Ahora Gorge, with the village of Ahora in the foreground. It is in the area of the gorge that the modern-day search for the ark is centered in the country of Turkey.

Insight: Romans reminds us, "God's kindness leads you toward repentance" (Romans 2:4, NIV). It should not be mistaken for weakness or unwillingness to judge sin.

The table of nations
Genesis 10

The names are ancient, but some of the seventy peoples listed here have been identified by archaeologists. Among those known is Mizraim, modern Egypt. But not all ancient peoples are listed in the table of nations.

The tower of Babel
Genesis 11

The tower mentioned here was probably a ziggurat. Usually temples were built on top of these stepped towers. Thus the phrase "reaching to the heavens" may suggest the tower of Babel was to house a place for worship in an attempt to influence pagan gods and thus "reach" the heavens.

Noah's deliverance gave mankind a fresh start. But sin, introduced by Adam, continued to find expression. Spiritual death remained the heritage of mankind.

5 The Patriarchs

Genesis 12–25

Genesis 1-11 relates God's dealings with the whole human race and thus prepares for his intervention in human history, through Abraham, to save people from sin. Now the focus shifts. God chose a single individual to father the family through which salvation would one day be offered to all.

About 2100 B.C. God spoke to a man named Abram, a wealthy trader in the dominant city-state of Ur. God called Abram to abandon his homeland and travel to a land the Lord would reveal. In return, God made a covenant with Abram. This covenant confirms special divine promises, which are vital to our understanding the Old Testament itself.

But Abram, whose name God changed to Abraham, is important in himself. The New Testament holds Abraham up as the Bible's prime example of a person who trusts God.

MASTERY KEYS to Patriarchal times:

- What was unusual about the covenant God made with Abraham?
- What are the six promises confirmed to Abraham in God's covenant?
- What do Abraham's three tests of faith teach us about trusting God?
- Why are the stories of Isaac and Jacob included in the Old Testament?

Abraham left Ur to live a nomadic life in Canaan. But he remained a wealthy man, who traveled with thousands of animals and hundreds of servants.

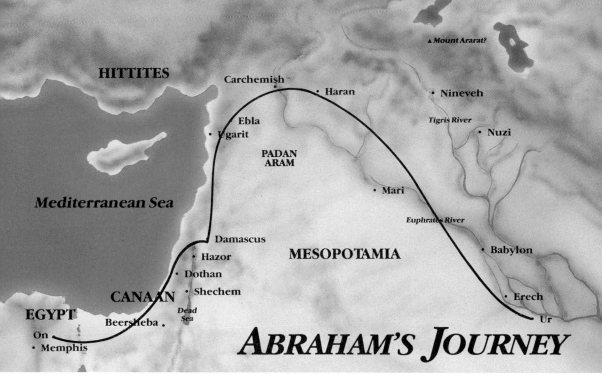

ABRAHAM'S JOURNEY

Map labels: HITTITES, Carchemish, Haran, Nineveh, Mount Ararat?, Ebla, Ugarit, Tigris River, Nuzi, PADAN ARAM, Mediterranean Sea, Mari, Euphrates River, Damascus, Hazor, MESOPOTAMIA, Babylon, Dothan, Shechem, CANAAN, Erech, EGYPT, Beersheba, Dead Sea, Ur, On, Memphis

Life 4,000 years ago

Archaeology has taught us much about the exciting world in which Abraham lived. Well-established trade routes were etched between the rich cities that lay in that half circle of well-watered lands known today as the Middle East's "fertile crescent" (see map).

Caravans carried many fine goods: gold, pottery, metal tools, clothing; even lumber and grain moved along these ancient highways.

The world Abraham knew was far from primitive. Although nomads and traders might live in tents, Egypt had pyramids long before Abraham lived. Astronomers had studied the stars, and doctors had written medical textbooks. One city, Ebla, which was destroyed in a war 500 years before Abraham's time, had contained a library of thousands of clay tablets. Ebla had maintained a population of 260,000 people, making it about the size of Albany, New York, and twice the size of Lansing, Michigan.

Archaeology has done more than help us realize the high level of civilization reached 4,000 years ago. Excavations at Nuzi have uncovered some 20,000 clay tablets written in Babylonian, which explain laws and customs reflected in these Old Testament chapters.

For instance, childless people might adopt a slave to be their heir, but if they later had a son, he would become chief heir (see Genesis 15:2-4). Customs and even laws that were in effect in Mesopotamia (The Code of Hammurabi) permitted a childless man to take a secondary wife, which Abraham did when he was urged by Sarah to take her handmaid, Hagar (Genesis 16:1-2). Those same laws, however, insisted that the handmaid could not rank with the primary wife — and if she tried to supplant her, she could be reduced to slavery! So when Sarah treated Hagar harshly, she was within her legal rights (Genesis 16:6). However, those ancient laws provided protection: the offspring of a secondary wife was not to be expelled.

No wonder Abraham, a truly moral man according to the laws and customs of his time, hesitated to cast out Hagar and Ishmael as Sarah insisted (Genesis 21:8-13)!

What do we know of Ur, the city of Abram? That city, lying beside the Euphrates River (see map), had sewers, wide streets and two-story houses. The city maintained careful records of business contracts and dealings. Golden dishes, found in the royal tombs, show the great skill of Ur's metalworkers. This was the city of Abram, whose wealth suggests that he may have been a successful merchant, who certainly enjoyed the best the great city could offer.

Insight: Archaeology has taught us much about the time in which Abraham lived, and all we learn demonstrates the Bible's historical accuracy.

God's promises
Genesis 12

In Ur, before God called him, Abram had possibly worshiped the city deity, Nanar the Moon God. Yet when God told Abram "Leave your country . . . and go to the land I will show you," Abram obeyed. This was Abram's first test of faith. Would he trust God's word enough to abandon all and set off on a journey toward the unknown?

Joshua told God's people to remember that once Abraham lived in a pagan land and worshiped idols (Joshua 24:5). It's good sometimes to remember where we were when God found us — and to be thankful about where our spiritual journey has brought us!

At that time God gave Abram six promises. These promises are the core of what is called the Abrahamic Covenant.

Notice that in each promise God states what he will do, not what Abraham must do.

As we read through the Bible, we see time after time how important these promises were to the Hebrew people.

The Promise	Its Fulfillment
■ I will make you a great nation.	The Old Testament tells of that nation and people.
■ I will bless you.	God blessed Abram all his long life.
■ I will make your name great.	Jews, Christians, and Muslims all honor him.
■ I will bless those who bless you and curse those who curse you.	Throughout history those welcoming Jews prospered; persecutors have declined.
■ All peoples will be blessed through you.	The Bible and Jesus himself were given through this family.
■ To your offspring I will give this land (Canaan).	The Old Testament tells of the Jewish people and of that promised land.

Why a covenant?
Genesis 15

In Abraham's day important commitments were confirmed by a "covenant" (Hebrew, *berit*). A *berit* was a formal, binding agreement, like a contract or treaty. There were six basic elements of ancient suzerainty covenants: the preamble, which identified the parties; the historical prologue, which told the previous relationship of the parties; the stipulations; the list of witnesses and the curses and blessings.

The basic covenants in the Bible are the bilateral and unilateral covenants. In a bilateral (or party) covenant two equal parties mutually agreed on a pact. Negotiation and compromise were often involved. Read about the bilateral covenants of David and Abner in

2 Samuel 3:12-14 and Abraham and Abimelech in Genesis 21:22-34. A unilateral or suzerainty covenant was used by a king to a subject people. The ruler laid down the terms, with no bargaining. The covenant was either accepted or rejected. God's covenants with man are of this type (Exodus 24:3-8).

To assure Abraham and his descendants of his commitment to them, God entered into the most binding of ancient covenants: a covenant of blood. This is described in Genesis 15, which pictures God passing between pieces of sacrificial animals.

Normally both parties to a covenant performed this ritual. Here God alone passed between the pieces, a fact which emphasizes the unconditional nature of God's commitment to keep his promises.

The New Testament explains. Because God "wanted them to understand clearly that his purposes never change. So God proved his promise by also making an oath" (Hebrews 6:17). You and I can put complete confidence in God's promises to us, too.

Abram's tests of faith
Genesis 12,15,17,22

The Bible records three incidents in which Abraham demonstrated great trust in God.

Genesis 12. At God's command Abraham left the comfort of his home in Ur to live the life of a nomad in an unknown land (see p. 30). Abraham was willing to take a risk in order to be obedient to God's word.

Genesis 15 and 17. Although Abraham was old, and Sarah had ceased menstruating, Abram believed that God would keep his promise and give them a son of their own. This faith "was credited to [Abraham] as righteousness" (15:6, NIV). Abraham was convinced that God could and would do what was humanly impossible.

Genesis 22. After the birth of the promised son, Isaac, God commanded Abraham to offer him up as a sacrifice at Mount Moriah. Many Bible scholars believe that this Mount Moriah is the same mountain where

centuries later Solomon's temple was constructed.

Abraham set out immediately! And Abraham told his servants, "My son and I will go over there and worship. Then *we* will come back to you" (22:5). The New Testa-

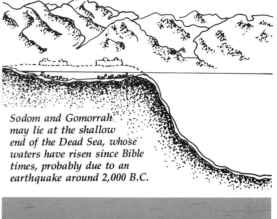

Sodom and Gomorrah may lie at the shallow end of the Dead Sea, whose waters have risen since Bible times, probably due to an earthquake around 2,000 B.C.

Because of the great amount of salt in the Dead Sea, animals and fish cannot live in and around it, but swimmers find its salty waters give great buoyancy for floating.

ment explains. Abraham was confident God would keep the promise that Isaac would carry on his line. "Abraham believed that God could raise the dead" (Hebrews 11:19). Abraham's trust led to complete obedience.

Abraham's example leads us to a clear definition of "faith." Faith is having such confidence in God that we count on and act on his word.

Today a Muslim mosque stands in Jerusalem on the traditional site of Mount Moriah, where Abraham prepared to sacrifice Isaac.

Insight: There are two ways to know if "faith" is real. One way is to test faith's object: is what we believe in true and trustworthy? The other way is to test faith's product: is the believer changed? Abraham's faith was real. He trusted the true God, and he did what God said. Your faith is real if you trust Jesus Christ and obey him.

Where are Sodom and Gomorrah?

Today many believe the ruins of Sodom and Gomorrah lie under salty waters near the south end of the Dead Sea (see drawing). God destroyed these cities with fire. Some think God caused an earthquake and an explosion of petroleum gases mixed with the sulphur and asphalt of the area. Israel's first oil well was drilled in this area in 1953.

Abraham's two names
Genesis 15

Bible names often have significance. "Abram" means "father." "Abraham" means "high father" or "father of a multitude." It must have been hard for Abram to tell his name to visitors and then admit he was childless. Yet when God changed "Abram" to "Abraham," inviting even more ridicule, Abraham faithfully adopted that new name.

Faith has its big tests and little tests too. Sometimes it is harder to obey in the little things, like facing ridicule, than in the greater challenges of life.

A pattern for prayer
Genesis 18

Abraham begged God to spare Sodom if only a few righteous persons could be found in it. His request led God to promise to spare the city for fifty, then forty-five and finally for the sake of ten. Abraham was concerned that God might be angry with him over these requests. God was not angry. In fact, God was more concerned about the people of Sodom than Abraham was. When the Lord found only one righteous person, Lot, God took steps to deliver him. God is never angry when our prayers involve pleas for others.

Insight: What if you don't know how to pray for others? Remember, you can pray for their salvation, for God does not want anyone to perish (2 Peter 3:9). And you can use Paul's prayers in Ephesians 1:17-20 and 3:16-19 as models to help you pray for fellow Christians.

6 Journey to Egypt
Genesis 25–50

Genesis continues the story of Abraham's family, focusing on his grandson Jacob and on Jacob's son, Joseph. God used the jealousy of Joseph's brothers to place him in Egypt, where Joseph rose to become a ruler in that great civilization. When famine came, Joseph was able to feed his family and bring them to Egypt, where the Hebrew people would remain for 400 years.

MASTERY KEYS to the journey into Egypt:

- Why was the "birthright" so important to Jacob and worthless to Esau?
- What was Egyptian civilization like in the time of Joseph?
- In what ways do these chapters of Genesis illustrate God's providential care?

Esau's birthright
Genesis 25

In Old Testament times the firstborn son was his father's heir and received twice as much as any brothers. The firstborn received double because he had the responsibility for taking care of his father's widow and unmarried daughters. According to custom, any special rights of the father would also pass to the oldest son, just as a royal title has historically passed to the eldest son. All this was included in the "birthright." And the most important of Isaac's special rights was the covenant (*berit*) God had made with Abraham and his descendants.

Israel's family moved to Egypt where Joseph had become a powerful ruler.

This helps us understand how significant it was that Esau, Isaac's oldest son, unhesitatingly traded his birthright for a bowl of stew. Esau had no concern for spiritual things. His momentary hunger seemed more important to Esau than the promise of God's blessing. The Bible adds, "so Esau showed how little he cared about his rights as the firstborn son" (Genesis 25:34).

Genesis portrays Jacob as a man with many faults. But he at least placed a high value on God's covenant promise.

Insight: Trading something eternally important for a momentary physical satisfaction is always a mistake.

Failure to trust
Genesis 27

Although Esau was born before Jacob, the Lord had told Isaac's wife, Rebekah, that "the older will serve the younger" (Genesis 25:23). Yet over the years Rebekah and Jacob realized that Esau was Isaac's favorite. What if Isaac should "bless" Esau and by this act pass the birthright on to him?

As Isaac drew near death, mother and son conspired to win the birthright by deceit. They still had to deceive Isaac, because as father he had the right to give the birthright to whomever he chose. Esau had sold it, but this was not binding on Isaac. Whether he knew about it or not, he was planning to bless Esau, which was equivalent to passing on the birthright.

Jacob pretended to be Esau, and the now blind Isaac gave the younger son the older son's heritage. Genesis 27 tells of Rebekah's and Jacob's plot to win Jacob the blessing. When their deceit was discovered, Isaac did not withdraw the blessing but confirmed it (27:33). Jacob's trickery caused hatred, and Esau determined to kill his brother when their father died. Frightened, their mother sent Jacob away to relatives in Haran, where Jacob would remain for twenty years.

The story illustrates how a lack of faith can lead to hasty action and to disaster. God had promised Rebekah that Jacob would have the birthright, so there was no need to plot or to deceive. The failure to wait on God resulted in hatred and bitterness in the family and years of exile for Jacob.

No goal justifies adopting wrong means. We need to do what is right and trust God to work through circumstances to accomplish his good purposes in us.

The dream at Bethel
Genesis 28

"Bethel" means "house of God." The city lies about twelve miles north of Jerusalem and is mentioned in the Bible more times than any other city besides Jerusalem. When the Lord spoke to Jacob there, God confirmed the continuation of his promises from Abraham to Jacob. Jacob made a pillar of stones to commemorate the experience. He promised to worship God and to give the Lord a tenth of all he possessed.

Jacob's reaction indicates an initial fear of God, but also gratitude to God.

Insight: Jacob's commitment to give a tenth to God came *before* the Law that decreed a tithe was given. His action shows that giving has always been an appropriate way to express appreciation to the Lord.

Jacob's wives and children
Genesis 29–30

The Muslim religion permits a man to have four wives, claiming that Jacob sets the divine pattern. Jacob clearly desired only one wife, Rachel. But now the deceiver was a victim of another's tricks, as his father-in-law gave him a heavily-veiled Leah, Rachel's sister. The other "wives" were servants that Rachel and Leah gave him in a jealous competition to provide their husband more sons and thus hopefully win his affection.

Although polygamy is not God's ideal, we should be understanding of Jacob who was following the customs of his land.

Yet this Genesis story of jealousy and bickering in the family illustrates how wise and good God's ideal of monogamous marriage really is. God's ideal is always his best, and we stray from that ideal at our peril.

Jacob's new name: Israel
Genesis 31–32

After twenty years Jacob left Haran, sneaking away out of fear of his father-in-law. According to law at that time, Laban had a right to control not only the life of his adopted son-in-law, Jacob, but also his twelve grandsons. Also, Genesis tells us that Laban pursued his household gods, which Rachel had stolen (31:33-37). These household gods were images that were placed on a small altar in the home. Rachel took these not necessarily out of religious zeal, but out of economic interest. In that day possession of the household gods gave a person a claim on the family property. Rachel probably took the gods to establish her sons' future right to Laban's wealth. This probably explains why Laban was so anxious to recover his family gods.

On the journey Jacob wrestled with a stranger, whom he later identified as a representative of God. That night Jacob was given a new name, Israel, which means "he struggles with God" or "a prince with God."

The sons of Israel

Jacob had twelve sons by his four wives. Each of them had a large family. These family lines were preserved, and the forefather's names were kept as the names of the Hebrew "tribes" or "clans." There were actually thirteen rather than twelve tribes. Ephraim and Manasseh, Joseph's sons, are often called "half tribes" because they divided Joseph's portion of land.

At this point in Bible history the covenant promise given to Abraham passed, not to one person, but to all of Israel's sons.

Jacob meets Esau
Genesis 32–33

Jacob, now named Israel, still had not learned that he could trust God completely. On his return to Canaan, he sent herds of animals on ahead as gifts (bribes) to Esau. Jacob must have been stunned when Esau arrived with 400 men and kissed him! Esau saw no reason to be angry. He had the material prosperity that had mattered to him so much. He still did not care about the stolen birthright, as his remark to Jacob displays: "I already have enough . . ." (Genesis 33:9)!

Egyptian writing, called **hieroglyphics,** *was often carved into stone tablets; therefore, much of it is preserved even today.*

EGYPT

Mediterranean Sea

• Damascus

Jordan
River

• Jerusalem

• Memphis

Nile River

• Thebes

Red Sea

Insight: The descendants of Esau prospered and built an impregnable city carved out of rock cliffs at Mount Seir. For centuries this city prospered because it controlled vital trade routes.

Ancient trade routes
Genesis 37

Joseph's jealous brothers sold him to traveling Midianite merchants to be resold as a slave. For centuries a well-established trade route, called the Kings' Highway, had led from Egypt, east of the Jordan river, and on through Damascus. There it led further north, finally swinging back south and east to Mesopotamia, where Babylon and Ur lay. Camel caravans were familiar sights in the semi-arid desert where Jacob's flocks now fed. Egyptian records list many slaves, and also many soldiers, who bore Semitic names. Like Joseph they had come from the area around Palestine. So the sale of Joseph was not an unusual event for that time.

Egypt in archaeology

Egypt is a narrow country, surrounded by desert and sea. Only the land close to the Nile River grew crops, so most of Egypt's population was clustered near the river. Napoleon's invasion of Egypt in 1798 aroused interest in that ancient land. The Rosetta Stone, which contained an inscription in three languages, led to the deciphering in 1822 of Egyptian hieroglyphic writing. In the past 150 years thousands of inscriptions and documents have enabled scholars to reconstruct Egypt's history for some 5,000 years! Along with the history, scholars have recovered treatises on religion and many other texts that, with wall art, permit us to reconstruct a fascinating picture of life in Egypt during biblical times.

Joseph's time

By 3200 B.C., more than a thousand years before Abraham, Egypt was unified into a nation. Magnificent pyramids were constructed, great artists worked and fascinating books were written. By Joseph's time Egyptians had produced short stories and adventure books, and even a book on the *Pleasures of Fishing and Fowling!*

Egyptian women used cosmetics much like those used today, lipstick, eye shadow

Abraham bought the cave of Machpelah from the Hittites as a burial place for his wife Sarah. Later, both Abraham and Jacob were also buried in the cave.

and rouge. Egyptian scientists studied mathematics, and astronomers mapped the stars. Egyptian traders traveled on land and sea to bring wealth to Egypt's cities. Often Egypt's military made her the strongest nation in the ancient world.

The Egyptians, however, were a pagan people whose many gods were often represented in the forms of animals. The most important gods were Ra, the sun god, and Osiris. The Egyptians believed in life after death, and Osiris was thought to rule the netherworld.

Insight: Like other ancient peoples, the Egyptians buried tools, weapons, food and even model boats with the dead. These were for use in the next world. The Hebrews did not follow this practice. They knew the body returns to dust, but the spirit to God who gave it (Ecclesiastes 12:7).

Wealthy persons and royalty had their dead dried and wrapped as mummies. The Egyptians believed that the soul was part of the body, so the body had to be preserved after death. The poor who could not afford expensive funerals had no hope. In fact, ordinary people were not even allowed into the great temples that Egyptian pharaohs built.

Egypt had a great and powerful civilization when Joseph was taken there as a slave. Yet in just thirteen years the teenage slave would rise to become the second most powerful person in the kingdom.

Was Joseph a type of Christ?
Genesis 39

A "type" is a biblical person, institution or event that foreshadows another that is to be revealed later. For biblical examples see Hebrews 9:1-10. Many people view Joseph as a type of Christ because of his high moral character, his innocent suffering, his ultimate exaltation as ruler and his ready forgiveness of his brothers. Surely Joseph's behavior in the household of Potiphar and in prison were Christlike.

We can also appreciate the anguish of the teenager, torn from his family to become a slave in a strange land. We can feel the hurt as Joseph was falsely accused. Joseph's steadfast faith, expressed by his commitment to trust God and do right, serves as an example to us as to how to respond when we, too, may suffer unjustly (see 1 Peter 2:13-25).

God's word about Joseph is a comfort, too. "The Lord made Joseph successful in everything he did" (Genesis 39:23). In difficult times we may not sense God's presence. But he is at work in our circumstances, too.

Dreams
Genesis 40–41

In many cultures dreams are thought to convey information from supernatural sources. So it was not surprising for Pharaoh's baker and cupbearer, then in Joseph's prison, to think that their dreams had meaning. When Joseph correctly interpreted their dreams, they were impressed. Two years later, when Pharaoh had strange dreams that none of his advisors could interpret, the cupbearer remembered Joseph.

Insight: "Cupbearer" was the title of a very high official in ancient kingdoms. It was an honor, rather than a duty, to serve wine to the ruler. The cupbearer's access to the ruler made him particularly influential.

Pharaoh believed Joseph's interpretation that his dreams foretold seven fruitful years followed by seven years of famine. Impressed by Joseph's wisdom, Pharaoh made the thirty-year-old Joseph the second most powerful man in his kingdom and placed him in charge of preparations for the coming famine.

7 The Exodus

Exodus 1–15

Sometime during the 430 years the Israelites spent in Egypt, they were made slaves. But they also multiplied. When the time was right, God unleashed his miracle-working power and through Moses led his covenant people out of slavery to freedom.

MASTERY KEYS to the Exodus:

- What do miracles tell us about God?
- What were the three purposes of the miraculous judgments God brought on the Egyptians?
- What is the prophetic significance of Passover in Scripture?

Israel enslaved

Exodus 1

About 150 years after Joseph brought his father and brothers to Egypt, a people called the Hyksos (HUK-sos) invaded Egypt and began to rule. These people came from the same part of the world as the Israelites.

By about 1570 B.C. the native Egyptians drove the foreign Hyksos from Egypt. It is

By the time Moses was born, about 1526 B.C., the number of Israelites was so great that Pharaoh ordered all newborn boys killed. This reaction supports the estimate of millions who later left Egypt under Moses.

Moses' birth

Exodus 2

Moses' parents did obey the king's decree and cast their son into the Nile. But they placed him in a basket first! God led Pharaoh's daughter to adopt the baby and hire his own mother to rear him. To be the "son of Pharaoh's daughter" suggests Moses had a claim to be next in line to Egypt's throne. Moses' faith in God was later expressed by rejecting this position (see Hebrews 11:24-29).

Brick making was a part of daily life as shown in this illustration of a panel from Thebes.

possible that the ". . . new king . . . (who) did not know who Joseph was" was Ahmose (1584-1560 B.C.), the ruler who freed his land from the Hyksos. It would be natural for the Egyptians to fear Israel. It is likely that there were more Israelites in Egypt than Hyksos, and Ahmose feared the Israelites would fight beside their racial relatives. So the Egyptians made the Israelites slaves out of fear.

Insight: The Egyptians made swift, banana-shaped boats by tying together bundles of papyrus reeds. Moses' basket boat was made of reeds and may have had that shape.

Moses' choice

Despite his position as son of Pharaoh's daughter, Moses chose to identify with

The Israelites used chopped straw mixed with mud and sand from the river to form bricks by hand.

God's people. He demonstrated his commitment by killing an Egyptian foreman who was beating a Hebrew. When the deed was known, Moses fled. The New Testament says that "It was by faith that Moses, when he grew up, refused to be called the son of the king of Egypt's daughter. He chose to suffer with God's people instead of enjoying sin for a short time" (Hebrews 11:24-26).

Insight: Egyptian records tell us that teams of brickmakers could turn out about 65 bricks per man a day. Modern brickmakers produce about 3500 per man per day.

Moses' next forty years were spent in obscurity as a shepherd, trudging across the arid Sinai desert. The Sinai had supported a small population for hundreds of years, and the Egyptians had once opened jewel mines there. But it was a desolate backwater.

Moses' commitment seemed to have cost him everything.

Yahweh
Exodus 3–4

When God called the now 80-year-old Moses to go back to Egypt and deliver Israel, he hesitated. In the dialogue that followed, God revealed the name *I AM* to Moses. God told Moses, "This will always be my name. That is how people from now on will know me" (Exodus 3:15).

In Hebrew the name is *Yahweh.* Most names of God, such as Lord of Hosts or the Almighty, are descriptions. But *Yahweh* is God's personal name, taken from the verb "to be." It means "The One Who Is Always Present."

Insight: English versions indicate the name Yahweh by printing LORD in small capital letters.

Moses: God's leader

Moses is rightly revered by the Jewish people as their Lawgiver. The Bible, too, holds Moses up as an example. He is commended as humble in Numbers 12:3. Here "humble" means submissive to God and ever ready to respond to him. Hebrews 3:2 says Moses was "faithful in all God's house." Studying the life of Moses can be an enriching experience for every believer.

Moses' early life (Exodus 2:1-25). Although raised as a prince, Moses dreamed of freeing his people from slavery. We, too, need to evaluate our life goals and make a full commitment to what is important to God.

Moses' lost years (Exodus 3:1-6). Any pride Moses may have felt was lost during his forty years as a mere shepherd. When God spoke to him from the burning bush, Moses held back. It is better to recognize our weaknesses and trust God than to rush ahead in false self-confidence.

Moses' hesitancy (Exodus 3:11–4:17). Moses doubted that God could solve the problems he foresaw. God provided a helper in Aaron, his brother. At times the presence of others may help us learn a more complete trust.

Moses' confrontation with Pharaoh (Exodus 7–11). Moses confronted Pharaoh's worldly power with complete confidence that God would and could act in space and time. We, too, can trust a God whose freedom to act is without limits.

Moses' praise (Exodus 15). When God opened the Red Sea for Israel and destroyed the pursuing Egyptian army, Moses led Israel in a song of praise. How good it is to praise God for what he does in our lives.

Moses' followers rebel (Exodus 16–18). The Israelites grumbled and complained and even threatened to return to Egypt. Almost driven to despair, Moses turned to God. When others disappoint us, we need to look to God and remain faithful to him.

Moses' anger at Sinai (Exodus 32). When Moses returned to the camp after receiving the Ten Commandments, he was angry because the Israelites had made an idol to worship.

Our character is as often revealed in the things that make us angry as in the things that make us glad.

Moses' prayer for Israel (Exodus 32). God offered to let Moses' children replace the Israelite people. Moses prayed for Israel, not because they deserved mercy, but because Moses was concerned for God's glory. Nothing must suggest that the Lord did not keep his promises. Concern for God's glory should have an important place in our prayer requests, too.

Moses' readiness to discipline (Numbers 16). When rebelliousness continued after God gave Israel the Law, the rebels were punished. Moses called on God to act, because he knew that sin in the congregation was contagious. We must be willing to take a stand against sin and to discipline those who will not respond to instruction.

Moses' personal failure (Numbers 20). Moses was an exceptional person, but he was not perfect. In a moment of irritation he also failed to obey God fully. How carefully we need to guard ourselves, so that after we have instructed others, we ourselves do not fall short.

Moses' encouragement (Deuteronomy 1–4). When a new generation of Israelites had matured and was ready to enter the promised land, Moses reminded them of how God had helped during the wilderness years. We bless others and ourselves when we relate how much the Lord has done for us in the past.

Moses' challenge (Deuteronomy 29). God had established a covenant relationship with the children of Israel. But each generation had to make its own commitment to the Lord. Moses, about to die, challenged the new generation to follow the Lord. How important it is for us to encourage others to make a conscious, personal commitment to obey Jesus Christ.

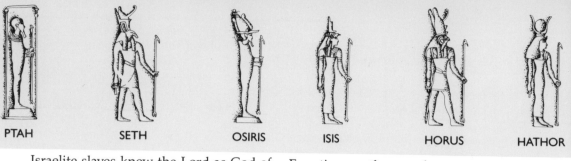

PTAH SETH OSIRIS ISIS HORUS HATHOR

Israelite slaves knew the Lord as God of Abraham, but they had not experienced his presence with them. Soon in mighty acts of power, God would show that he truly was with his people.

The words "This will always be my name" call us to view God as present with us, too.

Straw in bricks
Exodus 5

For years people wondered why Israelite slaves used straw in making bricks. Today we know that there are chemicals in chopped straw that, when mixed with river mud and sand, help the bricks dry more quickly and make them stronger. An Egyptian papyrus records a foreman's complaint: "I am not provided with anything. There are no men for brickmaking, and no straw in the district."

Judgment on Egypt

The Bible gives three reasons for the terrible plagues that God visited on Egypt. (1) God's mighty acts would be evidence to Israel of God's power and his love. Memory of his acts on Israel's behalf would be vital to future generations' understanding of God (Exodus 6:7). (2) By those same acts of power Pharaoh and the Egyptians would learn that the Lord is the only true God (Exodus 7:5). In biblical times people measured the power of supposed gods by the wealth or might of the people who worshiped them. Egypt, the most powerful nation on earth, was, at first, unimpressed when Moses demanded the release of Israel in the name of a god of slaves! How quickly the plagues of judgment would change that evaluation! (3) The plagues were also directed against specific gods in the Egyptian pantheon, who were supposed to control natural forces linked to life along the Nile. In addition to worshiping the Nile, the Egyptians worshiped frogs as a fertility symbol of their goddess Heqt. They also believed certain bulls were sacred to Apis, certain cows were sacred to Isis and certain rams were sacred to Amon. But God judged the deities of Egypt (Exodus 12:12). The display of God's power fully answered Pharaoh's question, "Who is the Lord?"

Pharaoh's hard heart

Many have been troubled by the verses in Exodus which say God "hardened Pharaoh's heart" (Exodus 7:3; 9:12, NIV). How could God punish Pharaoh for refusing to let Israel go if God caused Pharaoh's hardness? It hardly seems fair.

To understand, we need to note that the Bible also says that Pharaoh hardened his own heart (Exodus 8:15,32, NIV). So Pharaoh is portrayed in the same passage as responsible for his own stubborn refusal to respond to God.

But, most importantly, we need to ask, "What did God do to harden Pharaoh's heart?" The answer is, in each judgment God revealed more of himself and more of his power. Yet the more Pharaoh learned about God, the harder Pharaoh became. An analogy helps us understand. The hotter the sun, the harder clay becomes, while wax melts. The more God revealed of himself the harder Pharaoh's claylike heart became. While God's self-revelation was itself the direct cause of Pharaoh's hardening (and thus "God hardened Pharaoh's heart"), God was not responsible for Pharaoh's response (Pharaoh hardened his own heart).

The many gods of Egypt

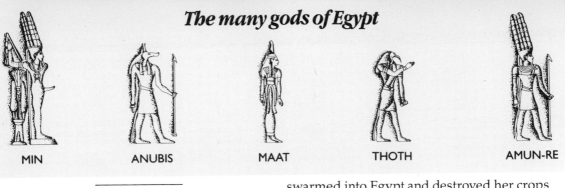

MIN   ANUBIS   MAAT   THOTH   AMUN-RE

Insight: We need to pray that our hearts be more like wax than clay, so the more God shows us of himself the more we respond to him.

The miraculous plagues

Many of the ten plagues that Exodus describes were not unique. Egyptian magicians could imitate the first two miracles, but none beyond that. At times Egypt had known too many frogs (the second plague). Cattle had sickened before (the fourth plague). Hail storms had killed animals in the field (the seventh plague). Great clouds of locusts had swarmed into Egypt and destroyed her crops (the eighth plague). These were in one sense "natural disasters." Some have even suggested that the darkness (the ninth) might have been caused by great clouds of dust raised when the Santorini Islands were destroyed in a volcanic explosion during this century. Does identification of the plagues as "natural disasters" rob them of their miraculous character?

It doesn't if we understand the nature of a "miracle" in the Old Testament. The Hebrew words are *pala'* (a marvel, a wonder), *mopet* (a wonder) and *'ot* (a sign). Thus a miracle is a special sign from God, something

The king of Egypt gave Joseph's family the land of Goshen in which to live.

Located between northeast Africa and the Arabian Peninsula, the Red Sea is approximately 1,450 miles long and up to 225 miles wide in places.

Dates from Abraham through Joshua

- Abraham born about 2166 B.C.
- enters Canaan about 2091 B.C.
- Isaac born • about 2066 B.C.
- Jacob born • about 2006 B.C.
- Joseph born • about 1915 B.C.
- sold to Egypt • about 1898 B.C.
- made ruler • about 1885 B.C.
- moved family to Egypt • about 1859 B.C.
- Hyksos rule • 1730 B.C.
- Israelites made slaves by Ahmose • about 1570 B.C.
- Moses born / Thutmose I • about 1526 B.C.
- Moses moved to Midian / Thutmose III • about 1486 B.C.
- The Exodus / Amenhotep II • about 1446 B.C.
- Conquest of Canaan about 1390 B.C.•

| 2200 | 2100 | 2000 | 1900 | 1800 | 1700 | 1600 | 1500 | 1400 | 1300 |

difficult or wonderful that God causes in order to accomplish his purpose. Looking into the text we see that (1) each plague was announced ahead of time, (2) each plague began and ended at Moses' command, (3) each plague was much worse than normal disasters and (4) most of the plagues struck the Egyptians and left the Israelites untouched.

The plagues in their timing, in Moses' exercise of control over nature and in their focus on Egypt were so clearly supernatural that the Egyptians themselves were totally convinced. They urged Pharaoh to let Israel go so that the Lord, this God of slaves, would not destroy their land.

Passover
Exodus 11–12
The final divine judgment was the death of each firstborn son of the Egyptians. The Hebrews were instructed to kill a lamb, to eat it and to sprinkle its blood on their doorposts. The blood on the doorposts was "a sign for you," (NIV) and God passed over such houses: no one there would die.

The symbolism is striking and a clear reference to the "lamb of God" who would one day die to pay for humanity's sins (see John 1:36; 1 Corinthians 5:7).

But Passover also had another significance. Each Israelite family was to eat a memorial meal on the anniversary of that first Passover and to explain to the children that the ceremony "is the Passover sacrifice to honor the Lord. When we were in Egypt, the Lord passed over the houses of Israel. The Lord killed the Egyptians, but he saved our homes" (Exodus 12:27).

In this ceremony each Israelite was to sense that God had delivered him or her personally, not just the ancestors, from slavery.

Insight: Later the Levites were not given a separate territory in Canaan as the other tribes were. They were scattered throughout the tribes in cities of their own. Christians too have no lasting interest in this world, but live among its peoples to share the good news of God's love.

The firstborn
Exodus 13
The firstborn sons of the Egyptians were killed in the final plague, while the Israelite firstborn were spared. God then claimed the firstborn Israelite male as his own. Later God set aside the tribe of Levi to serve him by doing the work of the tabernacle (the Israelites' worship center). The Bible explains, "I am choosing the Levites from among all the Israelites. They will take the place of the all the firstborn children of Israel" (Numbers 3:11-13; see Numbers 1:47-53). Those God claims are privileged to live and serve him forever.

The Red Sea
Exodus 13–14
What English Bibles translate as the "Red Sea" are the Hebrew words *yam suph*, which mean "sea of reeds." Some scholars believe that this body of water was actually a deep, ancient lake north of the Bitter Lakes (see map, Desert Wanderings, page 55), rather than the Red Sea itself.

Whatever the body of water, what happened there was clearly a miracle. God caused the waters to divide so that Israel passed through "on dry land. A wall of water was on both sides" (Exodus 14:22). When the Egyptians pursued, the Lord delayed them until the entire army was between the water walls, and then God released the waters. Not one soldier survived, and the Israelites saw the dead bodies of their oppressors washed up on the shore (Exodus 14:30).

How can we praise God?
Exodus 15
Moses taught Israel a praise poem to "sing to the Lord." The song recounts what God had done for Israel, and many of its stanzas are addressed directly to the Lord.

Every believer needs to learn to praise God, speaking directly to him and giving him glory for all he is and all he has done.

8 The Law of Moses

Exodus 16–40; Leviticus

God led Israel down the Sinai peninsula to Mount Sinai. The people camped there for a year, as God gave the Law to Israel through Moses. Included in that Law are not only the Ten Commandments, but also regulations regarding worship and the structure of Jewish society.

God gave his law to the Israelites through Moses. The law of Moses contained the Ten Commandments. The first four commandments are rules about man's relationship to God. The last six are his rules about man's relationship to other men.

MASTERY KEYS to the law and Tabernacle:

- What experiences show Israel's need for a law?
- What is the core meaning of each of the Ten Commandments?
- What are some of the spiritual lessons taught by the plan of the Old Testament Tabernacle, or Tent of Meeting?

An undisciplined mob
Exodus 15:22–17:7

The Israelites who left Egypt had been slaves for many generations. They had had no experience with freedom or the responsibilities associated with freedom. Three incidents show they were not ready to respond to God with trusting obedience.

Exodus 15:22-27 reports Israel's grumbling when they came to a place where the water was bitter. God purified the water.

Exodus 16:1-36 reports grumbling over lack of food. Moses warned them that this was "against the Lord," but God provided bread and meat.

Exodus 17:1-7 reports quarreling with Moses over water, to the extent that the people were ready to stone Moses and return to Egypt. God again provided water.

"Grumbled" and "quarreled" are strong words in Hebrew and indicate rebellion, not simple complaint. This people needed law to establish what God required. The law would also provide a basis for discipline when the people disobeyed. It may be foolish to drive out on a main highway without looking, but it is not criminal unless there is a stop sign at the corner. The law was God's "stop sign" for Israel. It told Israel what to do, and it es-

Moses received the Ten Commandments on Mount Sinai. One possible location of Mount Sinai is in northeast Egypt between the Gulf of Suez, the Gulf of Aqaba and the Strait of Tiran. This mountain is over 8,500 feet high.

tablished a basis for punishment when it was violated.

Insight: Paul suggests that law was given because the people of God were in spiritual childhood (see Galatians 4:1-7). People who are spiritually mature will do God's will without needing a written law to say "stop" (see Romans 8:4).

Mount Sinai
Exodus 19

Sinai lies on an arid peninsula between Egypt and Canaan (see map, The Desert Wanderings, p. 55). Mount Sinai is also called Mount Horeb in the Bible. It was the site of two important revelations. Here God revealed the name *Yahweh* (I AM) to Moses, and here God gave Israel his law through Moses.

The law is called a covenant in Scripture because it was a *berit*, a formal agreement containing promises. But unlike the Abrahamic covenant (see page 31), this covenant was conditional. God promised to bless Israel if they obeyed the regulations contained in the Mosaic law, and he also promised to punish them if they disobeyed.

Yet when the Bible uses the term "law," more is included than divine commands. The Old Testament law also established a priesthood and a sacrificial system, so that those who sinned might be restored to fellowship with God.

Theologians speak of three functions of God's law. (1) Law reveals God's own character. (2) Law sets high standards that prove human beings to be sinners. (3) Law shows those who love God how to please him.

How to treat God

1. Put no gods before me.	Trust God only.
2. Have no idols.	Worship God only.
3. Do not take God's name in vain.	Use God's name in ways that honor him.
4. Keep the Sabbath holy.	Rest and think about God.

How to treat people

5. Honor father, mother.	Respect and obey parents.
6. Do not murder.	Protect human life.
7. Do not commit adultery.	Be true to your husband or wife.
8. Do not steal.	Don't take what belongs to others.
9. Do not give false testimony.	Don't lie about others.
10. Do not covet.	Be satisfied with what you have.

Insight: The Sinai peninsula was desert that received only slight rainfall. It had been inhabited for centuries by small groups who used cisterns to preserve rain water. But there was no way that the millions of Israelites who came there could be supplied without God's miraculous provision of manna for food and unusual water sources.

The Ten Commandments
Exodus 20

The core of Old Testament law is expressed in the familiar Ten Commandments. These ten can be divided into two parts: the first four, which showed Israel how to show love to God, and the next six, which showed Israel how to show love to others. Jesus once commented that the whole law can be summed up in two commands: "Love the Lord your God with all your heart, soul and mind" and "Love your neighbor as you love yourself" (Matthew 22:37-39). Martin Luther once said, "Love God and do as you please." He meant that a person who truly loves God and others will obey God's law (see Romans 13:8-10).

Case law
Exodus 21–23, Leviticus

There are many specific regulations in Old Testament law. One count identifies 644! Why are there so many?

Certain laws, like the Ten Commandments, express general principles. The central idea or core meaning of each of the Ten Commandments is summed up on page 49. But general principles are not enough. These must be illustrated and explained.

This is the reason for many of the Old Testament regulations: they are "case law," which illustrate the principles expressed in the basic commandments by providing examples of how they apply to a variety of situations.

Characteristics of Old Testament law

Old Testament law regulates worship rituals. Law deals with social and criminal matters and establishes moral principles. The law shows a striking concern for individuals. The wages of hired men are to be paid on time, no one is to be slandered, and no favoritism is to be shown to the rich over the poor (see Leviticus 19:15).

Crime in the Old Testament is viewed as

Shown above is the Ur Nammu Law Code. In Bible times such law codes were often written on stone or clay tablets.

an offense against the victim, and the criminal is to repay the victim directly. If a person is injured, money is to be paid to support him until he can work again. If an animal is stolen, the thief is not only to return it but also must pay the victim double or triple (see Exodus 21–22).

In contrast, in American society, crime is viewed as an offense against the government, and the criminal pays by being punished (jailed). Thus our concept of criminal justice is very different from the concept that underlies Old Testament law.

Much in Old Testament law deals with the needs of the poor. The wealthy were to loan money to the poor without charging interest, and if the poor were unable to pay the debt back, the wealthy were to forgive it. Poor persons could pick up any fruit or grain that fell to the ground in another person's fields. In addition special tithes were collected to meet the needs of the fatherless and widows, and even destitute foreigners (see Leviticus 25:35-37, Deuteronomy 14:28-29 and 15:7-11). A law code proclaimed by the Assyrian ruler Hammurabi (c. 1792-1750 B.C.) covers many of the same issues as the Mosaic Code and thus provides an interesting comparison.

The Code of Hammurabi imposed the death penalty for homicide, theft, bearing false witness, kidnapping, house-breaking and other infractions. In Old Testament law the death penalty is limited to crimes which threaten life or the religious and moral structure of the community.

The Mosaic code was more humane, and unlike Hammurabi's, did not prescribe different penalties based on different social classes.

In every way God's law was compassionate and caring to an unusual degree.

The Tabernacle
Exodus 25–30, 35–40

God gave Moses specific blueprints for a portable house of worship 45 feet long, 15 feet high and 15 feet wide. Each object in this Holy Tent where Israel would come to meet God taught a spiritual lesson.

- Just inside the single doorway in the wall that surrounded the Tabernacle was an altar on which animals were sacrificed. There is only one way to approach the Lord, and that way requires blood sacrifice (see Hebrews 9:28; 10:11-18).
- Within the second room inside the Tabernacle stood the Ark of the Covenant. There, once a year, the High Priest sprinkled sacrificial blood. On the basis of this

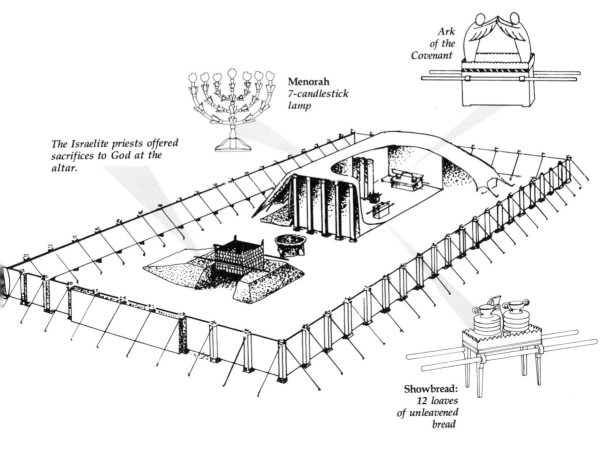

Ark of the Covenant

Menorah
7-candlestick lamp

The Israelite priests offered sacrifices to God at the altar.

Showbread:
12 loaves of unleavened bread

blood, God covered the sins of his Old Testament people (Leviticus 16). But the blood was symbolic, a picture of the blood Jesus would give on Calvary to pay the price of human sin (Hebrews 9:11-22).

- Other symbolic furnishings included the lampstand, incense altar and a table on which loaves of fresh bread were placed daily. These picture Christ as the source of our guidance, Christ as our avenue of approach to God in prayer and Christ as provider of our daily bread.

The priesthood

Old Testament law set aside the family of Aaron from the tribe of Levi to serve as Israel's priests. Other Levite families assisted.

These Mosaic books of the Old Testament define the duties of priests. Priests alone could offer sacrifices to God. In this they held the door to the Lord open for Israel. The priests were also to examine worshipers to be sure they were free of any disqualifying disease. Because purity was needed in approaching God, worshipers could not enter who had infectious skin diseases, mildew in their clothing, bodily discharges, recent sex with an "unclean" woman, or recent childbirth (Leviticus 13–15). In addition, the priests taught God's Law in Israel (Deuteronomy 33:8-10) and served as judges in difficult cases (Deuteronomy 17:8-9).

The priesthood is one of the major institutions in Old Testament faith, and the priests alone were able to approach God in his tabernacle.

Insight: Descendants of Aaron who had any physical defect were not allowed to serve as priests. But no one was morally perfect. Priests made sacrifices for their own sins before they offered sacrifices for the sins of the people.

Only the sons of Aaron could serve as priests. The color blue was set aside for priestly garments (Exodus 28). Yet every Israelite was to wear tassels on his or her clothing which contained a blue thread or cord (Numbers 15:37). The tassel reminded each Israelite of God's call and of the destiny of Israel to become a kingdom of priests.

The message of history
Exodus 20–30

In Bible study it is important to note the sequence and timing of events. The sequence of events at Sinai is especially important. God gave the law, but violating it made people guilty (Exodus 20–24). So God gave Israel a tabernacle, where sinning people could approach him (Exodus 25–26) through sacrifice

What is in Leviticus?

The book of Leviticus is a book of laws, not a book of stories. Here is what you can find in Leviticus.

Rules for worship	Chapters 11-15
The Day of Cleansing	Chapters 16-17
Rules for holy living	Chapters 18-22
Rules for special holidays	Chapters 23-25
More rules and promises	Chapters 26-27

(Exodus 27). Then God gave Israel a priesthood to offer the required sacrifices and teach the law so that Israel might better learn how to live in fellowship with the Lord (Exodus 29–30).

Insight: God provides for our forgiveness, but his goal for us remains holiness.

Leviticus

Leviticus is a book of laws rather than a narrative history. It has been rightly called God's handbook for holy living under the Mosaic Covenant. Its contents are summarized above.

9 The wilderness years

Numbers; Deuteronomy

After a year at Mount Sinai, the people of Israel were led out toward the promised land. Numbers tells the story of how that first generation rebelled against God and refused to enter. That generation was condemned to wander for forty more years until everyone over age twenty died. Then their children were again led by Moses to the edge of Canaan. Moses' great sermons to this new and faithful generation are found in Deuteronomy.

MASTERY KEYS to the wilderness years:

- How can you explain the difference in God's response to rebelliousness before and after the law was given?
- How does the New Testament explain Israel's rebelliousness?
- What concepts of living in harmony with God are emphasized in Deuteronomy?

The fiery cloud
Numbers 9

From Sinai God led his people in a visible way. The Hebrew *shekinah*, which means dwelling, refers to God's presence on earth. The Ark is his *shekinah* (Numbers 10:35-36); also God's presence came down in a cloud to talk with Moses in the tent (Exodus 33:7-11), led Israel to Sinai (Exodus 13:21-22) and continued with the Israelites toward Canaan (Exodus 33:1 8). Daily when the people were to move, this fiery cloud that hung over the Tabernacle rose up and led the way. If the community was to stay camped, the cloud was still. This unmistakable evidence of God's presence should have produced confidence and obedience, but it did not. Again and again, Israel rebelled against God's commandments. The pattern of disobedience seen here reveals the hearts of the Israelites and sets the scene for the events which follow.

Discipline
Numbers 11; 15

If we compare incidents before and after the giving of the law, we make a fascinating discovery. Before, complaints against God, such as despising the food he provided and breaking of Sabbath laws, seem to have been ignored (see Exodus 15:22–17:7). After, when the people complain, fire falls from the Lord (Numbers 11:1-3). Then a plague strikes thousands who had craved meat (11:4-34), and a Sabbath-breaker is stoned to death (15:32-41). What can explain this difference? When the law had been given, the people had promised to obey. Breaking the law was now sin in its clearest, intentional sense. Now God had a basis for punishing sinners, and he did so.

Yet even these severe punishments were gracious and were intended to encourage future obedience. They occurred before God commanded his people to enter Canaan. They should have learned from the discipline they experienced that they must obey God or suffer punishment. Fear as well as love sometimes motivates us to do what is right.

Canaan was a lush and fruitful land.

Today Israel is again becoming a rich and beautiful land.

What was Canaan like?

Around 1400 B.C. many strongly walled city-states existed in Canaan. In that age Canaan was marked by fertile valleys, a beautiful land that produced rich crops. It was truly a land of "milk and honey" (Numbers 13:27; Deuteronomy 6:3, NIV). Yet travelers in Palestine during the last century have described it as a barren, desert land. What has happened?

Over hundreds of years of wars, trees and other ground cover have been cut down, allowing the rich soil to erode. This devastation was predicted in the book of Deuteronomy should Israel not obey God's law (see Deuteronomy 28:15-68).

Yet today Israel is again green as modern Israelis irrigate the ancient land.

The Israelites rebel
Numbers 13–14

How can we explain the rebellion of this people who had been rescued from slavery and had seen so many evidences of the real-ity and power of their God? The book of Hebrews says that when the Israelites heard God's voice, they hardened their hearts (Hebrews 3:7-10, NIV). Disobedience is often evidence of the hard heart. But the cause of hardened hearts is a failure to trust God. Lacking simple trust in God, the Israelites were afraid to obey him and were terrified by the strong cities and inhabitants of Canaan.

Israel's refusal to obey brought divine judgment. Everyone twenty years and older would now die in the wilderness. It would be forty more years before the children of the disobedient generation could enter the land that was their heritage.

The wasted years
Numbers 15–19

Numbers 33 gives a list of places where the Israelites camped after leaving Egypt. Many of the locations are unknown, but those that have been identified are shown on the map on page 55.

During those years everyone who had

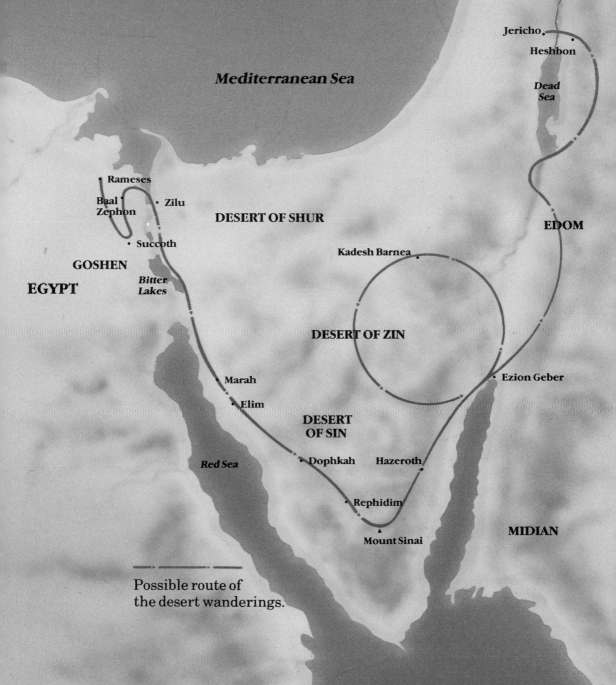

THE DESERT WANDERINGS

Jordan River

Mediterranean Sea

Jericho

Heshbon

Dead Sea

Rameses

Baal Zephon

Zilu

DESERT OF SHUR

EDOM

Succoth

GOSHEN

Kadesh Barnea

EGYPT

Bitter Lakes

DESERT OF ZIN

Marah

Ezion Geber

Elim

DESERT OF SIN

Red Sea

Dophkah

Hazeroth

Rephidim

MIDIAN

Mount Sinai

Possible route of the desert wanderings.

been over the age of twenty died. But a new generation was born and grew to maturity! It is striking that at the end of this time, there were 601,730 fighting men in Israel, in place of the 603,550 who would not fight forty years before.

The book of Numbers

Numbers is the Bible book that tells the story of the two generations. It looks back on the first generation and tells the story of their disobedience. But it also looks ahead and tells of the early victories won by the new, obedient generation.

A glance at an outline of Numbers shows us both the look back to disobedience and the look ahead to victory. Knowing the story of both generations, we can now see the significance of the major themes found in this pivotal book of Old Testament history.

Numbers

I.	At Sinai	1–9
	A. Organizing the people	1–4
	B. Culminating worship	5–9
II.	The Lost Generation	10–19
	A. The journey	10–12
	B. Disobedience	13–14
	C. Years wandering	15–19
III.	Preparation for Victory	20–36
	A. Warfare	20–21
	B. Balaam	22–25
	C. The new generation	26–31
	D. Victory preview	32–36

Victory and defeat
Numbers 20–21

Israel had not attacked Canaan when Canaanite and Amorite kings attacked them! In each case Israel fought and won. Yet during this same period some Israelites continued to rebel and were punished by God.

What a series of lessons! Israel ran from battle, but the enemy pursued. Israel's armies won; God could have given total victory if the people had only obeyed. And, while no external enemy defeated God's people, Israel's own lack of faith brought death to thousands.

The bronze serpent
Numbers 21

The danger of death from the poisonous snakes God sent could be avoided simply by looking at the bronze serpent Moses raised on a pole in the middle of the camp. Jesus linked this event with his own crucifixion (John 3:14-15). How are the two events alike? In each case (1) the issue is life or death, (2) the object raised up on a pole is easily visible to all, and (3) looking to that one is an act of faith. Those in Moses' day who scoffed at looking to a bronze serpent for deliverance died. And, today, those who scoff at the crucified Savior as God's only way of salvation likewise perish (John 3:16-17).

Balaam's curse
Numbers 23–24

Balaam, a man believed to have magical powers, was recruited by King Balak to curse Israel. The pagan "curse" was thought to be magic and to give persons power over others by draining their strength. But in the Bible God's "curses" are moral rather than magical. A divine "curse" is God's announced punishment for a violation of our relationship with him.

Balaam tried to use magic against God's people but failed. Finally Balaam was forced to tell King Balak, "No tricks will work on the people of Jacob. No magic works against Israel" (Numbers 23:23). In fact, Balaam was forced by God to pronounce a blessing, the opposite of a curse (23:24)!

Insight: Evil spiritual forces do exist (Ephesians 6:12). But no magic or supernatural powers can overcome those who are faithful to God (see 1 John 4:4).

Balaam's sins

The New Testament warns against three sins that Balaam illustrates. The "way Balaam went" (2 Peter 2:15) is using religion as a means to make money. The "wrong that Balaam did" (Jude 11) is wanting money so badly that we are willing to disobey God to get it. And the "teaching of Balaam" (Revelation 2:14) is false moral teaching that causes others to sin. When Balaam could not curse Israel, he suggested that Balak send women to Israel's camp to draw Israelites into immorality and idolatry. They tried and succeeded (Numbers 25)! But those who sinned were killed, and the community was cleansed. Later when Israel invaded Canaan, Balaam was killed (Joshua 13:22).

Victory preview
Numbers 32–33

The new generation which replaced the old had defeated enemies across the Jordan from the promised land. Two tribes asked for possession of that land but volunteered to go across the river and fight for Canaan for their brothers. The land was given to them, expanding Canaan's promised borders.

Levitical cities
Numbers 35

The tribe of Levi had been dedicated to God for his service. This tribe provided the priests and worship assistants. Only the Levites of Israel's tribes were not to be given their own district in the promised land (see map, page 69). By virtue of their work at the central sanctuary, they were in the service of Israel as a whole. For this reason they were to live scattered throughout Israel, in groups in the various tribal territories. They were given cities within the territory of the other tribes and were to be supported by tithes paid to them.

Insight: The principle seen here is important. The Levites were charged with teaching others (see 2 Chronicles 17:9). To reach all the other tribes, they had to be scattered among them rather than isolated. Christians, too, are "in the world" (John 17:18) so that we can have contact with persons who need to know God.

An outline of Deuteronomy

Deuteronomy means "second law." The book is a series of three sermons in which Moses restates the law for the new generation which is about to take Canaan.

This book is arranged in the order of a covenant document of the ancient world with its typical five or six parts:

Historical prologue	1:6–3:29
Basic stipulations	4:1–11:32
Detailed stipulations	12:1–26:19
Ratification statement	27:1-26
Blessings and curses	28:1-68
Recapitulation	29:1–30:20

Deuteronomy has a distinctive vocabulary. Many expressions are used repeatedly: "the place the Lord your God will choose" (21 times), "remember that you were slaves in Egypt" (5 times), "the land [or rest] the Lord your God is giving you" (30 times), "fear the Lord" (21 times).

The book is in the form of an ancient "suzerainty treaty," a *berit* which defined the relationship between a ruler and his people. This treaty form emphasizes that the Old Testament portrays God as Israel's living King.

The Old Testament word for king is *melech*. The ruler in those times exercised all functions of government. He was the legislature, establishing laws. He was the executive, running the nation. And he was the judiciary, enforcing his laws. In addition, the king was the military leader of his people. God was to be all things for his people, Israel.

Success guaranteed
Deuteronomy 4:39-40

Having reminded Israel of how God delivered them from Egypt and cared for them in the wilderness, Moses gives his prescription for guaranteed success. "Know and believe today that the Lord is God. He is God in heaven above and on the earth below. There is no other god! Obey his laws and commands, which I am giving you today. Obey them so that things will go well for you and your children." Our commitment to follow the Lord will have a positive impact on our children.

Law and love
Deuteronomy 5–11

Moses calls on Israel to love God as a response to God's love. God's love was demonstrated in his choosing Abraham and promising to give his children a flourishing land. He brought them out of Egypt "by his great power" (6:21). None of this was done because Israel was better than other nations, but "because he loved you. And he kept his promise to your ancestors" (7:8). Then in love God gave Israel the law to show his people how to live in harmony with him "for your own good" (10:13). When Israel did live in harmony with God's holiness, the Lord would be able to bless them.

Love for God was to be demonstrated by obeying "his orders, rules, laws and commands" (11:1). Worshiping God only and responding to his commandments were not to be just rituals but the response of a heart filled with love.

Insight: The strongest Hebrew word for love is *hesed*. It describes a deep bond of loyalty between persons. This kind of biblical love is not just a feeling of affection, but is an active commitment to another person. God shows his *hesed* for us by forgiving and sustaining us (Exodus 34:6-7). We show *hesed* for God by worshiping and obeying him.

Worshiping God
Deuteronomy 12–13

Israel was (1) to worship the Lord only, and (2) to worship God as he commanded, rather than in a pagan way. Some think that they can approach God any way they choose. But God says that people today can approach him only through his Son, Jesus Christ (see John 14:6).

Fearing God

This book speaks of fear of God. What does "fearing God" mean? This Old Testament phrase means taking God so seriously and giving him such respect that we respond to him obediently. Thus "fear" is closely linked with love. Fear does not imply terror at the thought of possible punishment but indicates a respect that motivates obedience.

The Bible calls such fear the "beginning of knowledge" (Proverbs 1:7, NIV).

The occult
Deuteronomy 18

The Bible forbids believers to be involved in any occult practice. Such things as astrology ("interpreting omens") and channeling (consulting a "medium or spiritist"), as well as witchcraft, are called "detestable ways." We are to depend completely on God and look only to him for help. Looking to the occult is looking away from God.

Blessings
Deuteronomy 28:1-14

Moses concludes by listing the benefits that obedience would bring to Israel. If the people would only obey, God would make the land fruitful and prosperous, Israel's armies would be victorious, and other nations would honor the Lord because of Israel.

Warnings of punishment
Deuteronomy 28:15-68

Moses also lists the results of disobedience. God would bring on a rebellious Israel military defeat, plagues and sickness, poverty and fear. Ultimately, continuing disobedience would lead to exile from the promised land itself. In graphic terms the consequences of disobedience are laid out for Israel to ponder.

Moses' death
Deuteronomy 34

Moses was given a glimpse of the promised land, and then he died. God himself laid Moses' body to rest.

10 Conquest of Canaan
Joshua

Led by Joshua, the Israelites crossed the Jordan River. The conquest took some seven years. Israel's victory was keyed by a series of decisive battles that demonstrated Joshua's military skill as well as his faith.

MASTERY KEYS to the conquest of Canaan:

- What was the significance of Jericho and Ai?
- What was the relationship between God's active involvement in battles and Israel's own military efforts?
- What lessons might this period have taught future generations of Israelites?

Joshua, the man

Joshua 1

Joshua had long been a leader under Moses. He had served as general of Israel's armies from the beginning (see Exodus 17:10). Some believe Joshua had been an officer in Pharaoh's army, because archaeologists have found Egyptian army records which list officers with Israelite-sounding names.

Joshua was one of the twelve spies who had entered Canaan 40 years earlier and with Caleb had urged Israel to attack then (see Numbers 13–14).

Joshua now faced two challenges. He needed to retain full confidence in God, and he needed to win the full confidence of his

Trumpets used in Bible times were often made by hollowing out a ram's horn.

people. God spoke to Joshua and promised victory: only "be strong and brave. Be sure to obey all the teachings my servant Moses gave you" (1:7). Joshua did exactly this and kept Israel close to God.

Insight: The "book of the law" that Moses left Joshua and Israel was the Pentateuch, the first five books of the Old Testament. Since the conquest took place about 1390 B.C., these books in our Bible are about 3,400 years old!

Rahab
Joshua 2

Everyone in Jericho, the strong, walled city that blocked access to Canaan, had heard of God and was terrified (2:8-11). But only in Rahab was fear transformed to faith. The book of James points out that it is not our knowing about God that saves us but our responding to him as Rahab responded (James 2:25-26).

Memorials
Joshua 4

By parting the flooding Jordan River to let Israel pass (vs 18), God confirmed Israel's confidence in Joshua, but Joshua quickly refocused their attention on the Lord.

He ordered twelve stones to be taken from the now dry Jordan and piled together on the land. These were to be a *zikkaron*, a Hebrew term which we translate "memorial." When future generations would ask their parents the meaning of the stones, parents were to say, "the Lord your God dried up the Jordan."

Zikkaron implies more than "memorial." It means identifying with a past event so well that we see ourselves as participating in it. The sign's function will be active, not remote or inoperative. Each future generation was to realize that God opened the Jordan so they could enter the land. This remembering in Hebrew is more than a calling to mind. It involves a remembering with concern; it also implies loving reflection and, where called for, a corresponding degree of action.

Insight: The Lord's Supper is to be viewed by Christians as a *zikkaron*. Each time we partake we are to sense our personal participation in Christ's death.

Jericho
Joshua 6

Jericho was a strong, walled city which controlled the mountain passes that led up into Canaan (see map, page 55). The site was settled about 8000 B.C. In Joshua's time it

Memorials (zikkarons) are often established in memory of an important event or person. In Bible times zikkarons were often a pile of stones or a large stone set up on its end.

Jericho was an ancient city in Palestine. It was located in the Jordan Valley, north of the Dead Sea. Jericho is likely the oldest known city in the world today.

was a walled city of about eight acres. The walls had a base 11 feet high. Then they sloped upward at a sharp angle for some 35 feet before the main walls rose even higher.

Commanded to march silently around this fortress, the Israelites obeyed. The seventh day after circling the city seven times, they gave a great shout, and the walls fell. It made no military sense to simply march around Jericho. The people must have wondered, yet they remained silent and marched as they had been commanded. Spiritual victories, too, are won by faithful obedience to God.

Jericho today

Archaeologists have excavated Jericho and found massive blocks of stone which may have once been part of the ancient city's walls. From the ruins of the area, scholars have reconstructed the contents of the typical home, including beds, tables, pottery vessels and food. On the whole, life in Jericho was simple with only very few items of value.

Achan

Joshua 7

Achan disobeyed Joshua's command and took loot from Jericho. As a result of this sin,

Jericho was sometimes called "The City of Palms."

an Israelite force was defeated at Ai with the loss of 38 men. Achan was put to death with his family. Why such a severe penalty? Achan's disobedience had led to the defeat, and many of his fellow soldiers had died. The death penalty was appropriate.

And why did Achan's family have to die with him? Many see the fact that Achan hid his loot "in his tent," where family members would have known, as the reason they died, too. They knew of and participated in Achan's sin.

These events taught Israel important lessons. Jericho showed that complete obedience would guarantee divine blessing. Ai showed that even one individual's disobedience could bring harm to the nation.

God's "choice" of Achan

Joshua 7 speaks of God as choosing Achan's tribe, clan, family and finally the individual himself. How did God "choose"? The Jewish high priest wore a Urim and Thummim as a sort of vest. These stones were used in divining God's will. Probably the Urim and Thummim contained three stones, indicating yes, no, and no answer. God guided the high priest's hand to choose the correct stone. Here in verse 16, the stone would indicate yes or no as each tribe, clan and family group passed before Joshua. Finally the stone indicated yes; Achan had sinned.

The Gibeonites
Joshua 9

People of a nearby Canaanite city, terrified by the invaders, tricked Joshua and the elders into making a peace treaty with them. Because Israel had sworn in the name of the Lord, the commitment could not be broken, even when the deceit was uncovered.

Joshua's mistake was not in being faithful to a fraudulent treaty, but in failing to inquire of God before making it.

Genocide?

God commanded Joshua to destroy utterly the Canaanite civilization (Joshua 6:21; 9:24). This has been condemned as genocide, the wiping out of a whole race. How can such apparent brutality be justified?

First, God was using Israel as his agent to punish these pagan people for sin. Centuries before, God had told Abraham he would not drive the Canaanites and Amorites from the promised land because they "are not yet evil enough to punish" (Genesis 15:16). Archaeology has revealed how morally depraved Canaanite religion was, even permitting infant sacrifice and temple prostitution. God used Israel to purge such evils from the land.

Second, God intended to protect the purity of Israel. If Amorites and Canaanites were left in the land, they would surely turn the Israelites away from God.

While Joshua did break the military

power of the Canaanites, he did not drive these pagan people completely out. In the next centuries the Israelites were, in fact, corrupted by the people and their religion.

The military conquest
Joshua 9–12

Joshua's military campaigns against Canaan are still studied in the Israeli War College. The discovery of Egyptian diplomatic correspondence, called the Amarna letters, gives a fascinating picture of Canaan around the time of Joshua. These letters were found in the ruins of the capital city of Pharaoh Akhenaton (1379-1362 B.C.), the ancient city of Akhetaton at the modern location of Tel El-Amarna. At the time the letters were written Canaan was divided into small city-states that had been clients of the now weak Egyptian empire. Individual cities were often walled and relatively strong. But the land was not united and had no single leader. A number of familiar cities are mentioned specifically in the Amarna correspondence. Among them are Jericho, Bethel, Jerusalem and Eglon.

One of the stronger cities was Hazor. This 175-acre city, surrounded by 50-foot walls, had a population of around 40,000 people.

Hazor and other Canaanite city-states had a high level of military skills. Their forces included chariots, the tanks of ancient warfare. The wheels of these chariots were equipped with great knife-blades which would cut down foot soldiers. Israel had no chariots.

How did Joshua's battle plan take advantage of Canaanite weaknesses? Before the city states could assemble a united army, Joshua led a forced march into the central highland. There he defeated several kings and cut the country in two (Joshua 10).

The gods of the Canaanites

By biblical times Baal was the chief god, whose realm was the sky. He wrestled with his enemies: Yamm, god of the sea, and Mot, god of death. The Canaanites believed that if Baal won, the rains would come that year and the land would be fertile. Baal's wife was A-nath, goddess of war as well as of sensuality. Together they combine two striking features of Canaanite religion: cruelty and lust.

The cruelty of the Canaanites is reflected in a poem celebrating Anath's slaughter of Baal's enemies.

> Anath swells her liver with laughter
> Her heart is filled with joy
> For in Anath's hand is victory
> For knee-deep she plunges in the
>   blood of soldiers
> Neck high in the gore of troops
> Until she is satisfied.

This bloodlust is the reason that later priests of Baal cut themselves with knives when praying (see 1 Kings 18:28). The priests hoped that the odor of blood would attract the attention of their bloodthirsty god!

The gods of the Canaanites had overpowering sexual appetites. Myths picture El, Baal's father, creating women in order to have sex with them. Baal himself is even portrayed having sex with a young heifer. In the religion of Canaan, sex is associated with fertility. Worship of Baal often involved sex acts intended to excite the gods and goddesses so they would have intercourse and guarantee the fertility of the fields. In Canaanite religion the designation "holy ones" is used of homosexual priests and priestesses who served as prostitutes in order to excite their gods.

The more we learn about the religion of the Canaanites, the brutality and the gross immorality that they practiced, the more we understand God's command to Joshua to "exterminate them without mercy" (Joshua 11:20).

The enemy was now divided, and Joshua turned south to crush the smaller remaining enemy force. Then he turned and attacked the northern coalition. In this campaign he totally destroyed the major city of Hazor.

While many Canaanites remained in the land, their power to defeat Israel was broken.

The Canaanites were a rich and powerful people. But spiritually and morally they were depraved, with a religion obsessed with fertility and sex. Writings recovered on clay tablets at Ras Shamra show just how brutal and licentious Canaanite worship was and helps to explain why God commanded they be exterminated, rather than simply driven out.

Dividing the land
Joshua 13–19

With Canaanite power broken, Joshua distributed land to the tribal groups and the clans within the tribes. The general areas allotted to each tribe are shown on the map on page 69. Not all the land allotted was occupied immediately. Each tribe became responsible to drive out any remaining Canaanites in its territory. The word "allotment" used for the land given each tribe and family describes how the land was distributed. Lots, much like our dice, were thrown to determine who received each area. This was not gambling, but a means sometimes used in Old Testament times to determine God's will. Proverbs 16:33 says, "the lot is cast into the lap, but its every decision is from the Lord."

Insight: An allegory is a story in which each element stands for something other than itself. There have been many allegorical interpretations of Joshua's conquest. Some say it represents Jesus, who on the cross broke Satan's power, but calls on us to face and overcome daily many foes until he returns and victory is complete. Allegorical interpretations are interesting, but it is best to try to understand Bible events in terms of their meaning in the context of history, and only then to try to draw lessons for living from them.

A permanent possession

A vital concept in the Old Testament is permanent possession of land. No family was to sell its land to others. While use of the land might be sold, every fiftieth year was a year of Jubilee, and land was to be returned to the family to which Joshua had originally given it (see Leviticus 25).

This system guaranteed that no family's basic wealth could be squandered by one person and so impoverish all descendants. This rule of law reinforced the truth that the promised land truly was God's gift, given not only to Israel, but given as well to each individual and family.

Similarly, no fellow Hebrew might be permanently enslaved. He or she must be freed after seven years.

Recommitment
Joshua 23–24

In his farewell address the now-aged Joshua challenged Israel. He recounted all that the Lord had done for Israel and called on the people to serve God.

Joshua also warned Israel: God is holy and jealous; he cares fiercely for his own and insists that they remain faithful to him. And the people promised: "We will serve the Lord our God. We will obey him" (24:24).

11 God's judges

Judges; Ruth

The Israelites settled down in the land that God promised them. But the next centuries were filled with suffering. The people often turned from the Lord and abandoned his law to worship false gods. God then permitted foreign enemies to oppress his people until the Israelites turned to him again for deliverance. It was then that God sent them the judges.

MASTERY KEYS to God's judges:

- What was the true role of a judge in this era?
- What are the names and exploits of at least three of the judges?
- What important spiritual lessons from this time can be applied by Christians today?

The biblical judge

Old Testament judges should not be confused with a member of the modern judiciary. The Hebrew word *shapat* and the poetic din mean "ruler" or "governor." The "judges" who appeared after Joshua were not simply persons who decided legal disputes but were leaders of the nation in every sense.

Like other ancient rulers the judges did decide disputes. But they also had legislative and executive responsibilities and typically led armies as well.

The judges of the Bible were not hereditary rulers but leaders because of a special call from God. Most, but not all of the judges, had a significant spiritual impact on Israel and kept the people faithful to the Lord during their lifetime. Most judges, however, served only one or two of Israel's twelve tribes. The people were never united into a single nation during this period.

The Spring of Harod (shown above) is the spring where Gideon's men were tested by God prior to their battle with the Midianites.

Characteristics of the age

Between about 1350 to 1050 B.C. some twelve judges appeared in Israel. The time of the judges extended from the death of Joshua and the elders of that time until God crowned Saul as Israel's first king.

During this period Israel shared a common language and worship. But there was no central government. There was a loose association of the twelve tribes, but most governmental functions were carried out in local villages and towns.

Insight: A pattern is found in the story of each judge that sums up the experience of God's people during this era:

Sin	The Israelites turn to idolatry.
Servitude	Neighboring people oppress them.
Supplication	Israel confesses and turns to God.
Salvation	God delivers them through a judge.
Silence	A period of peace ensues, during which the judge keeps the people faithful to the Lord.

Causes of decline

Judges 1–3

Joshua had destroyed the walled cities which were centers of Canaanite power, but many Canaanites remained in the territory given to each Israelite tribe. Each tribe was responsible to drive out the remaining peoples and to take full possession of its inheritance. Removal of the Canaanites was a religious duty, commanded by God because of the moral depravity of the Canaanites, whose worship of Baal and Ashtoreth incorporated sexual orgies and ritual prostitution by both sexes. God intended these sins to be purged from the land, not only as a divine judgment, but also to protect Israel from apostasy and adultery.

Each tribe failed. Some tribal groups were afraid to attack those Canaanites who lived on the plains because they had iron war

Baal was the primary god of the Canaanites. He was thought to control rains and fertility. They considered Baal to be the owner of the local lands.

chariots (1:17-21). Others defeated the Canaanites, but rather than driving them out of the promised land, they "forced the Canaanites to work as slaves for them" (1:27-36). This was in direct disobedience of God's command, and divine judgment was passed. God would not "force out the people in this land" (2:3). The result was that the remaining Canaanites intermarried with the Israelites and did draw them into immorality and idolatry.

Insight: Incomplete obedience still leads to disaster. It is dangerous to take that first step away from God. In contrast, Genesis 7:5 says, "Noah did everything that the Lord commanded him." And 9:1 says the result was, "Then God blessed Noah and his sons . . ."

Baal and Ashtoreth

Baal was the Canaanite name for their primary god. Baal was thought to control rains and fertility and was thought of as the owner of local lands. Ashtoreth was the goddess-consort of Baal.

The Canaanites worshiped their gods and goddesses in groves of trees and on hilltops, the "high places" referred to in the Old Testament. The religion was explicitly sexual as men and women engaged in intercourse to stimulate their gods into sexual acts, which were thought to guarantee fertility to crops and herds.

Further insight into Canaanite religion is gained from a reference in Jeremiah 19:5, which speaks of building "the high places of Baal to burn . . . sons in the fire as offerings to Baal" (NIV). Hundreds of years later the Carthaginians, who descended from the peoples who lived on Canaan's Mediterranean coast, still practiced child sacrifice to the goddess Tanit. Near the ruins of Carthage is a Topheth, or sacrificial area, like the one mentioned in Jeremiah 19. There thousands of urns marked by clay images of the goddess contain the remains of children from age two to twelve. They were burned alive as offerings to the goddess while the beating of drums kept the children's screams from their parents' ears.

No wonder God condemned the Canaanite civilization and commanded Israel to destroy its people completely. And no wonder the Israelites were judged severely when they were drawn away from the Lord into the practice of Canaanite rites.

Insight: The myth of the carefree pagan being free of the restrictions imposed by the Bible's strict God is just that, a myth. Only within the moral framework provided by faith in the one true God can an individual or society be truly happy and free.

Israel's important judges

Twelve persons are identified as judges (see chart page 71). Longer stories are told of Deborah, Gideon, Jephthah and Samson, each of whom probably led only a few tribes.

Deborah
Judges 4–5

Israel was a patriarchal society. The family line was carried on through men, and family inheritance went to sons. Leadership, too, was primarily male. Deborah is an exception who shows us that women were not excluded from leadership roles. The text says

This man is threshing grain. He throws the grain and chaff together into the air. The wind blows away the chaff, and the heavier, good grain falls back to the threshing floor. Gideon was threshing wheat when God called him.

Deborah was a prophetess as well as judge (4:4-7). She was so highly regarded that Barak, whom God called to command Israel's forces, refused to go into battle unless Deborah went with his army (4:8-16).

It is also significant that the chief enemy of Israel, Sisera, was killed by another woman, Jael.

Deborah's victory song (Judges 5) is recognized as one of the most beautiful poems ever written in any language.

Insight: The Bible contains other examples of women leaders. Among them were Esther, Priscilla (Acts 18), Lydia (Acts 16) and Phoebe, who was a deaconess (Romans 16:1-2).

Gideon
Judges 6–8

Judges 6:1-16: The name Gideon means "great warrior." But when we meet Gideon, he is hiding, trying to thresh a little wheat without being discovered by the oppressing Midianites.

Threshing in Bible times was usually done on hilltops, where the wind would blow away chaff tossed in the air while the heavier grain fell to the ground. But hilltop threshing might have been seen by the enemy who infested the land. Gideon's attempt to thresh grain in a winepress, which would have been constructed in a sheltered valley, shows how vulnerable the Israelites felt.

Gideon also felt his personal insignificance. As the least member of the weakest clan in Manasseh, how could he save Israel? God answered, "I will be with you" (6:16). Today, too, success does not depend on who we are, but on who is with us.

Judges 6:17-40: Even though Gideon had been given a sign by the angel who commissioned him, he begged God for signs. This was not an evidence of unbelief. Gideon had already acted on God's command and destroyed the local altar of Baal. His request was instead an admission of personal inse-

curity, and God gave him the signs for which he asked.

Insight: Obedience despite doubts is a sign of great faith.

Judges 7:1-25: God reduced the size of Gideon's army to make it very clear who had really delivered Israel. Though the release of thousands may have strained Gideon's faith, he continued to approach the enemy.

Judges 8:22-27: An ephod is a garment covering the chest, which in Old Testament times was used almost exclusively in worship. The golden ephod which Gideon made to commemorate his victory was quickly perverted into an object of worship for Israel and for Gideon's own family.

Insight: The Bible says that God is spirit (John 4:24). The Greek word *pneuma* means "wind." The acts of God are visible, but he can no more be seen than the wind. Jesus taught that our worship of God should not depend on visible aids, like the ephod, but should be "in spirit and in truth" (John 4:23).

Jephthah's daughter
Judges 10–12

Jephthah was an outcast recruited to lead Israel against an Ammonite oppressor. His constant references to the Lord in these chapters suggest he was a devout man. But what has troubled God's people is the vow he made to sacrifice "the first thing that comes out of my house to meet me" after victory. The first to come out was his only child, a daughter (11:29-40). Heartbroken, Jepthhah said, "I have made a promise to the Lord, and I cannot break it!" So, did Jephthah burn his daughter as an offering to the Lord?

While some have thought Jephthah did offer his daughter as a sacrifice, the weight of the evidence suggests that he did not. (1) Human sacrifice was forbidden in God's Law (Leviticus 20:2-5). (2) All burnt offerings must be made by a priest; no priest would offer a human being. (3) God also had a right

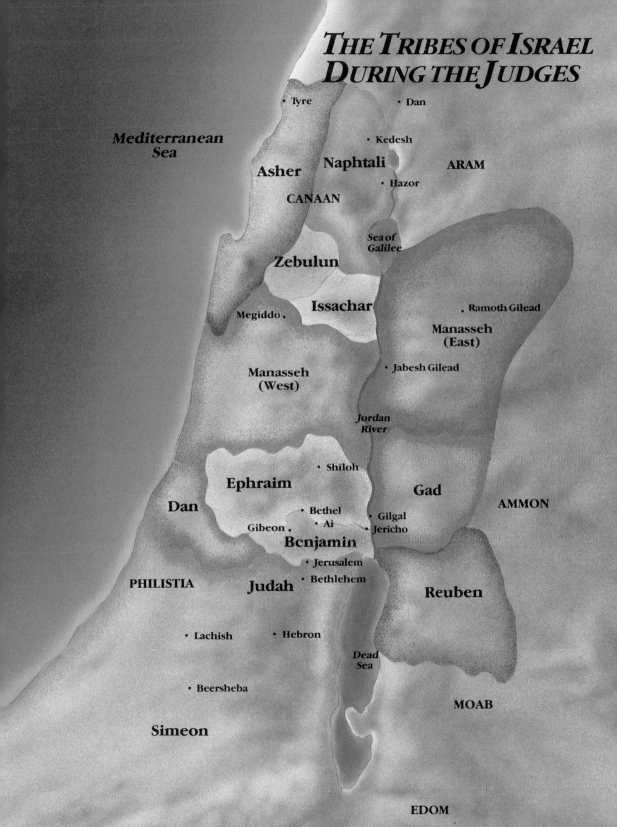

THE TRIBES OF ISRAEL DURING THE JUDGES

Mediterranean Sea

• Tyre

• Dan

• Kedesh

Asher

Naphtali

ARAM

CANAAN

• Hazor

Sea of Galilee

Zebulun

Issachar

• Ramoth Gilead

Megiddo •

Manasseh (East)

Manasseh (West)

• Jabesh Gilead

Jordan River

• Shiloh

Ephraim

Gad

AMMON

Dan

• Bethel

• Gilgal

• Ai

• Jericho

Gibeon •

Benjamin

PHILISTIA

• Jerusalem

• Bethlehem

Judah

Reuben

• Lachish

• Hebron

Dead Sea

• Beersheba

MOAB

Simeon

EDOM

to the firstborn of every human and animal. The animals were slain in sacrifice, but God took the Levites to serve him forever in worship (see Exodus 13). (4) A parallel exists in Samuel's dedication to God by his mother (1 Samuel 2:22). (5) Judges says the girl was given two months to lament because "I will never marry" (Judges 11:37). Our conclusion must be that she was dedicated to a life of service at the Tabernacle and was not killed as a blood sacrifice.

The Philistines

The Philistines were members of a sea people who invaded the southern Mediterranean from Crete. They crushed the Hittites and around 1200 B.C. attacked Egypt itself but were thrown back. These people controlled the coast of Palestine and built five major cities on the Mediterranean plain: Gaza, Ashkelon, Ashdod, Gath and Ekron. The Philistines, whom we meet in the story of Samson, were Israel's major enemy for the two hundred years between 1200 and 1000 B.C.

The warlike Philistines maintained military superiority because they held the secret of smelting iron. They made iron weapons, while the Israelites could not even sharpen iron-edged tools themselves (see 1 Samuel 13:19-22). The Philistines' superiority is shown by the fact that archaeologists have located Philistine outposts deep in Israel's territory not far from the Jordan River itself.

It was not until the time of King David (1010-970 B.C.) that Philistine power was finally broken, and their influence disappeared.

Samson

Judges 13–16

Samson is honored as history's strongest man. These chapters tell many of his exploits against the Philistines, but Samson's story is actually a tragedy. He was morally flawed, and his sexual passions led to his downfall. Samson's feud with the Philistines clearly was more of a personal vendetta than an effort to help his countrymen. While Samson killed many Philistines, he is the only judge

of which it is not said that he brought his people rest.

Samson's strength

Judges 16

Most city gates were made of two solid wood doors reinforced with metal bands and studs, and were locked with sturdy wood or metal bars. Gates were typically ten or more feet high. Samson tore this whole structure from the stone walls of Gaza and carried it on his back to the top of a hill that is 30 miles away!

Samson's hair

Numbers 6 describes the Nazirite vow, to be made as an act of special commitment to God. Not cutting one's hair was one element of this vow. Samson was under this vow from his birth (Judges 13:1-5). When Samson's hair was cut, the vow was violated and his God-given strength was withdrawn.

Israel's decline

Judges 17–21

Three incidents are reported in the final section of Judges. These incidents are not in chronological order but are intended to demonstrate how far the Israelites had declined since the days of Joshua.

Judges 17–18: Micah's idol. This story illustrates religious decline. Old Testament law forbade the making of idols. It ordained that sacrifices should only be offered at the Tabernacle and that only men of Aaron's line should serve as priests. Yet, here we see a householder, Micah, who is sure that God will bless him when he hires a Levite as priest to lead his family in worship at an idol's shrine!

Judges 19: The Levite's concubine. A concubine was a legal wife, but lacked the rights of a man's first or primary wife. Levites were members of a tribe set apart to serve God and teach his word. The homosexual rape intended by the men of the town at which they stayed called for the death penalty under Old Testament law. Yet the Levite's readiness to turn his concubine over to them probably shows his own moral bank-

The Twelve Judges

Name	Passage	Enemy	Years of suffering	Years of rule
1. Othniel	3:7-11		8	40
2. Ehud	3:12-30	Moabites	18	80
3. Shamgar	3:31			
4. Deborah	4,5	Canaanites	20	40
5. Gideon	6–8	Midianites	7	40
6. Tola	10:1,2			23
7. Jair	10:3,5			22
8. Jephthah	10:6–12:7	Ammonites	18	6
9. Ibzan	12:8-10			7
10. Elon	12:11-12			10
11. Abdon	12:13-15			8
12. Samson	13–16	Philistines	40	20

ruptcy. In the time of the judges even most religious leaders cared little for others or for what was right.

Judges 20–21: The Benjaminites. This story illustrates the decline of justice. Representatives from the other tribes called on the tribe of Benjamin to surrender those guilty of the rape and murder. Instead, the Benjaminites chose to defend them, and civil war erupted. The whole tribe was nearly wiped out in that war.

It is clear from these three incidents that during the era of the judges the people of Israel first lost their spiritual bearings and then the very foundations of morality.

Insight: Proverbs 9:10 says "the fear of the Lord is the beginning of wisdom." In Scripture "wisdom" is the ability to make right moral choices. Only when a society has a healthy respect for God will its people make right moral choices.

Ruth

The book of Ruth stands in bright contrast to the dark tales of the judges. Ruth lived during this same era, and the moral climate is reflected in Boaz's concern that Ruth might be harmed if she gathered grain in an other person's field (2:8-9). Yet Ruth, who made a commitment to Israel's God, is herself a godly person as is her mother-in-law Naomi and the man who married her, Boaz. Their presence shows that even in a sinful society godly people can live and remain faithful to the Lord.

The Book of Ruth also illustrates the important concept of the *go'el*, or kinsman-redeemer. A person who was a near relative could redeem, or buy back, possessions which another family member had lost. The kinsman-redeemer gives a picture of Christ, who became a true human being so that as our relative he might redeem us from the grip of sin.

12 Age of transition
1 Samuel

Samuel was Israel's last judge, and in his old age the people demanded a king. Israel's first king was Saul (1050-1010 B.C.), a man who was tragically flawed. This book of the Bible tells Saul's story and also introduces David, who was destined to become Israel's greatest ruler. This book also tells of Saul's jealousy at David's growing reputation and Saul's many efforts to kill his younger rival. Yet through it all, David remained faithful to his king and to his God.

MASTERY KEYS to the age of transition:

- What led the Israelites to ask for a king?
- How do Saul's responses to pressure reveal the weaknesses which made him an unsuitable ruler?
- What responses of David under pressure reveal strengths which made him suitable to be a ruler of God's people?

Hannah's prayer
1 Samuel 1–2

When the childless Hannah wept out her bitter prayer in the Tabernacle at Shiloh, she promised God that if he gave her a son, that boy would serve the Lord at his house. Some have criticized her for "bargaining" with God. Yet, in Hannah's prayer she surrendered to God the one thing that was most precious to her, the child she yearned for so much. Full surrender often must precede answers to our own prayers.

Samuel's childhood
1 Samuel 2–3

Hannah brought Samuel to the Tabernacle when he was three to be brought up by the priest, Eli. God began to speak to Samuel while he was still a child, and as he grew, all Israel realized that he was a prophet.

When Saul was king of Israel, God's Tabernacle was located at Shiloh. This was where God granted Hannah's prayerful request for a son.

The Ark
1 Samuel 4–6

The Ark was a special chest kept in the Tabernacle's inner sanctuary. It was the most holy object in Israel's religion and is often called the "Ark of the Covenant." It was at the Ark where God told Moses, "I will meet with you there . . . I will give you all my commands" (Exodus 25:22). Once a year, on the Day of Atonement, blood was sprinkled on the cover of the Ark to cleanse the Israelites from their sins (Leviticus 16). But Levi's sons and the people had a magical view of God and the Ark. They supposed that by taking it into battle God must war on their side. Instead, Israel lost, and the Ark was captured.

Later, God caused a plague that forced the Philistines to return the Ark. To underline his holiness, God struck dead seventy Israelites who violated God's Law by looking inside it. Any relationship with God must be based on obedience. We cannot "use" God, but rather we must submit to him.

Israel's call for a king
1 Samuel 7–9

Throughout Samuel's adult life Israel bested the Philistines in battle. God thus demonstrated that he was able to protect his people. Yet, when Samuel grew old and his sons proved ungodly, Israel demanded "a king to lead us, such as all the other nations have" (8:5). Deuteronomy 17 had foretold a time when Israel would have a king, but the motivation of this generation was wrong. Their request constituted a rejection of God as their ruler. God gave them a king but warned Israel that their kings would exploit and fail them.

Young Saul
1 Samuel 9–12

Saul was physically impressive, and before he became king, he was appropriately humble. Saul also gave credit to the Lord for his first military victory (11:13). Despite all this, Saul could not withstand the pressures of leadership.

1 Samuel 13: Facing an overwhelming Philistine force, Saul watched his army desert as he waited for Samuel to come and offer sacrifice. Finally Saul, though not a priest, made the sacrifice himself. Samuel called his action "foolish." The Hebrew term indicates a moral, rather than mental, deficiency. Note that even after Samuel came, Saul still had 600 men left.

Insight: This was twice as many men as God used to deliver Israel under Gideon. Saul disobeyed because he had no spiritual vision and failed to realize that God could deliver with few as well as with many.

1 Samuel 15: Saul permitted his army to take flocks from an enemy God had commanded him to totally destroy. Finally Saul admitted the reason: "I was afraid of the people, and I did what they said." Again sacred history should have instructed Saul. At Jericho Achan disobeyed God and took spoils from a city that was to be totally destroyed — and he was executed. Any punishment God decreed for Saul would be just.

1 Samuel 18: Saul was consumed by jealousy and fear. Awareness that God was no longer with Saul made him feel inadequate and insecure. Each indication that God was with David made Saul more jealous and fearful. These feelings motivated Saul to try to kill David.

1 Samuel 28: Near the end of his life, Saul, whose prayers to God for guidance were now answered, turned to occult religious practices. The "witch," a medium, was more shocked than Saul when the dead Samuel appeared and announced Saul's death in the coming battle. Again Saul acted against the known warning in the word of God to avoid the occult (Deuteronomy 18:9-13).

Saul's reign

Saul ruled Israel for 40 years but was never able to break Philistine power or to draw the loose association of tribes together into a unified nation. As the years passed and Saul drifted further from God, he became a moody, angry man, subject to fits of

The twenty-third psalm of David reveals David as a young shepherd, imagining himself as a sheep being cared for by the loving Shepherd.

deep depression. Saul also became desperately jealous of David, his son-in-law and a commander of Israel's forces. Saul spent his last years attempting to hunt down and kill the man God had chosen to succeed him.

David

1 Samuel 16

Samuel was sent to the family of Jesse to anoint one of his sons as Israel's next king. God indicated that the youngest son, David, was his choice. Samuel was surprised; though David was handsome, he did not have the commanding stature of Saul. God's response to Samuel is one of the simplest, yet most profound, sayings in Scripture: "People look at the outside of a person, but the Lord looks at the heart" (vs 7). Saul had been tall. David was godly.

In the psalms that David wrote, the Bible preserves a clear insight into his heart. We see David as a young shepherd, imagining himself as a sheep cared for by the Shepherd, God (Psalm 23). We discover his wonder at the beauty in God's world and note that he is ever ready to praise (Psalms 8–9). We see David in his moments of anxiety and observe him share every emotion with the Lord (Psalm 31). We sense David's deep trust in and love of God's word (Psalm 119). Most of all we see the depth of David's appreciation for God himself and his conviction that God truly is good (Psalm 103). Because David expressed so openly what he thought and felt, we know David better than we know most Bible men and women.

David's early life
1 Samuel 17–26

A series of stories in 1 Samuel gives us additional insights into this youth who became Israel's greatest king.

1 Samuel 17:4: Goliath was truly an awe-inspiring individual, 9'9" tall. His coat of mail weighed 125 pounds, and his spear had a 15-pound tip. All Israel was terrified, including Saul, who was the tallest among his people (see 1 Samuel 10:23). Only David had spiritual vision to realize "the Lord does not need swords or spears to save people" (17:47). Studies by archaeologists of Israelite houses of this period suggest the typical Hebrew man was only about five feet tall. This helps us understand the Israelites' fears—and appreciate David's faith.

Insight: An ancient tradition identifies a tribe called the Anakim as giants. These are not only mentioned in the Old Testament. The Anakim of Palestine are also mentioned in Egyptian "execration texts" intended to curse Pharaoh's enemies, dating back to 2000 B.C.

---

1 Samuel 18–19: Saul became insanely jealous of David's many military successes. Reference to an "evil spirit from God" that moved Saul does not imply God directs evil spirits. Rather it underlines the fact that Saul, who had abandoned the Lord, was now vulnerable to Satan's temptations. God permitted this as a consequence of Saul's own wrong choice, just as God has ordained that any pattern of morally wrong choices will have painful consequences for the sinner.

1 Samuel 20: Jonathan is one of the Bible's most admirable men. He realized that God intended David to succeed his father, Saul. Rather than being jealous, Jonathan defended David against Saul's accusations and proved to be a firm friend.

1 Samuel 21: The extent of Saul's decline is seen in his execution of 85 priests because

their patriarch had aided David unknowingly when told David was on a mission for King Saul. David was devastated, aware of his own responsibility for the tragedy. The one son who escaped, Abiathar, joined David and became Israel's high priest after David was crowned king.

1 Samuel 25: Abigail's quick action and willingness to take responsibility saved her family and prevented David from an act of bloody revenge. David so admired her wis-

David hid in these caves near the town of En-gedi when he was running from King Saul who was trying to kill him.

dom and beauty that when God struck her husband dead, David married her. Her husband's name, Nabal, means one who has foolishly hardened his heart. Nabal deserved punishment, but private citizens, as David was then, could not take justice into their own hands.

1 Samuel 24,26: David twice spared Saul's life when the king was pursuing him. He refused to kill the one whom God had

David was first sent to King Saul to comfort him by playing a small harplike instrument called a lyre. Musical notations in the Psalms indicate they were often used as songs and accompanied by lyres and other instruments.

anointed ruler of his people. The Jews thought a person anointed to a ministry had been appointed to it by God. David was determined to do nothing wrong but to wait for God to keep his promise and make him king.

Insight: In other lands, and later in Israel, kings were often assassinated by those who wanted to take their place (see 2 Kings 8:7-15; 9:14-29). David was careful not to set such a precedent. No kings in David's family line were assassinated.

---

1 Samuel 27,29: David was not immune to depression. Finally he became so discouraged that he led his band out of Israel into Philistine territory. The king of Gath, a principal Philistine city, knew that Saul was trying to kill David, and so he welcomed David. In biblical times mercenaries from other nations were often recruited into military service. The Philistine king saw David as a fierce fighter who would battle against Saul.

When war did come, the other Philistine rulers refused to let David's forces accompany their armies for fear he would betray them in the battle. David pretended disappointment, but he must have been rejoicing within.

The occult
1 Samuel 28

The Bible makes it clear that there are supernatural or occult forces. Deuteronomy 18 condemns every sort of occult practice, including mediums and spiritists. Modern expressions of the occult include palmistry and astrology. These are associated with evil rather than with God. Saul violated God's known will concerning the occult by visiting the medium, for he had previously ordered all practitioners destroyed.

Saul and David

Saul and David stand in vivid contrast in this Old Testament book. As young men each seems admirable. Yet as the years pass, the character of each is clearly revealed.

Saul is blind to spiritual realities and unwilling to obey God. His weaknesses consume him, and his dark nature is expressed in jealousy, anger and murder.

David, under pressures even greater than those which caused Saul's collapse, retains a clear vision of God as a real and present help. David consistently tries to make choices that will please God, and even in his failures he is quick to admit his faults. It is this, David's sensitivity to the Lord, which marks him as a man after God's own heart, who is spiritually equipped to become Israel's greatest king.

13 The United Kingdom

2 Samuel; 1 Kings

The United Kingdom was the period of time when Saul, David and Solomon ruled over all Israel. After Solomon ruled, the nation was divided into a northern kingdom, Israel, and a southern one, Judah. Upon Saul's death, David was recognized as king by the tribe of Judah. Seven years later all Israel was united under his rule. During the years that David and his son Solomon ruled, Israel reached the pinnacle of national power and glory. David expanded Israel's territory some ten times by military conquest. Relying on diplomacy, Solomon retained that territory. Solomon's control of trade routes brought Israel untold riches. And Solomon constructed the great Jerusalem Temple of which his father David had dreamed.

MASTERY KEYS to the United Kingdom:

- What characterized Israel under David and Solomon?
- What was the significance of David's capture of Jerusalem?
- How do David's and Solomon's failings compare?

David's accomplishments

As king, David proved to be a military and an organizational genius.

First, David crushed the Philistines, destroying the power of this people who had been Israel's major enemy for 200 years. With his victory he also gained the secret of smelting iron for weapons and tools. David also at-

Israel captured Jerusalem from the Philistines under the reign of King David. This Arch of David is at David's fortress in Jerusalem.

tacked and defeated enemies on Israel's other borders, making them vassal states. With his borders expanded and secure, David set about unifying his kingdom.

He captured Jerusalem, which lay on the border between Judah and Israel's other ten tribes. David made this his capital, thus avoiding the charge of favoritism which might have been raised if he had chosen a site within a tribal area.

David then established Jerusalem as the religious and political capital by bringing the Ark of the Covenant there. He reorganized worship, setting up shifts of priests and Levites to offer continual praise to God. David himself contributed many of the praise psalms which were used in public worship.

David established a standing army with 288,000 trained soldiers. Each month 24,000 of them were on active duty while the rest worked their land.

In addition, David established a strong central government, with governors responsible for each national district (see 2 Samuel 8:15-18; 20:23-26).

Under David the twelve tribal territories were bound together into a single, united nation. David mastered virtually everything from southern Syria in the north to the Gulf of Aqaba in the south, and from the Mediterranean Sea to the desert on the east. Two exceptions were the city-states of Phoenicia and Philistia. Evidently David had friendly relations with the king of Phoenicia, and, though the Philistines were not actually subject to David, he certainly had them under control.

Significance of Jerusalem
2 Samuel 5

With its capture, Jerusalem became a key city in Bible history and prophecy. The Temple was built there. It served as the political and religious capital of the United Kingdom and later of Judah. Seventy years after its destruction by the Babylonians in 586 B.C., Jewish captives returned to rebuild the city and Temple. It remained the center of Jewish faith and life until it was destroyed by the Romans

in A.D. 70. Jesus taught in Jerusalem and was crucified outside its walls. The prophets promised peace in Jerusalem when the Messiah came (Jeremiah 33:15-16), and the book of Revelation speaks of a "new Jerusalem" that will be present in eternity (Revelation 21).

The death of Uzzah
2 Samuel 6

Events associated with transportation of the Ark of the Covenant to Jerusalem have troubled many Bible readers. The Ark had rested on the land of a man named Abinadab since it had been returned by the Philistines nearly 60 years earlier (see 1 Samuel 4–6). But David's people violated rules for transporting the Ark by placing it uncovered on a cart (see Numbers 4:1-20). When the cart tipped and Uzzah reached out to support the Ark, God struck Uzzah dead.

David was afraid and angry and for three months refused to have anything to do with the Ark. Yet when God blessed the man on whose land the Ark rested, David found the courage to try again. This time he must have consulted the law, for the Ark was carried and then placed in a worship tent David had prepared in Jerusalem. But why had Uzzah died? Numbers 4 warns that the holy things from the inner room of the Tabernacle were to be covered with skins before even the Levites assigned to carry them could approach. They should "not enter and look at the holy things, even for a second. If they do, they will die." If God's Old Testament people were to obey the Lord, they had to hold him in awe and deepest respect. Uzzah's death emphasized for David and for his people that the Lord truly is holy and always must be respected as such.

The Davidic covenant
2 Samuel 7

After David's kingdom was secured, he wanted to build a temple to the Lord. God did not permit this but, instead, promised to build David a "house." In this context "house" means family line. God promised that there would always be a descendant of David qualified to take Israel's throne. Psalm 89:3 calls this promise a covenant, a formal promise like God's early promise to Abraham.

During the centuries that followed, a descendant of David did rule in Judah. The New Testament takes great pains to show that Jesus was from David's line, thus establishing Christ's right to be Israel's king (see Matthew 1:1-16).

Insight: Is anyone today qualified to take the throne of David? Yes, of course. Jesus was raised from the dead, and he lives today as Lord of Lords and King of Kings, David's far greater son.

David's sins
2 Samuel 11–12; Psalm 51

Although David loved God, he was far from perfect. David's affair with Bathsheba and his plot to have her husband Uriah killed in battle were terrible sins. What made David different from Saul, who had been king before him? When confronted, Saul made excuses. But David immediately confessed. Because David's was a public sin, his confession was also public. It is found in Psalm 51, which the superscription indicates was set to music and used in worship! The psalm reveals David's anguish over his sin and his appeal to God for cleansing.

In Scripture, guilt is not a feeling. It involves: (1) personal accountability for our sin-

The City of David was built inside Jerusalem as a place of protection for King David. Eventually the entire city of Jerusalem was known as the City of David because it surrounded the citadel.

ful acts and their consequences, (2) a state of being guilty in God's sight and (3) liability to punishment. God deals with guilt by forgiving our sins. Psalm 51 makes it clear that guilt does affect our feelings, but it is the *fact* of guilt we must deal with, not just guilt feelings.

In contrast to David, Saul admitted his sin to Samuel only and then begged Samuel to "honor me in front of my people's older leaders. Please honor me in front of the Israelites" (1 Samuel 15:30). Only David was completely honest with himself, with God and with others in dealing with his sin.

Insight: What does it mean to "confess" our sins? The original words in Hebrew and in Greek mean "to acknowledge," to admit fault without trying to hide the truth.

Failure as a father
2 Samuel 13–19

David, so wise in public policy, was not wise in governing his own family. He failed to deal with the rape of Absalom's sister Tamar by her half-brother (13:21). When Absalom murdered the half-brother, David again failed to act. And when David did recall Absalom from exile, he failed to see him for either reconciliation or discipline (14:28). David loved his son, but his failure to deal with family problems as they arose surely contributed to Absalom's later rebellion.

Insight: First Chronicles 3 lists 22 sons of David by 9 wives "besides his sons by his concubines!" With that many children and a kingdom to rule, David could hardly find quality time to give to any of his sons or daughters.

Living psalms
2 Samuel 16; Psalm 3

David was understandably shaken by his son Absalom's rebellion. As David often did, he expressed his thoughts and feelings in poetry. Psalm 3 was written at this time.

From it we discover that David realized that many thought God had deserted him (Psalm 3:1-2). Many may have lost confidence in David when they realized the extent of his sin with Bathsheba. Yet David had experienced God as his shield and strength [the meaning of "lifts up my head"] (3:3,4, NIV). So David will lie down and be able to sleep despite the thousands who are against him. Even in the present danger "the Lord sustains me" (3:5-6, NIV).

Insight: Other psalms which speak against specific experiences of David include Psalm 34 (see 1 Samuel 21:10-15), Psalm 52 (see 1 Samuel 21–22), Psalm 54 (see 1 Samuel 2–3), Psalm 57 (see 1 Samuel 22,24), Psalm 59 (see 1 Samuel 19:11-23).

David in 2 Samuel

1. David is very sad for Saul (1:1-12)	11. David is kind to Jonathan's son (9)
2. David is made king of Judah (2:1-7)	12. David defeats the Ammonites (10:1-19)
3. David battles Ish-bosheth (3:6-21)	13. David sins with Bathsheba (11:1-17)
4. David kills two murderers (4:5-12)	14. David is warned by a prophet (12:1-14)
5. David is made king of all Israel (5:1-5)	15. David's son Absalom turns against him (15:1-12)
6. David conquers Jerusalem (5:6-12)	16. David's army kills Absalom (18:1-18)
7. David defeats the Philistines (5:17-25)	17. David lets Gibeonites have revenge (21)
8. David brings the ark to Jerusalem (6)	18. David counts his army (24:1-17)
9. David is promised the kingdom forever (7)	19. David makes Solomon king (1 Kings 1)
10. David defeats other enemies (8:1-14)	

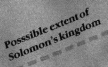

CYPRUS

Posssible extent of
Solomon's kingdom

SIDON   ARAMEANS
• Sidon
          • Damascus
• Tyre   • Dan

Mediterranean Sea

              *Jordan
              River*
  • Megiddo   • Ramoth Gilead

*Plain of
Sharon*   ISRAEL
Shechem •   *Jabbok River*

PHILISTIA Jerusalem
           •   AMMON
    • Ashdod
Ashkelon •
          • Lachish
                *Dead
• Gaza   Hebron Sea*
         •
    • Beersheba   MOAB
   JUDAH

  • Kadesh Barnea
      EDOM

DAVID AND
SOLOMON'S
KINGDOM

• Ezion Geber

Solomon
1 Kings 1–14

Absalom was killed in the rebellion, and after several more years as king, David passed his throne to another son, Solomon, whose mother was Bathsheba. How complete God's forgiveness is when we confess all to him.

When God appeared to the newly appointed king, Solomon asked only for "a discerning heart to govern your people and to distinguish between right and wrong" (3:9, NIV). God was pleased and not only gave Solomon wisdom but also promised him riches and honor.

Solomon's 40-year reign was a time of peace and prosperity. Solomon maintained a powerful army and built a number of fortified cities but fought no wars. Instead he wove a network of treaties with surrounding powers.

Solomon's wealth was legendary. He had copper mines at Ezion Geber. He built fleets that set out on three-year trading ventures, returning with gold, silver, jewels, ivory and animals (1 Kings 10:14-22). Solomon's businesses earned the king some 65,000 pounds of gold a year. At just $450 an ounce, that would be $468,000,000 a year!

Solomon's building plans were costly, and despite his wealth, Solomon taxed his people heavily. Thousands were pressed into service to work on his cities and buildings. This practice, called corvée, was common in the ancient world. Yet, the burden was felt by the Israelites and led to political unrest. When Solomon died, his kingdom was divided.

Solomon exhibited great intellectual curiosity throughout his life. The Bible tells us he wrote 3,000 proverbs, or wise sayings. Many of these are found in the Old Testament book of Proverbs. He also wrote 1,005 songs. Solomon studied plants and animals carefully. People came from all over the world to visit Solomon's court. One of the best known visitors, the Queen of Sheba, traveled 1,000 miles from what is now Yemen.

Yet, as Solomon grew older, he made a number of poor choices. To confirm his treaties with foreign powers, he married the daughters of pagan kings, who worshiped idols. Solomon permitted these idols to be put up in Jerusalem and even came to the point of worshiping them himself. Unlike David at the end of his life, Solomon lost sight of God.

The Jerusalem Temple
1 Kings 6–8

The Temple, built in 960 B.C., was to be the only place of worship and sacrifice for Israel. Unlike other ancient temples, the Jerusalem Temple was not viewed as a residence for God (1 Kings 8:27-30) but rather as a place where God and men might meet.

Solomon's magnificent Temple was overlaid with gold. At today's typical $450 an ounce, the value of the gold was around $35,742,857,000! Yet the spiritual value of the Temple far outweighed monetary considerations. Here Israel was to gather for the annual feasts commanded in the Law. Here sacrificial offerings might be made for the sins of the people. If God's people strayed, and God brought disasters on Israel, the people might come to the Temple to confess their sins and find forgiveness. The Temple was the visible symbol of God's presence and his forgiveness.

Solomon's Temple was destroyed by the Babylonians in 586 B.C. The second temple (or Zerubbabel's temple) was begun by the returned exiles under Zerubbabel's leadership in 536 B.C. It was finished in 516 B.C. (It lay incomplete for many of those years. The completion process began in 520.)

Herod's temple, a 46-year building project begun in 20 B.C., was a remodeling and magnificent enlargement of Zerubbabel's. It was Herod's temple that Jesus knew, a temple which was destroyed in its turn by the Romans in A.D. 70.

14 The books of poetry

Psalms; Proverbs; Job; Ecclesiastes; Song of Solomon

Four of the poetic books were largely written during the golden age of David and Solomon. Each has a different theme. Of the two best known, Psalms teaches the way to an intimate, personal relationship with God, while Proverbs teaches practical wisdom for living day by day.

MASTERY KEYS to the books of poetry:
- What is the distinctive theme and value of each of these five books?
- What characteristics help us understand Hebrew poetry?

Hebrew poetry

The verses of the Bible's poetic books do not rhyme as English poetry traditionally has. Yet the psalms and proverbs are poetry. While the stress placed on syllables in poetic lines is important, Hebrew poetry is really based on various patterns of expressing thoughts, rather than on patterns of sounds. Thus, rhyming words have no role in Hebrew poetry.

The basic unit of Hebrew poetry is the verse. In each verse the first line states a theme, and following lines develop that theme in one of three ways. This way of building thought upon thought is called "parallelism."

In *synonymous* parallelism the second line simply repeats the thought of the theme line:
"Lord, return and save me.
Save me because of your kindness."
(Psalm 6:4)

In *antithetical* parallelism the theme is emphasized by a second line, which contrasts with the thought expressed in the first line:
"Happiness makes a person smile.
But sadness breaks a person's spirit."
(Proverbs 15:13)

In *synthetic* parallelism following lines will amplify or develop the theme stated in the first line:
"The Lord does what is right, and
he loves justice.
So honest people will see his face."
(Psalm 11:7)

These are the ruins of an ancient farmer's house in Hebron. The home was the center of family life. The books of poetry and proverbs often used mnemonic devices to help parents teach their children God's law.

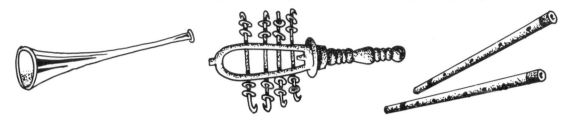

Some psalms have other distinctive features. In *acrostic* psalms the first letter of each verse starts with the succeeding letter of the Hebrew alphabet. Psalm 119 is a complicated acrostic psalm, and the words *aleph, bet,* etc., that separate its sections, are the Hebrew letters with which each verse in the section begins.

Insight: Poetry that relies on rhyme is difficult to translate. Because Hebrew poetry relies on images and patterns of ideas, it can be translated into almost any language without loss of power or beauty.

The psalms

Many of the psalms were written in the time of David, and 73 were written by David himself. Others were added later, with the final book (Psalms 107–150) probably added in the time of Ezra about 450 B.C.

There are many different kinds of poems in the book of Psalms:

(1) *Praise psalms,* which help us focus on God and express appreciation to him. Among these are Psalms 33, 103 and 139.

(2) *Historical psalms,* which review what God has done for his people. Among the historical psalms are 68, 78, 105 and 106.

(3) *Fellowship psalms,* which are about the loving relationship God maintains with believers. Among the fellowship psalms are 16, 20 and 23.

(4) *Imprecatory psalms,* which emotionally call on God to punish evildoers. Among these psalms are 35, 69, 109 and 137.

(5) *Confession psalms,* which express to God personal sorrow over failures and sins.

Among confession psalms are 6, 32, 51, 102, 130 and 143.

(6) *Messianic psalms,* which predict aspects of Jesus' life and ministry. Among the Messianic psalms are 2, 8, 22, 40, 45, 72, 89, 110 and 132.

(7) *Worship psalms,* which were sung during special worship festivals held in Jerusalem. Among these psalms are 30, 92 and 120–134.

As a whole the book of Psalms makes a unique contribution to our understanding of personal relationship with the Lord. As we read this wonderful book, we realize that our God invites us to share all with him. He delights to listen to our joys; he cares about our fears and troubles. We can share every emotion with the Lord and be confident that he will work within us and in our circumstances to guide us toward peace and rest.

Praise

One of the greatest contributions of the Psalms is as a model for our praise. Praise is spoken directly to God, to express our appreciation of who he is and what he has done. Note these elements in Psalm 108:3-4. "Lord, I will praise you among the nations . . ." [the psalmist speaks directly to God]. "Your love is so great that it is higher than the skies. Your truth reaches to the clouds" [the psalmist praises God for his qualities].

The practice of praise has many benefits. Praise focuses our thoughts on God. Praise draws us nearer to God. Praise stimulates inner joy. But more important than any of these, God deserves and wants our praise. The Bible says that God seeks people who will worship him (John 4:23-24).

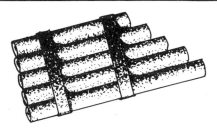

Proverbs

The book of Proverbs is filled with brief, pithy sayings on many subjects. The best way to outline Proverbs is by grouping its sayings:

I. Sayings concerning wisdom	1–9
II. Sayings of Solomon	10–22:16
III. Collected sayings	22:17–24:34
IV. More sayings of Solomon	25–29
V. Sayings of Agur and Lemuel	30–31

These sayings express general principles which apply to all persons and all times. But all general principles have exceptions. Thus, there is no conflict when Proverbs states the general principle, "when a man's ways are pleasing to the Lord, he makes even his enemies live at peace with him" (Proverbs 16:7), and Peter, who instructs the Christian how to respond when persecuted unfairly (1 Peter 3:13-18). Verses in Proverbs are *principles*, not *promises* made to God's own.

The sayings in the book of Proverbs cover many different subjects. Among them are attitudes toward work (10:45; 12:24; 13:4; 14:23; 18:9; 20:4,17), the dangers of desiring wealth (10:2,16; 11:4,16,18,28; 16:8) and instructions on our attitude toward the poor (13:8,23; 14:20, 31; 16:19; 17:5; 19:1).

Papyrus was a plant that grew along the River Nile in Egypt. Writings like Psalms and Proverbs were often done on paper made from the papyrus plant, such as the one below.

Job's visions of God

Job 38–41. In two powerful monologues, God confronts Job and demands that Job consider who God is. In each monologue God sets his own power and wisdom against the weaknesses of humankind. When Job realizes the truth of what God says, his attitude changes. He is now willing simply to trust God, rather than demand an explanation for his suffering. Job's vision of God is not intended to silence modern sufferers, but to help us trust. Who then is God?

God is Creator. He laid Earth's foundations, established its seas, and shaped its features (38:4-15).

God is Sustainer. He established light and darkness, the winds and the seasons (38:16-30).

God is Designer of the universe. He gave birth to the constellations, and established the laws that govern the heavens and the earth (38:31-38).

God is the Life Giver. He filled the Earth with animal life, each creature with its own unique beauty. He set the wild donkey free to roam the wastelands, designed the wings of the ostrich and stork, and gave the horse its strength. He taught the hawk to soar and implanted the instincts that lead the eagle to nest in the heights (38:39–40:30). All this displays the power and infinite wisdom of God.

God is Power. He designed creatures, like the behemoth (hippopotamus) and leviathan (crocodile), that no man can even subdue (40:15–41:34). Seeing God's greatness in creation, we are called to humility. The wonder is, this God of Creation has shown himself in Scripture to care for you and me, even as Job 42 demonstrates his care for Job.

Other topics discussed in this practical book include the use of the tongue (10:20; 15:1; 16:28; 21:23; 25:14) and personal qualities and character (11:22; 13:7; 22:3; 26:12; 30:33).

Insight: Jewish tradition says that Solomon wrote the Proverbs 31 praise of the noble wife in honor of his mother, Bathsheba. If so, this proverb casts special light on the character of the woman with whom David sinned.

Wisdom

The books of Proverbs, Job and Ecclesiastes are classified as "wisdom literature." In the Old Testament "wisdom" is a moral, rather than intellectual, trait. A person is wise if he or she makes right choices and in the process becomes a more godly person. In contrast, the "fool" in the Old Testament is one who is morally deficient and, therefore, chooses sinful paths.

Wisdom literature, then, focuses on the issue of making moral choices and is intended to help the reader evaluate and choose what is right. According to Proverbs 2:9, a person with wisdom will "understand what is honest and fair and right. You will understand what is good to do." And the expectation is that the truly wise will choose that good path.

Several psalms are also classified as wisdom literature. These are Psalms 19, 37, 104, 107, 147 and 148.

The book of Job may be the oldest book in the Bible. Its language is archaic. It makes no mention of either covenant or law. The name Job (*'iyyob*) was common in the second millennium B.C. Job may have been a contemporary of Abraham or the other patriarchs. If so, the book reveals how much ancient people knew of God before the Bible was written. From Job we learn that people saw God as a personal friend and as the Creator and Judge of men. The Lord was thought of as one who punishes evil and rewards those who do good. The book suggests people approached God through sacrifice and believed he would forgive sinners who repent. But there were many gaps in their knowledge of God. When Job experienced sudden tragedy, he and his friends were unable to reconcile what had happened with their ideas about God's justice.

Insight: Job wanted a logical explanation for his suffering, but what he received was an understanding of God's wisdom, resulting in a stronger personal trust in God.

Job Outline

Job explained

Job 1:1–2:10. Prosperous Job was "an honest man and innocent of any wrong. He honored God and stayed away from evil" (1:1). Satan challenged God to permit Job to suffer, cynically insisting Job would then deny the Lord. God permitted a series of disasters which devastated Job, yet Job did not deny God or "sin in what he said."

At this point Satan has been defeated and is not mentioned again in the book. But Job continues to suffer. Why?

Job 2:11–31. Three of Job's friends arrive to comfort him. For a long time they sit silent. Then the four begin to struggle with the why. The three friends are convinced that Job must have sinned to merit such punishment. God is the moral ruler of the universe; he does punish sinners. The enormity of Job's suffering must mean that Job has sinned terribly. But Job refuses to confess sin of which he is not aware. Yet Job has the same view of God that his friends have. Suffering has led Job to question his idea of what God is like, for Job

knows that his suffering is unprovoked.

Job 32–37. Now a younger onlooker speaks. Job and his three friends are all wrong, for they have assumed that suffering must always be punishment for sin. Elihu suggests that God may have other motives in permitting the godly to suffer: "He gets them to listen through their pain" (36:15). God may instruct through suffering and draw human beings closer to him.

Job 38–41. Then God himself speaks to Job "out of the storm." God does not explain his servant's suffering. Instead God points out how much greater in power and wisdom he is than a mere man. What Job must do when he suffers and cannot understand God's purposes, is acknowledge that God is God.

Job 42. This Job now does, withdrawing his foolish charge that God is unjust. God acknowledges Job as "my servant" (42:7) and gives Job "twice as much as he had owned before" (42:10).

Insight: The message of the book for those who suffer is this: do not try to understand God's motives but simply trust him to do that which is right and good. It is wrong to assume always that tragedy is God's punishment for sins.

Ecclesiastes

The book of Ecclesiastes was written by Solomon around 940-930 B.C. after he had wandered from God. In it Solomon sets out to discover, by reason apart from revelation, whether life has any meaning. It is important to understand that what Ecclesiastes reports is Solomon's reasoning, not God's teaching. Thus, such sayings as "the dead no longer think about such things. Dead people have no more reward" (9:5) is not God's word to us but is an inspired report of Solomon's conclusion.

How do we know this? Seven times Solomon says he "communed with my own heart" (KJV). Twenty-nine times he states that his conclusions are based on "what is done under the sun"; that is, on what he can observe in the physical universe.

Why, then, is this book in the Bible, and what does its inspiration imply? Inspiration guarantees that what is written is what God intended to communicate. And what the Lord teaches us through this book is that, apart from him, life has no meaning at all.

Yet, even human wisdom leads one to a vital conclusion. God must be acknowledged as Creator, and he must be remembered in the days of our youth. We must find God, for apart from him, all is meaningless indeed.

Ecclesiastes Outline

I. Prologue: All is meaningless   1:1-11
II. Proof of meaninglessness   1:12–6:12
III. If life is meaningless, then what?   7:1–12:8
IV. Epilogue: Conclusions   12:9-14

Wisdom from Ecclesiastes

"With much wisdom comes much disappointment. The person who gains more knowledge also gains more sorrow" (1:18).

"Anything I saw and wanted, I got for myself. I did not miss any pleasure I desired. I was pleased with everything I did. And this pleasure was the reward for all my hard work. Suddenly I realized it was just a waste of time, like chasing the wind!" (2:10-11).

"So I hated life. It made me sad to think that everything here on earth is useless. It is like chasing the wind. I hated all the things I had worked for here on earth. I hated them because I must leave them to someone who will live after me. Someone else will control everything for which I worked so hard here on earth. And I don't know if he will be wise or foolish" (2:17-19a).

"So I saw the best thing a person can do is to enjoy his work. That is all he has. No one can help a person see what will happen in the future" (3:22).

"The person who loves money will never have all the money he wants. The person who loves wealth will not be satisfied when he gets it. This is also useless" (5:10).

"I also saw all that God has done. Nobody can understand what God does here on earth. No matter how hard a person tries to understand it, he cannot. Even if a wise man says he understands, he really cannot. No one at all can understand it" (8:17).

"Enjoy life with the wife you love. Enjoy all the days of this short life God has given you here on earth. Whatever work you do, do your best. This is because you are going to the grave. There is no working, no planning, no knowledge, and no wisdom there" (9:9-10).

"Now everything has been heard. Here is my final advice: Honor God and obey his commands. This is the most important thing people can do. God knows everything people do, even the things done in secret. He knows all the good and all the bad. He will judge everything people do" (12:13-14).

Song of Solomon

King Solomon (970-930 B.C.) wrote this famous love poem. It has been interpreted by some as an allegory picturing the relationship between God and Israel or between Christ and his church. However, it has also been understood as a celebration of married love, affirming the beauty of the husband/wife relationship.

Insight: Song of Solomon is a dramatic poem. One effective way to study the Song of Solomon is to assign parts to different people in a group and read it aloud as a play. The drama unfolds in the following story.

Song of Solomon Outline

The bride longs for her groom. They meet and praise each other.   1:1–2:7

The bride praises her groom with figures from nature.   2:8–3:11

The groom comes and praises the bride.   4–5:1

The groom has gone away and the bride expresses longing for him.   5:2–6:3

The groom returns, the marriage takes place, and the new couple's happiness brings rejoicing.   6:4–8:14

15 Kings and prophets–Israel

1 Kings 12—2 Kings 18; Obadiah; Jonah; Amos; Hosea

Upon Solomon's death in 931 B.C., his great kingdom was divided into two hostile nations. For David's sake, and in keeping with the Davidic covenant (2 Samuel 7:11-16), Solomon's son Rehoboam ruled over Judah from Jerusalem. But the ten northern tribes of Asher, Zebulun, Naphtali, Issachar, Manasseh, Ephraim, Reuben, Simeon, Gad and Dan broke away to follow Jeroboam and to establish a nation called "Israel."

Every king of Israel did evil and led his people away from the Lord, despite the prophets sent from God. When the people refused to return to the Lord, Israel was finally destroyed by the Assyrians.

MASTERY KEYS to northern kingdom history:

- What were the religious foundations of Israel?
- Who were Israel's most significant kings, and what were their accomplishments?
- What prophets ministered to Israel, and what message did each bring?

Israel's religious foundations
1 Kings 12

Israel's first king, Jeroboam, had a problem. Every Jew was commanded by God to go to Jerusalem for three annual religious festivals—the Feast of Passover, the Feast of Pentecost (or Feast of Harvest) and the Feast of Tabernacles (or Feast of Ingathering). But

Assyrian soldiers are shown attacking the town of Lachish in this ancient relief.

Jerusalem was the capital of Judah, the southern part of Solomon's splintered kingdom. Jeroboam was afraid that his people's loyalty would revert to David's family if they made the required pilgrimages.

So Jeroboam established his own worship centers at Bethel and Dan. There he erected golden calves, on which the invisible Yahweh was supposed to stand or ride, and he appointed priests who were not from Aaron's family to offer sacrifices. He also developed his own religious calendar with new festivals. Jeroboam then set up shrines throughout the land for local worship. In every point Jeroboam's religious "reforms" counterfeited the religious observances commanded in God's Law. Every one of Israel's subsequent kings supported this perverted national religion. The people claimed to worship Yahweh, but even their worship was a violation of God's Law! No wonder Amos later delivered this message from God: "I hate your feasts. I cannot stand your religious meetings" (Amos 5:21).

God's warning
1 Kings 13–14

The day Jeroboam consecrated the altar of sacrifice at Bethel, God sent an unnamed prophet from Judah to pronounce judgment. In the future a king of Judah, to be named Josiah, would desecrate the evil altar by burning on it the bones of dead men. (This prophecy was fulfilled some 300 years later! 2 Kings 23:15-20) The prophet said, "This altar will break apart. And the ashes on it will fall onto the ground." As the prophet spoke, the altar cracked as a sign authenticating his words. Furious, King Jeroboam pointed to the prophet to order him killed, but the king's arm shriveled up.

The incident gives us insight into the office of the Old Testament prophet. These messengers from God carried warnings and instruction to the Hebrew people and their leaders. While they often announced things which would happen in the distant future, their message was typically authenticated by an immediate "sign." The sign might be a miracle but most often was a prediction which quickly came true, and which thus proved that God spoke or acted through them (Deuteronomy 18:14-22).

Kings and prophets of Israel

Kings ♛	*Prophets*	*Date*
☐ Jeroboam I	*Unnamed man of God*	930-909 B.C.
	Ahijah	
☐ Nadab		909-908 B.C.
☐ Baasha	*Jehu son of Hanani*	908-886 B.C.
☐ Elah		886-885 B.C.
☐ Zimri		885 B.C.
☐ Tibni		885-880 B.C.
☐ Omri		880-874 B.C.
☐ Ahab	*Elijah*	874-853 B.C.
	Elisha	
	An unnamed prophet	
	Micaiah	
	Obadiah (?)	
☐ Ahaziah		853-852 B.C.
☐ Joram	*Elisha*	852-841 B.C.
☐ Jehu	*Elisha*	841-814 B.C.
☐ Jehoahaz		814-798 B.C.
☐ Jehoash	*Elisha*	798-782 B.C.
☐ Jeroboam II	*Jonah*	793-753 B.C.
	Amos	
	Hosea	
☐ Zechariah		753 B.C.
☐ Shallum		752 B.C.
☐ Menahem	*Hosea*	752-742 B.C.
☐ Pekah		752-732 B.C.
☐ Pekahiah		742-740 B.C.
☐ Hoshea		732-723 B.C.

Mediterranean Sea

SIDON

ARAM

• Damascus

• Dan

Sea of
Galilee

• Megiddo
• Jezreel

• Ramoth Gilead

Jordan
River

• Samaria

KINGDOM
OF ISRAEL

• Succoth

AMMON

• Jericho

• Jerusalem

PHILISTIA

• Lachish • Hebron

Dead
Sea

• Beersheba

MOAB

Brook of
Egypt

KINGDOM
OF JUDAH

EDOM

• Kadesh Barnea

THE KINGDOMS OF
JUDAH AND ISRAEL

The prophet's death
1 Kings 13

The prophet who delivered God's warning was told not to eat or drink in Israel. He violated this command and was killed by a lion. Why did God cause the death of the prophet who delivered his message to Jeroboam? It was to demonstrate to all Israel and to us that God must be obeyed completely; no sin, and surely no sin like that of Israel at Bethel, would be ignored.

Jeroboam's judgment
1 Kings 14

The prophet Ahijah announced the death of the wicked king's ill son and the future death of every male in Jeroboam's line.

Without a biblical religious foundation, Israel was politically and morally unstable. King after king of Israel met a violent end; many were assassinated and replaced on the throne by their killers.

The ten "lost" tribes

Many have assumed that ten of the Hebrew tribes were "lost" when the Assyrians carried the people of Israel into captivity. The Bible never indicates a return of the Israelites. Were the ten northern tribes "lost"? No, but they were dispersed by the Assyrians. They moved some Israelites out and moved other conquered peoples in. This was the Assyrians' way of blurring national identities of subject nations. This new mixed breed of people in northern Israel became the Samaritans of the New Testament.

When Jeroboam I set up his false worship system, many Israelites who loved God left to settle in Judah (2 Chronicles 11:13-17). When the kingdoms divided Judah could muster only 180,000 fighting men (1 Kings 12:21). Some 20 years later the extent of the desertion is seen when Judah's army had swelled to 400,000 (2 Chronicles 13:3). Clearly thousands from each of the ten northern tribes had moved to Judah. So, no tribes were "lost" when the Assyrians took Israel's citizens into captivity; representatives of every tribe lived in Judah.

Prophets who ministered in Israel

The books that record the history of Israel mention many prophets God sent to his straying people. In the next chapter we look in depth at two prophets who left no writings, but who had a vital ministry during the years Ahab and Jezebel sought to replace worship of Yahweh with worship of Baal.

There were other prophets whose messages to Israel have been preserved as Old Testament books. Studying these books against the background of Israel's dark history helps us understand the depth of God's concern for his people despite their sins.

Obadiah

This brief, one-chapter writing may be the oldest prophetic book. It is a prophecy against the Edomites. These descendants of Esau had threatened Israel during the Exodus (Numbers 20:14-21) and had been subdued later by David's armies. After David's time, Israel and Edom continued to fight periodically for the next 200 years. The Edomites lived south of Judah in the area between the Dead Sea and the Gulf of Aqaba. The book announces God's judgment on Edom for their support of an attack on Jerusalem.

The attack referred to probably took place about 844 B.C. by allied Philistines and Arabians (2 Chronicles 21:16-17). God would be faithful to his promise to Abraham and bless those who blessed his people but curse those who mistreated them.

Jonah

Jonah was a patriot and a popular prophet during the reign of Jeroboam II. His early prophecies foretold the victories by which Jeroboam expanded his nation's borders and which led to unparalleled prosperity (2 Kings 14:23-25).

But then, around 760 B.C. Jonah was called by God to travel to Nineveh, the capital of the nation whose armies were destined to destroy Jonah's homeland. Jonah's book breaks naturally into four chapters.

Jonah Outline

Tarshish: 1:3. This city on the Spanish coast is in the opposite direction from Nineveh. Jonah wanted to get as far from Nineveh as he possibly could.

The great fish: 1:17. The Hebrew does not say "whale" or identify any species. The unusually large fish was prepared and placed by God to swallow Jonah when he was thrown overboard.

Jonah's "death:" 2:2,7. With his "life ebbing away" Jonah did call out to God. Jesus said that as Jonah was in the fish's belly for three days, so he himself would be three days in the grave (Matthew 12:39-41).

Nineveh: 3:1. With its suburbs Nineveh was a city of 120,000 people. As Jonah walked through it, he cried, "After 40 days, Nineveh will be destroyed" (Jonah 3:4).

Repentance: 3:6-10. The king led the people in repentance. Wearing sackcloth and sitting in the dust showed contrition. Most importantly, the king decreed everyone must "turn away from his evil life. Everyone must stop doing harm." Repentance involves not only a change of heart but a change of moral direction.

God relents: 3:10. Why did Jonah's words not come true? In Scripture prophetic warnings assume an "implied condition." The disaster of which a prophet warns will come unless those who are warned turn to God and change their ways. Jonah understood this principle and had taken a ship to Tarshish because he feared Nineveh might repent and not be destroyed.

Jonah's complaint: 4:1-2. Jonah also understood that God was compassionate. Yet Jonah was angry with God for having compassion on the city, its 120,000 people and many cattle.

The message of Jonah to Israel: What happened in Nineveh was an object lesson for Israel. God would soon send Amos and Hosea to Israel. If only Israel would repent, they too might be spared.

Amos

Amos lived in Judah when God called him to go to the centers of wealth in Jeroboam II's Israel and announce judgment. Amos' book reveals the oppression of the poor that marred a prosperous society. The word that identifies Amos as a "shepherd" means "sheep rancher," rather than simple shepherd. (Amos also means "burden" or "burden-bearer.") God may have sent a godly rich man to speak to the wealthy sinners of Israel.

Amos Outline

"For three transgressions, even for four:" 1:6,9,11,13; 2:4,6 (NIV). The repeated phrase means "for many sins."

Three sermons: 3–6. The first sermon (3:1-15) reminds Israel that all the prophets warn that sin (the cause) leads to judgment (the effect). The second sermon (4:1-13) details Israel's refusal to repent, despite judgments which God sent as warnings. The third sermon (5:1–6:14) is an urgent invitation to "seek God and live" (NIV). Amos teaches that seeking God will be demonstrated by a commitment of God's people to justice.

Visions of judgment: 7–9:10. The visions tell of past judgments delayed but warn that now judgment is certain and near.

Kingdom vision: 9:11-15. After the judgment God will yet restore David's line to the throne and through a descendant of David will bring peace to all nations and blessing to Israel.

Hosea

At God's command Hosea married a woman who was, or became, a prostitute. His pain reflected the pain of God, for the Lord had been like a husband to unfaithful Israel.

Hosea's book is made up of sermons that the prophet must have preached many times. Hosea ultimately bought back his straying wife from one of her lovers, but Israel refused to return to God. Israel continued her spiritual adultery by worshiping idols and engaging in the sexual sins which were then associated with idolatry. Yet the prophet foretells a coming day when Israel will be God's own: "My people," who with deep and renewed love will again confess, "You are our God" (2:21-23).

Hosea Outline

Israel's end

Despite God's patience and his love, and despite the prophets he sent, the nation of Israel lasted for only 200 years. Eight of her nineteen kings were murdered or committed suicide. Not one was considered good by God. And, finally, the terrible judgment, which it so pained God to send, did come. The Assyrian army swept into the land, devastated its cities and took away its population. The evil kingdom finally came to its end in 721 B.C.

Vision of a sin-cursed society. Many verses in Amos reveal the sins in Israel which so disturbed God. God can hardly be less disturbed when he sees such practices in our society. See, for instance, 4:1; 5:10,12 and 8:4-6.

When Amos prophesied, great social changes were taking place in Israel. Jeroboam II's military and political victories gave Israel control of trade routes and created a wealthy city class.

Old Testament law gave each family land to work and live on. Family land was not to be sold, but kept from generation to generation. Now high taxes forced farmers to borrow from the newly rich. The wealthy then foreclosed and took away family farms to build great country estates. Amos cried out against the injustice and the uncaring attitude of the rich, who resorted to bribery to cheat the poor and who would gladly sell a man into servitude for the price of a pair of sandals (5:12; 8:4-6).

He graphically pictures their wives, feasting daily as they recline on ivory couches, gaily crying, "Bring us some drinks!" as their countrymen starve (4:1). In Samaria, Israel's capital, archaeologists have found ivory inlays that may have been in the furniture of the very women Amos condemns!

Insight: What are marks of injustice in a society? Amos provides the following criteria: oppression of the poor (4:1); bias against the poor in the justice system (5:12); a denial of God (5:25-27); insensitivity of the wealthy to the needs of others (6:4-6); dishonest business practices (8:4-5); a passion for wealth (8:4-6).

16 Elijah and Elisha

1 Kings 17—2 Kings 13

The quarter century between 875 B.C. and 850 B.C. was critical in Israel's history. King Ahab, urged by his evil queen Jezebel, made a concerted effort to replace worship of Yahweh with the worship of Baal. God raised up two prophets, Elijah and Elisha, to spearhead the struggle against Baal worship. Their stories give us insight into the role of prophets in ancient Israel and into the spiritual battles waged in Old Testament times.

MASTERY KEYS to the time of Elijah and Elisha:

- How did the acts and teachings of the two prophets stimulate faith in Yahweh?
- What deeds most clearly reveal the character of Ahab and Jezebel and the "morality" produced by false religion?

Ahab

Ahab earned the reputation as Israel's most wicked king. Although a strong military and political leader, Ahab was a weak man, dominated by his wife Jezebel. She easily influenced him not only to worship the Canaanite god Baal but even to build a tem-

Elijah built an altar atop Mount Carmel where God defeated 450 prophets of the false god Baal.

The view from Mount Carmel today.

ple to Baal in his capital city, Samaria. The Bible says Ahab "did more things to make the Lord, the God of Israel, angry than all the other kings before him" (1 Kings 16:33). The prophet Elijah led the battle against Baal worship. The intensity of the spiritual battle is shown in the fact that this, with the Exodus and the time of Christ, is one of only three biblical periods when many miracles are recorded.

Elijah's miracles

God endowed Elijah with special powers for the struggle against Baal worship. The Old Testament reports seven of his miracles. Elijah stopped rain from falling on Israel for three and a half years (1 Kings 17:1). He kept the food of a widow with whom he stayed from being used up (17:7-16). He brought the widow's son back to life (17:17-24). He called down fire from heaven to burn up a sacrifice (18:16-40). He brought back rains to the parched land (18:41-45). He called down fire on Ahab's soldiers when they came to arrest him (2 Kings 1:13-14). And he parted the Jordan River (2:1-8).

These miracles are interwoven in stories of high drama, which not only display the confrontation of Elijah with Ahab and Baalism, but also reveal Elijah's own humanness.

On Mount Carmel
1 Kings 18

Elijah challenged Ahab and his priests of Baal to demonstrate their supposed supernatural powers. The text says the 450 prophets cut themselves. The odor of blood was supposed to arouse the god, noted for his violence and sexual appetite. But Baal kindled no fire to consume the sacrifice laid out on an altar. Yet as soon as Elijah prayed, fire from heaven not only burned the sacrifice but even consumed the stones and the water with which it had been drenched.

Where did Elijah get the water with which to soak his sacrifice after three and a half years of drought? Perhaps it came from the nearby Mediterranean or perhaps from nearby springs, which archaeologists have located, that do not dry up even during droughts.

The demonstration convinced the people. On Elijah's command they seized and killed every priest of Baal.

Insight: Why wasn't this contest conducted before the drought? It often takes years of suffering before people are ready to listen to God's word or to accept evidence of his existence and power.

Dealing with depression
1 Kings 19

Despite the great spiritual victory at Carmel, Elijah was terrified when Jezebel threatened to kill him. The prophet also fell into such deep depression that he begged God to take his life. Instead, God dealt gently with his prophet, giving us a model of how to help others who are depressed. What did God do? (1) While the depression was deepest, God simply offered support, providing Elijah with food. Earlier God had used ravens to bring Elijah's food, but here the food may have been cooked by an angel, a further sign of God's tenderness to a despondent person. God did not get angry and did not criticize Elijah. God even spoke in a gentle whisper (19:12). (2) God encouraged Elijah, who felt alone and deserted. He revealed that there were 7,000 others in Israel who had not worshiped Baal. Often depression makes things seem darker than they are, and facts are needed. (3) God gave Elijah a task to do. Depression brings lethargy. It is important for a person troubled by depression to remain active and to do necessary daily tasks. (4) God gave Elijah a companion. He told Elijah to find the younger Elisha, who would be with him and one day would take Elijah's place as Israel's leading prophet. Research shows that companionship, even of a pet, is important in overcoming depression.

Not alone
1 Kings 20

Elijah was not the only prophet of God active in Ahab's reign. An unnamed prophet confronted Ahab when he let the defeated Syrian ruler, Ben-Hadad, live. An official named Obadiah had hidden 100 prophets of the Lord during the earlier famine (1 Kings 18:4). Later Elisha led "the sons of the prophets." Some think this phrase simply means a group of prophets. Others think it refers to a sort of seminary, where young people

The East is laced with a variety of vineyards. The excellent grapes ripen in September and October when the people enjoy a season of happiness and celebration.

trained to become prophets. For every famous leader, there are hundreds who quietly serve God.

Naboth's vineyard
1 Kings 21

The incident at Naboth's vineyard illustrates an important biblical concept. Naboth refused to sell or trade away his vineyard-laced slope near Ahab's palace in Samaria. When the owner, Naboth, refused to sell or trade his vineyard to Ahab, he was being faithful to a law stated in Leviticus 25:14-18. Sections of the promised land had been allotted to each Hebrew tribe and family. The process of dividing by lot indicated that God himself (not chance) distributed the land. Naboth would not surrender what God had given his family. David uses this imagery in Psalm 16: "Lord, you have assigned me my portion and my cup (NIV)." God still sovereignly distributes his good gifts to his own.

Micaiah the prophet
1 Kings 22

Ahab formed a coalition with Judah to battle the Arameans. But the king of Judah insisted that a prophet of God be consulted. When Israelite prophets promised victory, Micaiah explained that a "lying spirit" from God had deceived the other prophets and that God had actually planned Ahab's destruction.

How could a lying spirit come from God? The Old Testament views each individual as responsible for his or her own actions. God permitted, but did not command, the spirit to deceive the prophets. The lying spirit was responsible for its act. God did not lie by permitting the spirit to lie. Also note that God did not suggest the lie, and that he, in fact, revealed the truth through Micaiah. When the kings of Judah and Israel went into battle, they knew that God had ordained an enemy victory.

Insight: Ahab was extremely strong militarily. Assyrian records report that Ahab was one of a coalition of kings who threw back an early invasion attempt in 853 B.C. Ahab provided 2,000 chariots to the allied force, while the Syrians mustered only 1,200.

Victory over Ben-Hadad
1 Kings 20

Throughout Ahab's reign Israel's major enemies were the Arameans, a powerful people, who controlled what is now Syria. God gave Ahab, the apostate king, a number of notable victories over Ben-Hadad, the Aramean king. Why? First, in this case Ahab did listen to God's prophet and do what he said (20:13-17). Second, Ben-Hadad discounted God after his first defeat, saying the Lord was a "God of the hills" (NIV). This view may be rooted in the fact that many Israelite shrines had been built on "high places," such as the tops of hills. God gave Ahab a second great victory to demonstrate his sovereignty over all. The victories Israel won revealed God both to Ahab and the Ar-

Elijah was taken away in a whirlwind by God. Whirlwinds are powerful forces of God's nature and can be highly destructive.

Leprosy *was a general term that described a variety of harmful skin diseases in Bible times. Some types of leprosy still exist.*

ameans. Both were without excuse for later disobeying the Lord.

Elisha
2 Kings 2

Elisha was Elijah's companion during the last years of his ministry. When it came time for Elijah to die, he was taken directly into heaven (2 Kings 2). At that time Elisha begged for a "double portion" of Elijah's spirit. The phrase "double portion" reflects Old Testament inheritance law. The primary heir received a double portion of his father's possessions. Thus, what Elisha meant was that he wanted to be Elijah's successor as God's chief spokesman to his people.

Elisha's miracles
2 Kings

Strikingly, the Bible records almost twice as many miracles of Elisha (13) as of Elijah (7). These serve as evidence that Elisha was a valid successor to the famous prophet and did receive the "double portion" for which he had asked!

Insight: While Elijah's miracles were often national in scope, Elisha's miracles seem much more personal, designed to meet the needs of God's people. After the intense struggle with Ahab and Baalism, in which Israel suffered a terrible drought, and then war with Damascus, a more personal ministry of healing was especially needed.

Elijah taken up
2 Kings 2

Elijah was one of two persons taken to heaven without experiencing death. The other was Enoch (Genesis 5:24). The prophet Malachi said Elijah would appear to announce the Messiah's coming (Malachi 4:5-6). Jesus said that John the Baptist fulfilled this prophecy (Mark 9:11-13).

Leprosy
2 Kings 5

The Hebrew word translated "leprosy" is used for many skin diseases, as well as what we call leprosy. A person with any of these

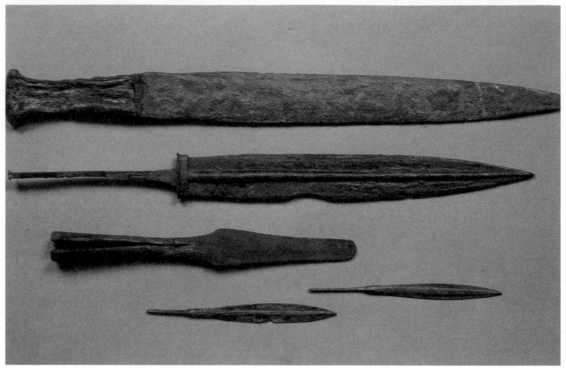

These bronze blades are typical of those used during the time of Elisha.

skin diseases was an outcast in Israel, forced to live away from others and unable to take part in worship rituals. Today we have medications that can fight leprosy, but no cure was known in biblical times.

Thus, when the king of Aram sent his chief general, a leper named Naaman, to Israel for healing, Israel's king supposed the Arameans were seeking a pretext for war. Elisha sent a message commanding that Naaman be sent to him. Apparently, Israel's leaders never even thought of looking to God!

Jehu

2 Kings 9–19

Elisha sent a young prophet to anoint an army commander, Jehu, as king of Israel. Jehu acted quickly: He killed every member of Ahab's family and ordered that Jezebel be thrown from her palace window. He then gathered all Baal worshipers together for "a holy meeting for Baal." When all Baal's de-

votees arrived, Jehu killed every one. This effectively ended the organized attempt to introduce the worship of Baal into Israel.

However, Jehu's mission had political, rather than religious, motivation. He killed Ahab's descendants so there would be no living rivals to the dynasty he intended to establish and eliminated Baal worship because it had been associated with Ahab and Jezebel. Once these steps had been taken, Jehu ignored God and his Law and continued the false religion that had been established by Jeroboam I when the kingdom was set up in 931 B.C.

Insights: Jehu used religion for his own ends. In the process he did perform God's will and was rewarded by the Lord. But Jehu's lack of commitment to God led ultimately to the end of his dynasty and to the destruction of his people.

17 Kings and prophets–Judah

1 Kings 14—2 Kings; Joel; Micah; Isaiah; Nahum; Habakkuk; Zephaniah; Jeremiah

When Solomon's kingdom was torn in two, David's tribe, Judah, and some of Benjamin's tribe remained faithful to David's descendants. This southern area became the kingdom of Judah. It was ruled by a series of nineteen kings, all from David's line. Eight of the nineteen were more or less godly kings. Even so, the nation experienced tragic spiritual ups and downs. Finally, the apostasy was so great that God used the Babylonians to punish Judah. The great conqueror, Nebuchadnezzar, destroyed Jerusalem and Solomon's Temple and carried the people of Judah away as captives.

MASTERY KEYS to southern kingdom history:

- Who were Judah's most significant kings, and what were their accomplishments?
- What impact did religious revivals have?
- What prophets ministered to Judah, and what message did each bring?

Judah existed as a nation for about 344 years, compared to Israel's survival for only 208 years. This is explained primarily by the fact that in Judah godly kings often led reli-

gious revivals, which turned the people back to God.

These revivals were marked by a fresh commitment to obey God's word and usually by a revival of religious festivals and Temple worship. In addition, some of the godly kings aggressively rooted out pagan practices and destroyed Judah's "high places."

Yet even the most godly kings were unable to turn the hearts of God's people completely to the Lord. The revivals were superficial, and Judah, like her sister Israel,

In the year 586 B.C., the city of Jerusalem and the beautiful Temple were destroyed by fire by the Babylonians.

became less responsive to the Lord and more committed to idolatry. When Judah's sin was too great to overlook, God unleashed Babylon.

Hezekiah, a godly king

2 Kings 18–19

Hezekiah illustrates the impact of a godly ruler on the population and history of the southern kingdom.

Hezekiah ruled Judah from 715-686 B.C., the tense era in which Assyria attacked and destroyed the northern kingdom, Israel. Hezekiah was totally committed to God. He actively destroyed pagan places of worship in Judah, and he "obeyed the commands the Lord had given Moses."

Yet, the Assyrian ruler Sennacherib destroyed Judah's border cities and seemed about to attack Jerusalem. The commander of the Assyrian armies stood outside Jerusalem's walls and ridiculed Hezekiah's dependence on God. Hezekiah humbly went to the Temple to pray and sent messengers to Isaiah, the prophet, to see if there was any word from God. There was. God promised

In an attempt to thwart his enemies, King Hezekiah built a secret, underground waterway into Jerusalem so that enemies could not cut off the city's water supply. The water formed the Pool of Siloam inside the city.

Kings and prophets of Judah

Kings ♛	Prophets ♟	Date
☐ Rehoboam		930-913 B.C.
☐ Abijah		913-910 B.C.
☐ Asaᵍ		910-986 B.C.
☐ Jehoshaphatᵍ		872-848 B.C.
☐ Jehoram		853-841 B.C.
☐ Ahaziah		841 B.C.
☐ Athaliah		841-835 B.C.
☐ Joashᵍ	*Joel*	835-796 B.C.
☐ Amaziahᵍ		796-767 B.C.
☐ Azariah (Uzziah)ᵍ	*Isaiah*	792-740 B.C.
☐ Jothamᵍ	*Isaiah* *Micah*	750-732 B.C.
☐ Ahaz	*Micah* *Isaiah*	750-715 B.C.
☐ Hezekiahᵍ	*Isaiah* *Micah*	715-686 B.C.
☐ Manasseh		697-642 B.C.
☐ Amon		642-640 B.C.
☐ Josiahᵍ	*Huldah* *Nahum* *Habakkuk* *Jeremiah*	640-609 B.C.
☐ Jehoahazᵍ	*Zephaniah* *Jeremiah*	609 B.C.
☐ Jehoiakimᵍ	*Jeremiah*	609-598 B.C.
☐ Jehoiachinᵍ	*Jeremiah*	598-597 B.C.
☐ Zedekiahᵍ	*Jeremiah*	597-586 B.C.

Note: Sometimes kings ruled at the same time as their fathers or sons. A ᵍ indicates good kings.

This stone carving dates back to 2,000 B.C. It pictures a god of the Babylonians.

the Assyrian king "will not enter this city or even shoot an arrow here" (2 Kings 19:32). God kept that promise. God struck dead 185,000 Assyrian soldiers, and Sennacherib returned home.

Sennacherib left a record of his invasion carved on a stone now called the Taylor Prism. There the Assyrian ruler bragged of taking 46 strong cities of Judah and many prisoners. But all he said about Jerusalem was that he shut Hezekiah up behind its walls "like a bird in a cage."

Sennacherib constructed a new palace in honor of his victories in Judah. The main room features carved reliefs showing the attack on Lachish and, according to one inscription, the ruler "sitting on his throne, while the spoil from the city of Lachish passed before him." Archaeologists' findings help make this era one of the best known in

Bible history. Nothing has been found which in any way contradicts the biblical account.

In preparation for the Assyrian invasion, Hezekiah had also cut a 1750 foot tunnel through the rock to supply water to Jerusalem (2 Chronicles 32:30). The tunnel was discovered many years ago and is called Hezekiah's Conduit. Engraved words in the Hebrew writing of Hezekiah's time tell how workmen, starting from opposite ends of the tunnel, met deep underground to complete it.

The Greek historian Herodotus adds written testimony. He tells of the Assyrians' retreat but credits it to mice who swarmed into the Assyrian camp and ate their bowstrings and shield handles. Some think a disease like Europe's Black Plague, which was carried by rats and mice, may have caused the massive casualties. Whatever it was, it was an act of God.

So Hezekiah's early commitment to God, his revival and the trust in God that Hezekiah exhibited, led to the delivery of Judah from the Assyrian invasion.

The godly kings of Judah did purify the land, and God honored them. No revival was lasting, however, so each godly ruler was forced to cleanse the land again of the same evils!

Prophets in Judah

The reforms of Judah's godly kings were supported by the ministry of several prophets whose writings are found in our Old Testament.

Joel

Nothing is known of Joel personally. His message on the principles of divine judgment was given sometime before the Babylonian captivity. This particular prophecy was stimulated by historic events. Joel's prophecy was stimulated by a swarm of locusts, grasshopperlike insects that destroyed all growing things in areas they invaded. Joel describes the literal locust plague, which he recognized as God's judgment (Joel 1:1–2:27). The latter part of the book shows some of the blessings that will come with repentance.

Locusts are destructive insects that resemble grasshoppers. They feed on green plants and can completely destroy a healthy crop.

Insight: Joel introduces the phrase, "The Lord's day of judging." This prophetic term is used for any time when God himself directly intervenes in human affairs, usually to punish or to judge evil. Peter uses it to refer to the second coming of Jesus (2 Peter 3:8-12).

Micah

Micah prophesied during the reigns of Jotham, Ahaz and Hezekiah (742-687 B.C.). He was a contemporary of Isaiah and dealt with many of Isaiah's themes. Micah warned both Israel and Judah against idolatry and oppression of the poor.

Outline

Gems in Micah include the promise of Jesus' birth in Bethlehem (Micah 5:2) and a beautiful image of forgiveness, portraying God as one who will "throw away all our sins into the deepest sea" (Micah 7:19).

Perhaps the most important verse is Micah 6:8, which summarizes God's call to the sinning people of both kingdoms: "The Lord has told you what is good. He has told you what he wants from you: Do what is right to other people. Love being kind to others. And live humbly trusting your God."

Israel ignored Micah's message and was destroyed. Judah heard, and judgment for the generation to whom Micah and Isaiah preached was delayed because of their response to the word of the Lord (see Jeremiah 26:17-19).

Isaiah

Isaiah, who ministered from 739-681 B.C., was one of the greatest of the Old Testament prophets. His book is quoted 50 times in the New Testament and referred to another 150 times. The book of Isaiah is often called the Gospel of the Old Testament because of its many and beautiful pictures of the coming Savior.

Outline

Insight: Perhaps a good way to read Isaiah is to begin with chapter 6 which tells of Isaiah's call. This chapter introduces many of the themes that will come up again later in the book: God's rule, man's sin, punishment as a means of redeeming his people, preserving a remnant. Isaiah's vision of God in chapter 6 helped him see himself, the Lord and other people in a new light.

Isaiah's images of God are linked with names given to the Lord. Various passages help us see God in various ways. To Isaiah God must be understood as the Holy One (5:15-16), and as Sovereign Lord (8:13-15). God is Judge (11:3-5) and he is our Salvation (26:1-4,12-13). God is the Everlasting God (44:6-8), the Living God (40:11; 41:10,13), and Lord of Glory (60:1-3).

Some of Scripture's most beautiful predictions about Christ are found in Isaiah 7:14; 9:1-8; and 11:1-12. In other passages, called the "servant songs," Jesus is seen as the servant of God who accomplishes his will and who wins salvation for human beings (42:19; 49:1-6; 50:4-11; 52:13–53:12).

The latter part of the book has a different thrust than the beginning. After the punishment of captivity, there's a brighter day. Besides physically returning home, there are promises of spiritual renewal (40:31). This hope for the future is climaxed by the great messianic prophecy chapter of the suffering servant who will bear "the sin of many" (52:13–53:12).

The Ishtar Gate, a part of the powerful Babylonian empire, is shown in this reproduction.

Nahum

Nahum is another unknown. His prophecy was given sometime between 663 and 655 B.C. and describes the fall of Nineveh, capital of the Assyrian empire. It portrays with total accuracy a flood which permitted the Babylonians to penetrate Nineveh's massive defenses in 612 B.C. The book was intended to comfort Judah in a time when her existence was threatened by Assyria.

Habakkuk

Tradition indicates that Habakkuk was a Levite, who took part in the religious revival led by King Josiah. He probably wrote about 620 B.C. Despite the revival, Habakkuk complains in his first chapter that "justice never prevails" and wonders how a holy God can permit such sin among his people.

Habakkuk 2 explains how God is judging the wicked even when they seem to prosper.

How? They are denied satisfaction, 2:4-5. Their acts create a hostility that will destroy them, 2:6-8. They are denied security, 2:9-11. Their accomplishments will not last, 2:12-14. They will be treated the way they treated others, 2:15-17. Never suppose that anyone "gets away with" sin.

God tells Habakkuk that he is preparing the Chaldeans (Babylonians) to devastate Judah. But Habakkuk is still troubled. How can God use an even more wicked people than Judah to discipline them? In their success the wicked will ridicule any personal need for God. God shows Habakkuk that despite success, the wicked are miserable and always make enemies who will destroy them. Finally, Habakkuk faces the personal anguish that invasion by Babylon will bring him and determines to live by faith.

Outline

The Babylonians

The city of Babylon was part of the Assyrian empire until 627 B.C. It rebelled then, and Nabopolassar not only set up a rival kingdom but also attacked Assyrian territory. By 605 B.C. Babylon, now led by Nebuchadnezzar, routed the last Assyrian army and took over that ancient empire.

All the countries of Palestine quickly submitted to the conqueror. But soon Judah and others rebelled. In a series of invasions and deportations, the Babylonians devastated the promised land. Finally, in 586 B.C. Jerusalem itself was destroyed, and the beautiful Temple built by Solomon was left in ruins. Most of the remaining population was deported to Babylon to join those who were exiled there earlier.

Habakkuk described the Babylonian military machine. Their "cavalry gallops head long" (1:8, NIV), and "Their armies march quickly like a whirlwind in the desert" (1:9).

When they come to walled cities, they "build earthen ramps and capture them" (1:10, NIV). Ancient armies used a variety of additional means to take walled cities. They might build fires at the base of the walls. The heat cracked the limestone so it could be scooped away. At times dead bodies were hurled by catapults into cities to cause disease. Ancient armies also used towers and battering rams to assault the walls. But the preferred Babylonian method was simple and straightforward. They put thousands of soldiers and prisoners to work piling up dirt to create ramps to the top of the city walls. Then their soldiers charged up these ramps and took the city by storm. People in the cities fought back with arrows, stones and by pouring hot oil on the enemy below. But the Babylonians could not be stopped.

Zephaniah

Zephaniah was a nobleman, a descendant of godly king Hezekiah. He began his ministry during the reign of Josiah. His blunt message, which was probably given before Josiah's reform began in 621 B.C., is recorded in his three-chapter book. Zephaniah announced that Judah's sins were so great that God must judge them. One day God would judge all people. But very soon God would judge sinning Judah. "The great day of the Lord is near—near and coming quickly" Zephaniah cried. And "that day will be a day of wrath" (1:14-15, NIV).

Jeremiah

Jeremiah was one of the Old Testament's four major writing prophets. He was born into a family of priests during the reign of Manasseh, who murdered many followers of God. Jeremiah began his 42-year ministry in the reign of Josiah about 627 B.C. He foretold, and then witnessed, the destruction of the Jewish homeland by Babylon. Jeremiah is often called the weeping prophet. He was unpopular and was often accused of treason because he urged his countrymen to submit to Babylon since God had raised this pagan power up to punish Judah for her sins. De-

The Bible compares God to a potter and Israel to the clay that he molds. A potter makes dishes and utensils from wet clay by molding it with his hands as it spins on a wheel.

spite times of deep despair, Jeremiah faithfully kept on warning Judah. He denounced the nation's sinfulness and warned that judgment must surely come. The sermons recorded in the 52-chapter book of Jeremiah give us insight into Judah's last, dark days.

Outline

Highlights from Jeremiah

18:1–20:18: **The potter.** As Jeremiah watched a potter at work, he saw him discard a marred project. "So the potter used that clay to make another pot. He used his hands to shape the pot the way that he wanted it to be." From this incident Jeremiah preached a powerful sermon to Judah. The marred nation must be shattered like a broken pot, and shaped anew.

28:1-17: **The iron yoke.** Jeremiah had preached that God himself placed the yoke of Babylon on Judah's shoulder. Another prophet, Hananiah, announced that God would break the Babylonian yoke within two years. But Hananiah was not sent by God; he was persuading God's people to trust in lies. Jeremiah confronted Hananiah. God had forged a yoke of iron which Judah could never break. As for Hananiah, "You will die this year. This is because you taught the people to turn against the Lord." Within two months Hananiah was dead. Despite this evidence that Jeremiah spoke the word of God, Judah still would not listen to his message.

Jeremiah 37–39: Imprisoned. When the Babylonians attacked, Jeremiah was charged with treason. He was beaten and locked in a cell. Many insisted Jeremiah be killed; his defeatist message was affecting morale. The old prophet was lowered into a cistern (used for water storage) where he sank into the muck and was left to die. But Jeremiah was rescued. Questioned in private by the terrified king, Jeremiah repeated his message of doom. The king, who had rebelled against Babylon in violation of God's words spoken through the prophet, would see his children and advisors executed. Then his own eyes would be put out.

Jeremiah 40–43: Flight to Egypt. With the city of Jerusalem destroyed, nearly all the people of Judah were deported to Babylon. The few who remained fled when the governor appointed by Nebuchadnezzar was assassinated. But first they begged Jeremiah for a word from God, promising to do what he told them. When Jeremiah told them it was safe to remain, the people accused him of lying! What is more, they announced they would no longer worship God but only the idols of their parents. So the last remnant of the people of Judah set off toward Egypt and destruction.

Jeremiah 30–31: The new covenant. The grim note of Jeremiah is brightened by one of the most important of the Old Testament's covenants of promise. Judah has sinned, and her people must be expelled from the land. But the expulsion is discipline, not divine rejection. God has not abandoned his ancient people or taken back his promises.

Jeremiah promises that one day a ruler from David's line will save God's chosen people (30:2-10). He will bring Israel back from the lands where they have been scattered as a judgment (30:11-24). When the Hebrew people have been regathered, the Israelites will also be purified and know God's blessing (31:1-22).

Now comes the heart of the new covenant. In that day the external Law of Moses will be replaced, and God's law will be so engraved on his people's hearts that they will both know and obey him (31:23-40).

Insight: The New Testament tells us that Jesus put the new covenant into effect when he died on the cross. The Holy Spirit is given to those who obey the Lord (Acts 5:32). This transforming power does what the old covenant could not (2 Corinthians 3:7-18).

Life in Babylon

Lamentations; Ezekiel; Daniel; Esther

The people of Judah were taken to Babylon. The early deportations were mainly the skilled artisans of the Jews. Many of them were settled near the rich and busy capital city. Life in Babylon was not hard, and many Jews prospered. Yet, others longed for their lost homeland, considered their sins, and turned to the Lord.

MASTERY KEYS to the Babylonian captivity:

- How did the captivity affect Jewish religious practices?
- What is the message of each Bible book associated with this period?

Babylon

The city of Babylon was the capital of the great empire of Babylonia and later Chaldea. The city was built along the Euphrates River, and its walled core covered over 3,000 acres. Archaeologists began their careful study of

This is a representation of the entrance to the Processional Street in Babylonia that led to the palace of King Nebuchadnezzar II.

its ruins about 100 years ago. Many of the careful records the Babylonians maintained have been found written on clay tablets. Included in the finds are plans of buildings, descriptions of festivals, records of business transactions and of money spent on public buildings, as well as Babylonian literature.

The great city itself was surrounded by miles of fields, irrigation canals and suburbs packed with homes and businesses. The Israelites were settled by one of these canals, called the Kebar River, about 60 miles from the central city.

The walled city was famous for its wealth and beauty. The outer walls ran for 42 miles, while the inner walls stood some 300 feet high and were 21 feet wide at the top—wide enough for chariot races! In the city was Nebuchadnezzar's famous Hanging Gardens, one of the ancient world's seven wonders. This manmade hill featured gardens planted on different levels, irrigated by water pumped up to them.

There was also a temple area dominated by the ziggurat, or temple tower, dedicated to the god Marduk, the supposed creator and chief god of the Babylonians. Nebuchadnezzar's boasts of piety have also been found: "I adorned [chapels] with lustrous silver . . . Giant bulls I made. I adorned them with jewels and placed them upon the threshold gate of the shrine."

The book of Revelation speaks of "Babylon the Great." There Babylon is a symbolic city that represents human efforts to build a religion and a civilization without reliance on the one true God.

Jewish life in Babylon

Three different groups of captives had been taken to Babylon. The first group, deported in 605 B.C., was drawn from the upper classes. The teenage Daniel was among them and was selected with several young friends for special training for future posts in the administration of the empire. Another group, taken in 597 B.C., likely included Ju-

The famous Hanging Gardens were one of the seven wonders of the world.

dah's artisans. The final deportation in 586 B.C. was the largest—probably about 70,000—and included all but the very poor.

Life in Babylon was not difficult for the captives. Most seem to have owned their own homes and possessed enough land to raise crops (see Jeremiah 29:4,7; 12:17). Babylonian records reveal at least one trading company owned by persons with Jewish names. The Jewish community was also largely self-governing with its own elders and leaders.

In fact, the city of Babylon continued to have a large and prosperous Jewish community over a thousand years into the Christian era. The "Babylonian Talmud," interpretations of biblical laws that were developed in Babylon, continues to influence Jewish life even today.

The spiritual impact of the captivity

Although life was good in Babylon, many Jews yearned for their homeland and their God. From the decades spent among their pagan captors, several vital religious reforms emerged in Judaism.

(1) The captivity purged the Jews of idolatry. So susceptible to idolatry before Babylon, the Jewish people were never again attracted to idol worship.

(2) The Temple, which had been the focal point of Jewish worship, was now destroyed. It is generally believed that in Babylon a new institution, the synagogue, developed. The word synagogue simply means "gathering." The Jews met in these local assemblies to study the written word and to worship God with collective prayers and to read the psalms in unison. Even after the Temple was rebuilt by those who later returned to Judah, the synagogue continued to be central in Jewish life. The Jewish encyclopedia suggests that the synagogue helped the people discover a new freedom to approach God personally without the intervention of priests. The Talmud reports that there were 394 synagogues in Jerusalem in the first century while the Temple was still standing.

(3) The Jewish people now spoke Aramaic, the common language of the Middle East. Soon a class of men developed whose mission was to study and to teach the law, which had been written in Hebrew. These men, called scribes, replaced the priests as the prime interpreters of the Scriptures. In the New Testament such persons, trained in the law and in religious tradition, were given the familiar title "rabbi," which means "teacher."

Emerging from the captivity, the Jewish community became a people of the Book, who studied the word of God not only to understand their destiny but also to learn how to please the Lord.

Insight: The Bible reminds us, "God punishes us to help us, so that we can become holy as he is." While discipline may be painful, "later . . . we have peace because we start living the right way" (Hebrews 12:10-11). The Jews had learned this lesson.

Lamentations

Tradition says that this Old Testament book was written by Jeremiah, who found his way to Babylon after leaving the remnant of people that went to Egypt. The five poems are dirges, whose dark mood reflects the pain of a people who at last realize all they have lost by being taken from the promised land.

Outline

Ezekiel

The prophet Ezekiel lived among the captives in Babylon, ministering both before and after Jerusalem's fall. Ezekiel had a unique approach and often acted out his messages. He built a toy army and lay on his side to represent a seige, thus prophesying what would happen to Jerusalem in the homeland (Ezekiel 4). To show final deportation, Ezekiel daily packed a few belongings and left his home then crept back in at night through a hole he had dug in the wall (Ezekiel 12).

Visions are another distinction of this book. It opens with the report of a vision of God himself (Ezekiel 1). One of the most important of Ezekiel's visions is found in chapters 8-11. In it the prophet was transported to the homeland, where he saw the elders of his people worshiping idols within the Temple area itself as others worshiped various pagan deities outside it. As Ezekiel watched, the "glory" of God (the visible sign of his presence) rose from the inner sanctuary and deserted Jerusalem. The Jews had wrongly reasoned that God would never permit the destruction of Solomon's magnificent Temple. Ezekiel's vision meant that God's presence was no longer there: The Temple had become an empty and meaningless heap of stone.

Outline

I. Prophecy against Judah   1–24
II. Prophecy against nations   25–32
III. Prophecies of restoration   33–39
IV. Prophecy of a new temple   40–48

Many passages in Ezekiel are justly famous.

Ezekiel 18:4: "the soul that sins will die" (NIV). In this passage "soul" is used in the sense of "person," as it is often used in the Bible. The "death" spoken of here is physical. In Judah the people had shrugged off warnings of judgment, saying that if God wanted to punish them for their parents' sins, there was nothing they could do. Ezekiel establishes an important principle. God deals with individuals as well as nations. The person who repents and does right will live through the coming judgment. Thus God will use the Babylonians to purge the wicked from among his people.

Ezekiel 37: the valley of dry bones. In a vision Ezekiel sees the dried bones of an army, scattered in a desert valley. Can the dry bones live? Told to prophesy, Ezekiel watches as the bones assemble and are covered with flesh. God interprets the vision. No matter how hopeless it may seem, his scattered people will be regathered to live as a united nation in the promised land, and "my servant David will be their king."

Ezekiel 40–48: a rebuilt temple. The book of Ezekiel concludes with the description of a magnificent temple to be built in the future.

The fate of Babylon

Babylon under Nebuchadnezzar replaced Assyria as the dominant world power. But Babylon was itself destined to fall to another conqueror, Cyrus. By 550 B.C., Cyrus controlled Persia and had added the larger Median province. He defeated King Croesus and added that territory to the growing empire. Then in 539 B.C. Babylon fell to Cyrus without a battle, and Cyrus took over administration of that great empire.

A series of rulers followed, including the famous Xerxes who was barred from Europe in 490 B.C. by the Greeks at the battle of Marathon. Xerxes, who is called Ahasuerus in the Bible, was the ruler who made the Jewish girl Esther his queen.

The Bible books of Daniel and Esther report events which take place in the center of power of these great empires. Daniel was a chief administrator under Nebuchadnezzar and Cyrus. Esther became Xerxes' queen and the instrument through which God saved the Jewish people from Haman, an implacable enemy.

Daniel

Daniel was one of the first group of captives taken to Babylon in 605 B.C. In his early teens Daniel was enrolled in training to become an administrator of Nebuchadnezzar's far flung empire. The first part of Daniel's book contains stories of his relationships with the rulers of succeeding empires. The second half of the book contains Daniel's visions and prophecies.

Outline

Daniel's date

Daniel accurately describes the succeeding world empires that dominated the Middle East from the time of Nebuchadnezzar to New Testament times. Critics who doubt the possibility of predictive prophecy have insisted that the book of Daniel must have been written in the second century B.C. Yet, archaeology has shown that Daniel was written by someone familiar with the royal court, who used technical terms like "Chaldean" correctly (Daniel 2:10; 3:8). Daniel's dates reflect use of the Babylonian calendar while Jeremiah uses the Hebrew system. Daniel also notes that Belshazzar was in Babylon when the city fell. For years this was a keystone of arguments against Daniel's authenticity until the fact was confirmed by archaeologists who located records showing he was co-regent with his father Nabonidus, who was in Syria when the city fell. Only a person who lived at the time portrayed in the book of Daniel, rather than in the second century B.C., could have known such details.

Insight: The accuracy of the Bible has been challenged. But every challenge has failed as new information about the past comes to light.

Stories of Daniel

Stories of Daniel are found in all children's books and Sunday school curricula. Most familiar are his commitment to Jewish law as a young man (Daniel 1), his interpretation of Nebuchadnezzar's dream (Daniel 2) and his night in the lion's den (Daniel 6). However, most students do not realize that when Daniel was thrown to the lions, he was some 80 years old.

Most striking in Daniel are stories of his relationship with Nebuchadnezzar. Daniel so influenced the mighty conqueror that in the end Nebuchadnezzar acknowledged God as king of heaven and Most High God (Daniel 4).

We see five important themes throughout the book of Daniel.

1. *God shows his power by being in control of kingdoms and individuals.* Even though the Babylonians put Shadrach, Meshach and Abednego into the fiery furnace (Daniel 3:17,

Official papers were sealed with hot wax into which was pressed a special symbol that represented its sender. Some seals were worn as signet rings; others were worn on a cord around the neck.

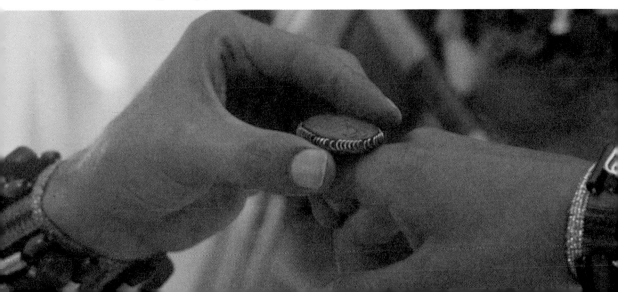

29), God delivers them. Nebuchadnezzar boasts of the great city of Babylon he has built, but God reduces him to the level of an animal because of his pride (Daniel 4:34-35, 37). Belshazzar dishonors God by using holy vessels for drinking mugs, but the Lord takes away his kingdom from him overnight (Daniel 5). Even though Daniel is cast into the lions' den, the Lord God protects Daniel by shutting the mouths of the lions (Daniel 6:16, 22).

2. *Ultimately, God's kingdom will prevail over all the kingdoms of men.* His kingdom, like a stone cut out of a mountain by no human hand, will bring down the greatest human kingdom (2:31-45). The nations of men only appear like fearful beasts, but the Lord's people will be given an everlasting kingdom (Daniel 7). Even though the Jerusalem Temple was desecrated, in a short time the evil monarch will be overthrown, and worship of God will be resumed (8:9-14, 23-25; 9:24-27; 11:30-35; 12:11).

3. *The heavenly struggle between good and bad angels is behind the earthly conflict between good and evil.* Gabriel was delayed three weeks from being able to come explain a vision to Daniel because he was fighting the prince of Persia. Because Gabriel was helped by Michael, Gabriel was able to come to Daniel (Daniel 10:13). Gabriel must return to finish this battle and meet the prince of Greece in a great conflict (Daniel 10:20). Michael will enable God's faithful people to be victorious over their enemies (Daniel 12:1-3). Similar passages are found in Ephesians 6:10-12.

4. *God must punish his people for sinning, but his grace delivers them.* Daniel realizes his own sin and the sins of his people which made the Babylonian captivity necessary, and he begs for forgiveness. Daniel, pleading for mercy for himself and his people, asks to be restored to the Lord and to their land (9:3-19).

5. *In spite of persecution and death, God's people must remain faithful to him.* Daniel and his friends will not eat the king's food and drink the wine because they would defile themselves by violating God's law (Daniel 1). Shadrach, Meshach and Abednego choose to die in the fiery furnace rather than worship an idol (3:17-18, 28). Daniel chooses to face death in the lions' den instead of worshiping a man as God, for he trusts in his Creator and Master (Daniel 6:10,22-23,26-27).

Esther

Cyrus replaced the Babylonian empire with the Medo-Persian empire. He reversed the Babylonian policy of removing people from their homeland and so offered the Jews a chance to return to Judah. While many did return, thousands of others set up small colonies in the empire's major cities.

Esther was an orphan girl who lived with her cousin, Mordecai, in the Persian capital of Shushan (Susa) in what is now Iran. The king in her time was Xerxes, and the events in this book took place between 483 and 471 B.C. The Greek historian Herodotus even tells about a banquet like the one mentioned in Esther 1:14. Herodotus explains that it was held to talk over plans for invading the Greek states. This book, too, uses technical terms and describes customs that would be known only by a person who lived in the political center of Xerxes' empire.

The book of Esther tells the story of a plot to exterminate the Jewish people. Through an amazing series of "coincidences," the young Jewish girl becomes queen and is able to save her people. The Feast of Purim, still held today, remembers Esther and her role in delivering God's people.

Returning home

Ezra; Haggai; Nehemiah; Zechariah; Malachi; Daniel

When Cyrus established his Medo-Persian empire, he permitted captive people everywhere to return to their homelands. Several thousand Jews eagerly returned to Palestine about 539 B.C. They went there to rebuild the Temple of God and to reestablish a Jewish people in the land God had promised to Israel.

MASTERY KEYS to the return:

- Who were the most influential leaders of this era, and what was the accomplishment of each?
- What was the message of each of the prophets of this era whose writings are found in books of the Bible?

The return prophesied

Before Jerusalem was destroyed, Jeremiah had predicted that the Jews' captivity would last 70 years (Jeremiah 25:11-12;

29:10). Even earlier, about 740 B.C., Isaiah had written:

> I will bring Cyrus to do good things.
>   And I will make his work easy.
> Cyrus will rebuild my city,
>   and he will set my people free.
> Cyrus has peen paid to do these things.
>   The Lord of heaven's armies says this.
>   Isaiah 45:13

Upon taking power in 538 B.C., Cyrus immediately ordered a return of the Jews to

This is a representation of the famous Jebusite Wall and Israelite buildings in the City of David.

rebuild the Jerusalem Temple. Cyrus even gave the Jews the golden articles taken from the Temple by the Babylonians. Surely, Cyrus did not act "for a price or reward!"

And so a first group of 42,360 Jews returned to Judah in 537 B.C. A second group followed eighty years later in 458 B.C., and an even smaller third contingent returned in 444 B.C.

Ezra

Ezra was a Jewish priest who also had an important post in the Persian court (Ezra 7:21-26). Early in his life he committed himself to study, to live and to teach the word of God. His book gives the history of the first return to the land, led by Zerubbabel and Jeshua. His book also relates the story of the second return, which Ezra himself led. Thus, this book of history divides naturally into two parts:

Outline

   I. The first return (538 B.C.)   1–6
  II. The second return (458 B.C.)   7–10

Ezra 2: Genealogies. The genealogical record was vital to establish the Jewish descent of each person and his or her right as an heir to God's ancient covenant promises.

Ezra 4: Opposition. The Jews refused the offer from the people living in the area to "let us help you build" the Temple. These people, who had been resettled in Israel by the Babylonians, claimed to worship God (Yahweh), too. When the Jews rejected the offer, they aroused serious opposition to rebuilding. Why were the settlers so adamant in refusing help?

Insight: In biblical times pagans thought of gods as local deities who "owned" a locality. When such peoples moved to a new area, they wanted to be on good terms with the god who "owned" that territory. The Jews were not interested in association with the half-pagan worshipers, and were also aware that God's covenant promises had been given only to those who descended from Abraham, Isaac, and Jacob.

Ezra 5: The prophets. In 520 B.C., after 15 years, construction of the Temple was resumed. The new burst of energy was stimulated by the preaching of Haggai and Zechariah. The opponents' appeal to the Persian emperor, Darius, was rejected, and the Jews' enemies were ordered to use government funds to pay for the rebuilding!

Ezra 7: The scribe. Fifty-eight years after the Temple was rebuilt, Ezra came to Judea with royal authority to administer justice according to "the law of your God and the law of the king" (7:26).

Ezra 9–10: Spiritual decline. Ezra was devastated to find that God's people had intermarried with the surrounding pagans. He led the nation in public confession of sin and insisted that foreign wives be divorced. They did, but a decade later Nehemiah would face the same problem.

Haggai

Haggai's message was clear: Complete the Temple. Each of Haggai's sermons is dated so that we know when it was preached.

Outline

    I. The call to rebuild   1:1-15
   II. A promise of glory   2:1-9
  III. Blessing promised   2:10-19
  IV. God to triumph   2:20-23

1:1-15: The first sermon, August 29, 520 B.C. The message was delivered against a background of poverty. Harvests had been poor. Each year the people seemed further behind. The Lord said this was "because you are busy working on your own houses. But my house is still in ruins!" The people responded and began to work on God's house on September 21st.

2:1-9: The second sermon, October 17. God promised to be with his people. A poor people will build a glorious Temple, for "the silver is mine, and the gold is mine." Ezra 6:8-12 tells us God met the need through the command of the Persian king that the Jews' enemies finance the rebuilding project!

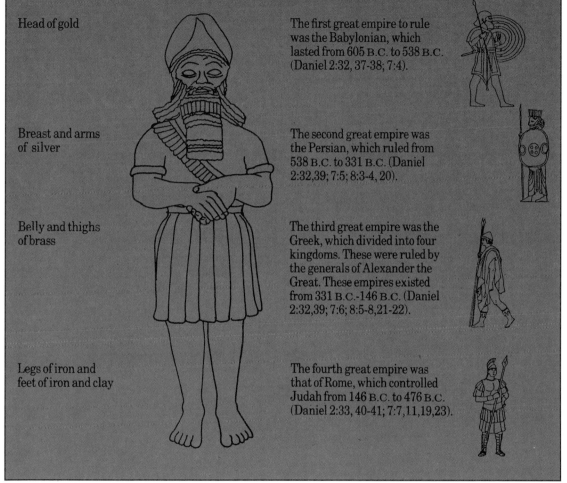

The centuries of waiting / Daniel 2, 7, 8

God gave Daniel special information about the empires that would rule the world. They would also rule his homeland until God acted. Then Jesus the Savior would be born. The future was made known in Nebuchadnezzar's dream and visions given to Daniel.

Head of gold

The first great empire to rule was the Babylonian, which lasted from 605 B.C. to 538 B.C. (Daniel 2:32, 37-38; 7:4).

Breast and arms of silver

The second great empire was the Persian, which ruled from 538 B.C. to 331 B.C. (Daniel 2:32, 39; 7:5; 8:3-4, 20).

Belly and thighs of brass

The third great empire was the Greek, which divided into four kingdoms. These were ruled by the generals of Alexander the Great. These empires existed from 331 B.C.-146 B.C. (Daniel 2:32, 39; 7:6; 8:5-8, 21-22).

Legs of iron and feet of iron and clay

The fourth great empire was that of Rome, which controlled Judah from 146 B.C. to 476 B.C. (Daniel 2:33, 40-41; 7:7, 11, 19, 23).

2:10-19: The third sermon, December 18. The law shows that a defiled object is not made holy by association with something that is holy. The Temple cannot make a sinful people clean, but God in grace will accept their obedient completion of the Temple and will bless this people.

2:20-23. Zerubbabel was from David's line. In this passage Zerubbabel represents the line; so, this mysterious promise is that one day a Davidic king will reign.

The times of the Gentiles

The book of Daniel contains several prophecies which predict the course of Gentile world empires between the time of Nebuchadnezzar and the appearance of Jesus. This era is known as "the times of the Gentiles" and is summarized in the chart on page 117. These "times" provide background for the book of Zechariah. The book of Zechariah is intended to encourage the people of Judah, who must now live for many centuries under Gentile control.

Zechariah

Zechariah was a contemporary of Haggai and preached his first sermon about the same time Haggai gave his second message to Judah (Zechariah 1:1-6). The structure of this book is very complex, as it adopts a literary form called *chiasmus*. In general, however, it is divided into two parts. The first eight chapters contain a variety of visions and messages from the prophet. The last five chapters look far ahead, to the time when God will personally intervene in human affairs.

Outline

PART I
I.	Introduction: return to God	1:1-6
II.	Eight visions and oracles	1:7–6:15
III.	Messages on fasting	7:1–8:19
IV.	Conclusion: longing for God	8:20-23

PART II
V.	The Lord intervenes: his Shepherd	9:1–11:17
VI.	The final intervention of the Lord: the suffering	12:1–14:15

There are many fascinating themes in the book of Zechariah, who has been called "the prophet of hope."

Fasting. Zechariah is asked if God is pleased when his people go without food and drink as a sign of sorrow for sin. God answers through his prophet, "Administer true justice; show mercy and compassion to one another. Do not oppress the widow or the fatherless, the alien or the poor" (7:9-10). God is not interested in mere religion, but in godliness.

Prophecies about Jesus. Israel's king will come, "righteous and having salvation, gentle and riding on a donkey" (Zechariah 9:9, NIV). Jesus entered Jerusalem on a donkey and was hailed as king (Matthew 21:5). The coming descendant of David will be pierced by his own people (Zechariah 12:10).

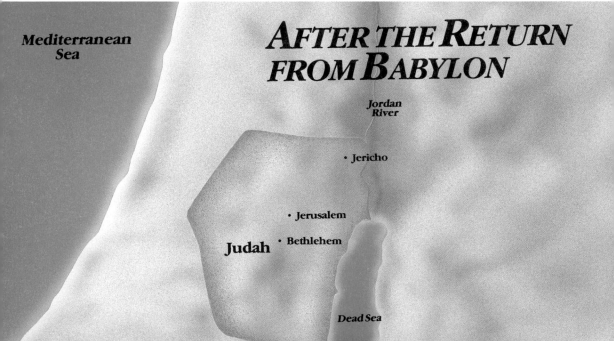

AFTER THE RETURN FROM BABYLON

Mediterranean Sea

Jordan River

• Jericho

• Jerusalem

Judah   • Bethlehem

Dead Sea

Jesus' hands and side were pierced on Calvary (John 19:34-37). The coming one is called a shepherd (Zechariah 13). Jesus called himself the Good Shepherd, who gives up his life for his sheep (John 10). The coming shepherd will be struck down and his followers scattered (Zechariah 13:7). When Jesus was taken, his disciples deserted him and fled (Matthew 26:31-32).

Nehemiah

In 444 B.C. Nehemiah, an official in the Persian emperor's court, led a small group of Jews back to Jerusalem. His motive was to rebuild the city's ruined walls and, thus, take away the reproach of the holy city. Nehemiah served two terms as governor of the district in which Jerusalem lay. He not only led construction of the city walls but also led a moral and spiritual reformation.

Outline

I.	The walls rebuilt	1–6
II.	The covenant renewed	7–12
III.	Sins purged	13

Nehemiah 1–6: Rebuilding. Nehemiah also faced opposition from local peoples and their leaders. Nehemiah encouraged his people to rely on God and have their weapons ready.

Nehemiah 8: The law read. With the wall built, Nehemiah had Ezra read and interpret God's law to all the people. The act emphasized the fact that all of God's people were to know and to be responsible for keeping the divine law.

Nehemiah 9:1-37: Revival. A spontaneous revival led to the confession of sins, expressed here in a worship liturgy (5-37).

Nehemiah 9:38–10: Covenant renewal. The people promised to keep God's law and committed themselves to abide by the rules laid out in the Mosaic covenant. No longer would this people marry pagans, buy or sell on the Sabbath or hold back the tithes owed the Temple for support of priests and Levites.

Malachi

Little is known of Malachi, whose name means "my messenger." He wrote this last

These are typical seals in ring form used by government officials, as well as in everyday life.

book of the Old Testament sometime between 465 and 430 B.C. The book reveals how quickly the people of Judah turned away from the Lord. Just a few years after Nehemiah's death, God seems to have played an insignificant role in the thinking and practices of his people. The book is organized around a series of charges against Judah.

Outline

I.	God chose Judah	1:1-5
II.	Judah neglects God	1:6–2:9
III.	Judah breaks commitments	2:10-16
IV.	Judah doubts God's presence	2:17–3:5
V.	Judah denies God	3:6–4:3
VI.	Closing exhortation	4:4-6

Insight: "I hated Esau" (Malachi 1:1-5). Esau and Jacob were twin brothers, grandsons of Abraham. Esau was just a few minutes older, and as the older son would be his father's heir. But God did not want Esau to be heir to the covenant promise given Abraham's family. One meaning of the Hebrew word for "hate" is to decisively reject. Here "hate" is used in this sense. God decisively rejected any claim of Esau to the covenant promise he gave Abraham. Ancient legal documents from this part of the world use "love" and "hate" in exactly this way, to designate one person as heir and to rule out another.

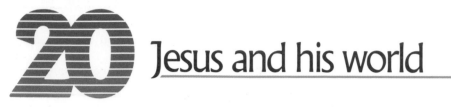

20 Jesus and his world

Jesus was born in the town of Bethlehem about five miles south of Jerusalem. At that time the land of the Jews was an insignificant district in the mighty Roman Empire. No one would have imagined that world-shaking events would take place there. Yet for hundreds of years, God had been shaping the world for a unique event, the birth of his Son.

MASTERY KEYS to the first century world:

- In what ways was the existence of the Roman Empire important to the development of Christianity?
- What was life like in Palestine in the time of Jesus?

Jewish politics

After the Babylonian captivity Judea and the promised land were under foreign rulers. The worst of these, Antiochus Epiphanes, stimulated a revolt in 168 B.C. when he ordered pigs sacrificed in the Jewish Temple. After three years of fierce guerilla struggle, the Jews were victorious. Jerusalem was taken, and on December 25, 165 B.C., the Temple was rededicated. Today the Jewish people still commemorate this event with Hanukkah, the Feast of Lights.

The Jewish revolt was led by the Maccabean family, who succeeded for a time in maintaining some semblance of independence. In 64 B.C. the kingdom was annexed by the Romans to their empire. In 47 B.C. Herod was made a Roman procurator in hopes of appeasing the Jews, so the Romans could control the region. Herod was made an administrative king under Rome's control in 37 B.C.

When Jesus was born, the land that God had promised Abraham was incorporated as a tiny province in the great Roman Empire. There were about 4,000,000 Jews in the

THE ROMAN EMPIRE IN NEW TESTAMENT TIMES

ISLAND OF BRITAIN

GALLIA

Rhine River

Danube River

ITALY

Black Sea

HISPANIA

CORSICA

• Rome

MACEDONIA

• Byzantium

SARDINIA

CAPPADOCIA

PHRYGIA

GALATIA

Tigris Riv

Corinth • Athens

LYCIA AND

Euphrates Riv

SICILIA

PAMPHYLIA CILICIA

Carthage •

CRETE

MESOPOTAM

Mediterranean Sea

JUDEA

AFRICA

CYRENE

Alexandria

• Jerusale

world, but most of them had settled in major cities of the Empire. Only some 700,000 Jews lived in their ancient homeland.

Insight: Many Gentiles in the cities of the empire were attracted by Judaism's high morality and monotheism. Later these Gentiles, who were called "God fearers," formed the core of most of the churches that Paul and other Christian missionaries established.

The empire

When Jesus was born, the Roman Emperor, Caesar Augustus, ruled a vast area (Luke 2:1). In his forty-year rule this first of the Roman emperors controlled all the lands along the Mediterranean Sea and also the island of Britain. His Roman armies, organized into well-armed legions of some 6,000 men, were the most powerful in the world. The Roman navy had put down piracy and had made travel safe throughout the empire. In addition, the Romans built a system of paved roads throughout the empire. Each of these accomplishments would later make it easier for Christian missionaries to spread the Gospel.

It was Roman policy to permit a great degree of self-government to the diverse peoples within the empire. The Sanhedrin, of which we read in the Gospels, was both a Jewish religious and secular court. In Palestine, Herod the Great ruled the combined lands of Judea and Galilee for Rome. Herod the Great was the ruler who ordered the wise men to betray the Christ child and, when they did not obey, commanded that hundreds of children be killed. Herod was a cruel and wicked man, who, when near death, brought all the leading men of his kingdom to Jerusalem and left orders that they be murdered the moment he died. He could not bear the thought that any might rejoice at his death! Herod's orders were not carried out.

Herod was also a builder. He beautified the Jerusalem Temple and built the Roman-style city of Caesarea on the coast.

When Herod died, civil war broke out. The Roman army stepped in. For some twenty years after the civil war, Palestine was at peace under three different Roman governors. Then Pontius Pilate became governor of Judea.

Insight: There are several "Herods" in the Gospels. The Herod who ruled Galilee when Jesus was an adult was Herod the Great's son. He had John the Baptist's head cut off. Later, Jesus was sent to Herod for trial. Herod ruled from 4 B.C. to about A.D. 39 (Matthew 14:1; Mark 6:14; Luke 23:6-7). His title was Tetrarch.

A Roman soldier in full dress uniform

Homes in Palestine today are often similar to homes built in that region in Bible times.

The dream of independence

The Jewish people yearned for freedom. But different political and religious groups disagreed about Judah's future.

The Zealots were a minor party who counted on an armed rebellion to win freedom by war. The Essenes, who maintained a community at Qumran, near the northwest coast of the Dead Sea, simply withdrew to an isolated desert community. This is the group that hid its library in jars in a nearby cave. Part of that library became the famous Dead Sea Scrolls found again in 1947.

But two major parties dominated Jewish life in Jesus' time. The Sadducees controlled the priesthood in the time of Christ. They

were the party of the wealthy upper class, which thought it best to get along with the Romans. This was because Rome supported their claim to power and enabled them to misuse the priesthood to gain vast wealth. Centuries later Jewish tradition still called down curses on the family of Annas, the high priest, for its greed and cruelty.

The Pharisees were a small group of less than 6,000 men in Jesus' time. They were the religious conservatives of the day. They were committed to keep every detail of God's law until the Lord sent the Messiah. They believed that the Messiah would free God's people, shatter Rome and make Israel powerful once again. Although they were a small group, the Pharisees were influential and were greatly respected by ordinary people for their commitment to God's law.

The Messiah

The true hope of the Jewish people was rooted in Old Testament promises about the Messiah, God's Anointed. The Jews believed that this person was destined to sit on David's throne, to destroy Israel's enemies and to restore the nation to prominence. But the people of Jesus' day failed to consider other Old Testament pictures of the Messiah. The promised Savior was destined to deliver his people from sin not just from foreign enemies. He was destined to suffer and die before he would rule. When Jesus did appear and begin to preach, the leaders of the Jewish people and most of the population refused to believe that the humble carpenter of Nazareth was the Savior promised long ago by God. He did not fit their image of a powerful, political Messiah.

Daily life in Jesus' day

Most people who lived east of the Mediterranean Sea shared a common lifestyle and language. Greek was the language of trade and daily life. Latin was also in use at least by some of the Romans. The sign on Jesus' cross was in Aramaic, Latin and Greek (John 19:20). Some translations use the word "Hebrew" in places like John 19:20-22; Acts 21:40. It was actually Aramaic. The Greek called it "Hebrew" because Aramaic was the language of the Hebrews. Jesus and his disciples may have spoken all three languages.

Houses in the land of Jesus were usually built of stone or sundried brick. In cities throughout the empire, poorer and middle class people often rented single rooms in large apartment buildings.

The homes of the wealthy were comfortable with many rooms constructed around an open court. Some homes had furnaces, with hot air carried through the house by pipes. Some also had running water. The wealthy in Jerusalem might even have had a *miqveh*, a special enclosed bath used for ritual purification.

But most homes in Judea and Galilee were one-story structures. The roofs were flat, made of tiles or layers of branches and mud. Stairs on the outside led to the roof, which was surrounded by a low wall. People often ate and slept there in the open air.

The Jewish people ate two regular meals, one at noon and the other in the evening. Most people ate fruits and vegetables, supplemented at times with fish and cheese. Meat was usually eaten only on festival days. Bread, made from wheat or barley flour and cooked in flat, round loaves, was the basic staple of life.

Jewish men wore white tunics, long skirt-like garments about knee length. They also wore a belt, called a girdle in some Bible versions. They wore shoes or sandals on their feet. The men wore their hair shorter than men of some other nations, and they grew beards. Women wore short tunics under a brightly colored outer tunic that fell to their feet. The veils worn by Jewish women covered the head but not the face.

In the Roman Empire as a whole, there were more slaves than free men. There were fewer slaves in the little land of the Jews.

People struggled to earn a living there. Many worked on small farms or herded sheep. Some had little shops or small businesses. There were fishermen, tanners, tentmakers and carpenters. Each of these last occupations is mentioned in the Bible. Archaeologists have also discovered evidence of a glass factory in first century Jerusalem.

But life was hard, and wages were low. Those who worked for others were paid daily, and a day's wage was just enough to buy food and shelter.

Insight: The reference in the Lord's model prayer, "give us this day our daily bread," reflects the hand-to-mouth existence lived by most people in Palestine.

Education

Proverbs 1:2-3 sums up the Jewish vision of education. Learning is "for attaining wisdom and discipline; for understanding words of insight; for acquiring a disciplined and prudent life, doing what is right and just and fair" (NIV).

The Jewish people valued education highly. Boys began their education at age six, going to their local synagogue. There a teacher paid by the community instructed them in reading and writing using the Scriptures as the textbook. The curriculum also included simple arithmetic and religious rituals. Boys with special promise went on to study with a rabbi. The goal of this higher education was a better mastery of the Old Testament. There was, however, no formal education for girls; training in domestic skills was taught at home by the mother.

Every Jewish boy was also taught a trade, to enable him to provide for himself and his family. Even those like the Apostle Paul, from well-to-do homes, were taught to earn a living with their hands. This reflects the Jewish ideal that every workman should be a scholar, and every scholar a workman.

The Jewish people had little interest in the education valued by the Greeks or Romans. There was nothing more important to the godly Jew than God, and no better way to learn to please him than to know the word of God. Thus, the true goal of Jewish education was holiness, which could be achieved by knowing God's law and living in full harmony with the law of God.

Jewish worship

In cities throughout the Roman Empire Jews gathered each Sabbath in synagogues. There they read and discussed the Scriptures, and joined together in ritual prayers and songs of worship. This practice took place in Judea and Galilee as well. In Jerusalem alone there were over 100 synagogues in the time of Christ.

Yet, Jerusalem had a unique role in Jewish worship. Jerusalem was the site of God's Temple, expanded and beautified by a forty-year building project initiated by Herod the Great. At the Temple, priests offered the animal sacrifices commanded by the Old Law. Jews from all over the world traveled to Jerusalem to take part in annual festivals, like Passover. On such occasions the city population might swell from an estimated 40,000 to some 200,000 persons! The Feast of Tabernacles was an especially joyous occasion. The people sang as they journeyed to the Holy City, chanting Psalms 145-150. All week they camped outdoors, in tentlike booths made of branches. Thus, they relived the journey of their ancestors from slavery in Egypt to freedom, and celebrated with dances and feasting.

This, then, was the land of Jesus. It was a tiny province in a mighty empire. But God was about to send his Son to this tiny land, to live a human life, and then to die a human death for the sins of all mankind.

21 Jesus: the baby, the boy

Matthew 1—2; Luke 1—3; John 1

The first four books of the New Testament are known as the Gospels. The word means "good news." These books tell the story of Jesus' life on earth, his death on the cross and his resurrection from death. What the Gospels say about Christ's birth makes it clear he is both the Old Testament Messiah and the Son of God.

MASTERY KEYS to the birth of Jesus:

- What is the significance of Jesus' virgin birth and the events surrounding it?

- What passages of Scripture teach Jesus' preexistence as God, coequal with God the Father?

Sources of the Gospels

Each of the four Gospels gives a distinct portrait of Jesus. Matthew is directed to the Jews and demonstrates Jesus' right to David's throne and his fulfillment of prophecy as Israel's Messiah. The Romans admired a man of decisive action, and Mark is directed to them, showing Jesus as a man with au-

It is likely that Jesus was born in a stable inside a cave much like this one near Bethlehem.

Nazareth in southern Galilee today. Jesus was raised in Nazareth.

thority and a mission; he also shows Jesus' great power as God. The Greeks idealized human excellence, and Luke is directed to them, to show Jesus as the perfect human being. These three Gospels are organized mostly in chronological order and are known as the synoptic gospels. The slight variations between them are explained by the fact that each writer selects incidents to report that demonstrate his particular theme. Only John's gospel is primarily topical rather than chronological. It is the universal Gospel, presenting Jesus to all men everywhere as the eternal Son of God.

John and Matthew were Jesus' disciples and write as eyewitnesses. Mark was a young teen when Jesus taught. Later Christian writers report that Mark tells what he heard from Peter. Luke was a careful historian who spoke to many of "those who from the first were eyewitnesses."

Jesus' birth
Luke 2:1-16

A study of Roman census records and records concerning the death of Herod in 4 B.C. suggests that Jesus was born in 5 B.C. The calendar we use today was introduced in A.D. 525; due to calendar inaccuracies from the time of Augustus, Dionysius, who prepared the calendar we use today, missed the actual date of Jesus' birth by about five years.

The virgin birth
John 1

Jesus came into the world by natural childbirth. Every other human being since Adam and Eve has originated in the union of a father's sperm and a mother's egg. The Bible teaches that the divine Christ existed before conception and that no human fathered him. Because Jesus had a human mother and a divine Father, he was both fully human and fully divine.

The doctrine of Christ's preexistence is directly taught by John, who identifies Jesus as "the Word" (that is, the one who has always expressed or revealed God). John says that "the Word was with God, and the Word was God" (John 1:1). This means that Jesus was, in fact, the Creator of the universe and all living creatures (1:3-4; Colossians 1:15-17).

In 700 B.C. Isaiah predicted that a child born of a virgin would be "Immanuel," a name that means "WITH US IS GOD" (7:14). The Gospel accounts stress the fact that Jesus was conceived by the Holy Spirit, so that the baby born to Mary was no ordinary human being, but "the Son of God."

Insight: How important to Christianity is the deity of Jesus Christ? The Bible says, "If anyone acknowledges that Jesus is the Son of God, God lives in him and he in God" (1 John 4:15).

Mary and Joseph
Matthew 1; Luke 1; 3

Mary and Joseph were ordinary Jewish people, living ordinary lives in Palestine. Joseph was a carpenter, so poor that he was not able to afford a lamb to offer in sacrifice at Jesus' birth. Instead, the couple was only able to offer two doves or young pigeons (Luke 2:24; Leviticus 12:8).

Yet both were extraordinary in their readiness to obey God. Mary joyfully accepted her role despite what must have been a deep concern that her fiance would refuse to marry a pregnant virgin. Mary's praise in Luke 1:46-55 is one of Scripture's most beautiful expressions of faith. Joseph, too, immediately accepted the angel's word that Mary had not been promiscuous but that her child was from the Holy Spirit.

Mary and Joseph were extraordinary in another way. Each was in the messianic line of David. Most biblical scholars believe that the genealogy in Matthew 1 is Joseph's, giving Jesus the legal right to David's throne, and that the genealogy in Luke 3 is Mary's, recording Jesus' biological descent.

Bethlehem
Luke 2:1-7

Joseph and Mary lived in Nazareth, a town in Galilee. But the promised Savior was to be born in Bethlehem (Micah 5:2). At just the right time, they had to travel to Bethlehem to be counted in a Roman census (Luke 2:1-2).

Insight: In some cases Romans required people to return to their ancestral home to give their tax report. But people who owned property in another town had to go there for the census. Since Bethlehem was Joseph's ancestral home, Joseph may have owned some property in Bethlehem that had been in his family. Joseph and Mary were required to go there when the census was taken. God even used Roman law to fulfill prophecy!

Many others were in Bethlehem for the census, and there was no room for Mary and Joseph at the local inn. Jesus was probably born in a cave behind the inn. Caves were often used to stable animals, and such caves are common around Bethlehem. See photo on page 125.

The shepherds
Luke 2:8-20

Jesus was born during the time of year when shepherds brought their flocks to the hills near Bethlehem. Scholars debate whether he was born in December or in March. The famous saying of the angels, "on earth peace, good will toward men" probably means "on earth peace to men who now receive God's grace."

The wise men
Matthew 2:1-12

The name given the wise men in the Bible is "Magi." This title was used for hundreds of years in Persia (present-day Iran). The Magi were a highly educated class of advisers in the Persian empire. They studied languages, astronomy, mathematics and many other sciences but often relied on astrology and other occult arts.

Daniel was one of this special group some 500 years before Jesus was born. Only Daniel was able to answer many of the rulers' questions, for God himself revealed truths to Daniel (Daniel 2, 4, 5).

How did the Magi know about Jesus' birth? Many believe they linked the appearance of an unusual star with the teaching of Daniel and a prophecy in Numbers 24:17.

It was natural for the Magi to seek a newborn king in the palace of Herod. But this king was born in humbler circumstances. After finding the child and worshiping him, the Magi went back to their homeland another way to avoid Herod.

Murder of the children
Matthew 2:13-18

Herod the Great had been ill for some time prior to his death in 4 B.C. He died just two or three months after the Magi came to Jerusalem. This cruel and jealous king had murdered his own sons when he thought they wanted his throne. He was now determined to kill the unknown child. (A Roman emperor once joked that it was safer to be Herod's pig [*hus*] than his son [*huios*]!)

When the Magi did not return, the dying king learned from the Old Testament that the promised ruler was to be born in Bethlehem. He had learned from the Magi when the star appeared. So, to be safe, Herod ordered that all male children (in the Bethlehem area) who were two years old and under should be put to death. Herod could not bear the thought that anyone should ever have his throne.

Ready for the Messiah

Several events associated with Jesus' birth suggest God was preparing the nation for the Messiah. Each event must have stimulated gossip and a heightened expectation in Judah and Galilee. Zechariah, the priest who fathered John the Baptist, had been struck dumb before John was conceived but, upon naming John, could speak again. Luke says that, "In all the mountains of Judea people continued talking about all these things" (Luke 1:65). The arrival of the Magi, the appearance of the unusual star and Herod's execution of the children must have also caused excited gossip. When Jesus was presented at the Temple, an aged man named Simeon and a prophetess named Anna both identified him to his parents and bystanders as the Messiah. All these events must have encouraged rumors in the tiny Jewish homeland, so that people expected something unusual to happen during their lifetime.

This photo shows a detailed model of King Herod's palace in Jerusalem.

Jesus' childhood
Luke 2:41-52

We know little about the childhood of Jesus. But we do know something about the way godly parents of Jesus' time trained their sons. Josephus, writing about A.D. 80, said, "Our ground is good, and we work it to the uttermost, but our chief ambition is for the education of our children. We take the most pains of all with the instruction of children, and esteem the observation of the laws, and the piety corresponding with them, the most important affair in our whole life" (*Against Apion*, 1:12).

On his birth the boy Jesus would have been given a life verse, a text from the Old Testament that began with the first letter of his name and ended with the last. His mother and father would have repeated Scripture verses to him even as an infant, and he would have been taught to touch the tiny box containing a Bible passage whenever leaving or entering the home.

Beginning school between ages five and seven, Jesus would have been taught for several hours a day by a teacher. The teacher would be chosen for his character and would use kindness and caring to motivate learning. In the school teaching would be oral; key passages of the Old Testament would be memorized.

Thus, Jesus' childhood must have passed pleasantly. He was nurtured by loving parents, taught the word by a dedicated teacher, worked beside Joseph and played with the younger brothers and sisters that were added to the family's home.

Jesus' Temple visit
Luke 2:41-52

At age twelve each Jewish boy became a "son of the law." The modern Bar-Mitzvah ceremony carries on this tradition which is thousands of years old. The ceremony is a "rite of passage" and means the individual is now considered an adult as far as responsibility to obey the laws of God is concerned.

Among the laws in force in Jesus' time was a commandment that all adult males go to Jerusalem three times a year to take part in worship festivals. The year Jesus was twelve, he went with his parents to Jerusalem for the seven-day Passover celebration. On these festival days it was the practice of religious teachers to hold public classes in the Temple court.

When the festival was over, and Mary and Joseph left for Nazareth, Jesus stayed behind, asking and answering questions. We learn two important things from Luke. First, the teachers were stunned that a twelve-year-old should have his understanding. And second, when Jesus was finally missed and then located by his parents, he told them, "I must be where my Father's work is!" (Luke 2:49)

Insight: This personal expression, "my Father," was not used by the Jews of their personal relationship with God. Even as a child Jesus understood his special relationship with God.

22 Jesus' baptism and temptation
Matthew 3—5; Luke 3—4; John 1—2

When Jesus was about thirty years old, John the Baptist began to preach in Judea. John called on the Jewish people to repent and warned them that the promised Messiah was about to appear. Jesus was baptized by John and then led by the Spirit into the desert. There he was tempted by Satan. Only after passing this test did Jesus begin his own ministry of preaching.

MASTERY KEYS to Jesus' baptism and temptation:
- What was the significance of Jesus' baptism?
- What do we learn about Jesus from his temptation, and what lessons can be applied to help us successfully meet our own temptations?

John the Baptist
Luke 3, Matthew 3

During Mary's pregnancy she had stayed for several months with Elizabeth, an older woman who was pregnant with John the Baptist. Luke 1:36 says Elizabeth was a relative, and many believe that Jesus and John were cousins. As the two boys grew up, their families may have spent time together.

John's birth had been predicted by an angel. His father, a priest named Zechariah, was told that John would be "filled with the Holy Spirit even from birth" and would "go on before the Lord, in the spirit and power of Elijah" (Luke 1:15,17, NIV). This was a reference to Malachi's prediction about 400 years earlier that Elijah would appear just before the coming of the Messiah.

Then, in young adulthood, John disappeared into the wilderness. There he ate only the simplest foods and wore rough clothes as had Elijah (2 Kings 1:8). When Jesus was nearly thirty years old, John appeared near the Jordan River and began to preach. John described himself as "the voice of a man calling out in the desert" (John 1:23). John's mission was to prepare the hearts of God's

people for Jesus' appearance and to ready them spiritually for the mission Christ would soon undertake.

John's message
Matthew 3, Luke 3

John's preaching was blunt and compelling. First, he confronted his listeners with their sins and called for repentance. The word "repent" indicates a change of both heart and life. John demanded that his hearers make an inner commitment which would be demonstrated by a holy life. Thus, tax collectors were told to collect only what the law allowed, while those with material possessions were told to share with those in need.

Second, John called on his listeners publicly to undergo water baptism. In Judaism water baptism was associated with cleansing and purification (Leviticus 14:7-8; 2 Kings 5:14). Jewish rabbis in Jesus' time taught that cleansings must be by immersion in running or 'living" water. John's baptism in the Jordan River met this criteria, and probably he, too, immersed those who came to him. Archaeologists have found special pools with containers to collect rain ("living" water) that were used by people in Jesus' time for rites of cleansing. But such cleansings were personal and private. John's baptism was different. It was conducted openly and was no ritual cleansing. Instead, John's baptism was a public commitment to repent of sin and to faithfully practice the law of God. Those who were baptized sought God's forgiveness and were ready to change their hearts and lives.

Third, John announced that very soon the promised Messiah would appear. The people must prepare themselves for his appearance, for he would baptize those who were ready with the Holy Spirit and, using a symbol of judgment, would baptize the unresponsive with fire (Matthew 3:11).

Insight: The baptism of the Holy Spirit and fire was shown dramatically at Pentecost (Acts 1:5,8; 2:1-13; 11:16).

John and Jesus

One day Jesus joined the crowds that listened to John and soon offered himself for baptism. John tried to stop him.

Why? At that time John may not have yet realized Jesus was the Son of God (John 1:31). But John did know his friend well and was so aware of Jesus' holy life that he said, "I should be baptized by you!" (Matthew 3:14). But Jesus insisted that he be baptized, explaining that "We should do all things that are right" (Matthew 3:15). By undergoing John's baptism, Jesus identified himself with John's message. Jesus showed that he trusted God's promises and that he himself was committed to obeying God.

Jesus identified
Matthew 3:13-17; John 1:29-34

As Jesus came up out of the Jordan River where John baptized him, God's voice was heard by John, saying, "This is my Son and I love him. I am very pleased with him." At that time, also, the Holy Spirit visibly settled on Jesus. John realized that Jesus was the one whom he had been called by God to announce. From that time on, John identified Jesus as "the Son of God" (John 1:34).

Temptation

The same Greek word that is translated as "temptation" is also rendered as "test" or "trial." In both Old and New Testaments a temptation situation lets the reader know the character or commitment of an individual.

Jesus was baptized in the Jordan River, perhaps near this spot.

Insight: James 1:13-14 says God "does not tempt anyone, but each one is tempted

Sometimes called the Wilderness of Temptation, it may have been here that the Devil tempted Jesus after he was baptized by John the Baptist.

when, by his own evil desire, he is dragged away and enticed'' (NIV). The difficult situations which God permits are not intended to cause us to fail, but rather to strengthen us and to demonstrate what God has been doing within us to release us from evil desires.

Jesus' temptation
Matthew 4; Luke 4

After his baptism Jesus was led into an empty wilderness. There he fasted for 40 days. Most people will use up all bodily resources in a fast of 30 days. It was only when Jesus was physically exhausted that Satan appeared to tempt him.

Each Gospel lists the same three temptations. Satan meets a hungry Jesus and challenges him to turn stones into bread.

In this test the pressure on Jesus is rooted in every human being's physical needs and hungers. Jesus rejected Satan's suggestion that he use his divine power and met the temptation in his human nature alone. This is the significance of Christ's first quotation of Scripture: ''A person does not live only by eating bread.''

Satan also challenged Jesus to throw himself from the ''pinnacle'' of the Temple. This was the highest point on its outer wall. In this temptation, too, Satan said ''if you are the Son of God.'' In the Greek language there are different ''ifs.'' In the first temptation the ''if'' means ''since you are the Son of God.'' In this temptation the Greek ''if'' is an ''if'' of uncertainty. It means ''if you really are God's Son.'' Satan added that Scripture promised angels would catch Jesus before he even bruised his foot (Psalm 91:11-12). Satan was asking Jesus to prove his relationship with the Lord by putting God to a test. Jesus knew exactly what Satan was doing. He went back to an incident in which Israel had tried to test God to make God prove, ''Is the Lord with us or not?'' (Exodus 17:1-7). Jesus answered by quoting Moses' comment on this experience: ''Do not test the Lord your God . . .'' (Deuteronomy 6:16). Jesus would trust God, despite the weakness and hunger he felt in his human nature.

Insight: Satan quoted Scripture when tempting Jesus. But Jesus knew the Bible well and was not deceived when Satan applied a passage wrongly. Bible study had been important to Jesus. Bible study is important for us.

For the third temptation Satan promised Jesus immediate authority over every kingdom of this world if only Christ would worship him. If Jesus ruled, surely wars and suffering would end. So Satan offered Jesus a truly "good" thing. But God's plan for Jesus led to the cross before the crown. Jesus refused to abandon the will of God even for something which might seem good.

Jesus' victory over Satan was nearly complete (Jesus' resurrection completed his victory over Satan). Christ had demonstrated his personal commitment to God.

This photo shows the Pinnacle of the Temple formed by a high corner of the Temple wall.

Jesus' first miracle
John 2:1-11

Jesus went to a wedding party in Cana of Galilee. When the wine ran out, Jesus turned more than a hundred gallons of water into wine (John 2:1-11).

The friends whom Jesus would soon invite to be his disciples observed this miracle and, the Bible says, "put their faith in him."

Insight: In New Testament times wine was mixed with three to seven parts of water. The rabbis taught that wine not mixed with water was to be considered unclean and should not be drunk.

The Beatitudes
Matthew 5:1-12

After his baptism and temptation, Jesus began his public teaching. His most famous sermon featured the Beatitudes, which explain how people are to be "happy" or "blessed."

Each of the beatitudes contrasts the basic kinds of attitudes with which persons can approach life. The blessed, who find true happiness, abandon the attitudes that pervade human society. Rather than being self-confident and self-reliant, they "know they have great spiritual needs . . ." and depend on the Lord. Rather than being satisfied with what this world offers, they hunger and thirst for righteousness. Rather than being self-willed, they are meek, that is, utterly responsive to God.

True happiness is not to be found in this world or its values but rather in the believer's commitment to the values of God and those things which are important to him.

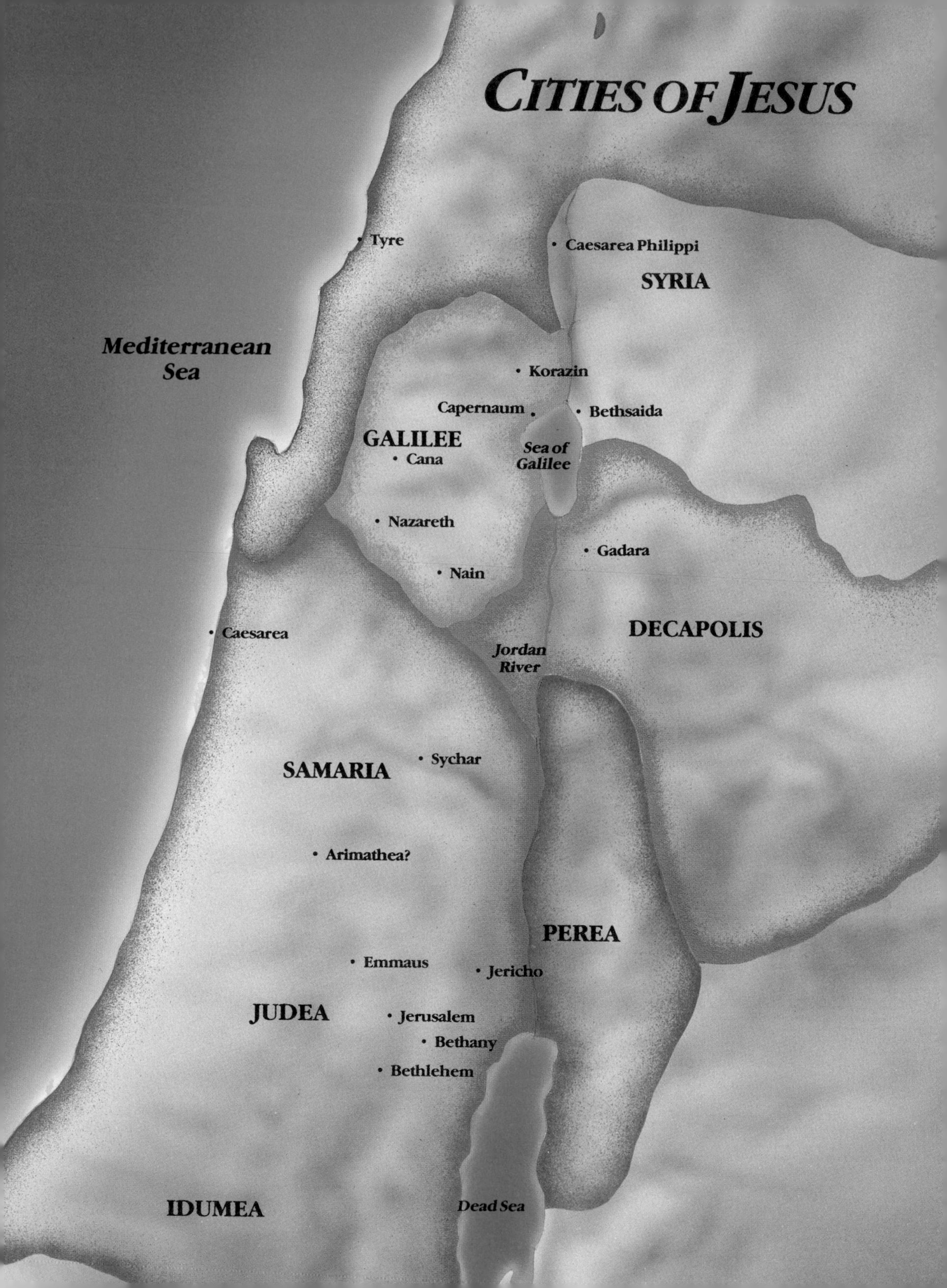

CITIES OF JESUS

Mediterranean
Sea

• Tyre

• Caesarea Philippi

SYRIA

• Korazin

Capernaum •   • Bethsaida

GALILEE
• Cana

Sea of
Galilee

• Nazareth

• Gadara

• Nain

• Caesarea

DECAPOLIS

Jordan
River

• Sychar

SAMARIA

• Arimathea?

PEREA

• Emmaus   • Jericho

JUDEA   • Jerusalem
• Bethany
• Bethlehem

IDUMEA   Dead Sea

The Beatitudes were given to the people by Jesus in his Sermon on the Mount on a mountain very near this scene.

The Beatitudes

Now when he saw the crowds, he went up on a mountainside and sat down. His disciples came to him, and he began to teach them, saying:

"Blessed are the poor in spirit,
for theirs is the kingdom of heaven.
Blessed are those who mourn,
for they will be comforted.
Blessed are the meek,
for they will inherit the earth.
Blessed are those who hunger and thirst
for righteousness,
for they will be filled.
Blessed are the merciful,
for they will be shown mercy.

Blessed are the pure in heart,
for they will see God.
Blessed are the peacemakers,
for they will be called sons of God.
Blessed are those who are persecuted
because of righteousness,
for theirs is the kingdom of heaven.

"Blessed are you when people insult you, persecute you and falsely say all kinds of evil against you because of me.
Rejoice and be glad, because great is your reward in heaven, for in the same way they persecuted the prophets who were before you.
— Matthew 5:1-12, NIV

23 The miracles of Jesus
The Gospels

The Gospels report a number of miracles performed by Jesus. In each case these helped others. The miracles had at least two distinct purposes. They clearly demonstrated the love of God. And they also authenticated Jesus as one who came from God and who acted in God's name. Both Jesus' words and works showed him to be the Son of God.

MASTERY KEYS to Jesus' miracles:
- How do biblical miracles differ from magic?
- What do the different kinds of miracles that Jesus performed teach about his authority?
- What is the relationship between Jesus' miracles and faith?

Miracles and magic

People in Christ's time believed in magic. Pagans used spells and incantations in attempts to influence their gods and to control other people. They firmly believed that magic could harm their enemies. The Jewish people were commanded to avoid the occult (Deuteronomy 18:9-12), but they recognized

Sick people lay on the five porches that surrounded this pool. The water in the pool was sometimes stirred up. Many people believed that the first person into the troubled water would be healed.

Many of Jesus' miracles were performed on and around the Sea of Galilee shown above, where stormy winds come up quickly and around which daily life hummed.

the existence of the spirit world. Many Jewish religious writings from the two centuries before Christ show a preoccupation with demons and evil spirits. The book of Acts mentions several incidents involving persons who possessed real or pretended occult powers (see Acts 8:9-23; 13:4-12; 19:11-20). Interestingly, modern books on magical arts are strikingly similar to ancient books of magic. The Bible tells us that when those who believed in magic became Christians, they burned their books of spells (Acts 19:19).

Jesus' miracles were not magic. He used no incantations. Instead, Jesus simply spoke, and his word alone accomplished the wonder he intended. Instead of seeking to gain power over others, Jesus used his power to help. In healing the sick and feeding the hungry, he demonstrated God's limitless love.

Even Jesus' enemies acknowledged his acts as miracles. As Nicodemus, a member of the Sanhedrin, admitted, "We know that you are a teacher sent from God. No one can do the miracles you do unless God is with him" (John 3:2).

Miracle overview

The New Testament reports four distinct types of miracles that Jesus performed: (1) Jesus exercised power over nature, seen in such miracles as stopping a storm, walking on water and multiplying bread to feed the hungry. (2) Jesus exercised power over illness, healing the lame and giving sight even to those born blind. (3) Jesus exercised power over evil spirits. Demons who oppressed or possessed human beings were forced to leave at Jesus' command. (4) Jesus had the power to recall the dead to life, as he showed in the case of a young girl and of Lazarus, who had been dead for four days.

Jesus' power over nature
Matthew 8:23-27

The Sea of Galilee is subject to sudden wild storms as winds sweep down the Jordan

River valley. Jesus slept in a boat during one such storm, which was so severe even his fishermen disciples were terrified by the heaving seas. When the frightened disciples woke Jesus, he commanded the wind and seas to cease, and it suddenly became calm.

Jesus performed few nature miracles. Even this one had as its purpose saving the lives of the disciples. Yet, knowing that Jesus can exercise control over the material universe remains a source of comfort to us to-day, as does Jesus' promise, "I will continue with you until the end of the world" (Matthew 28:20).

Jesus' power over sickness

Jesus performed more miracles of healing than any other kind. There are a number of things we can learn from a study of these miracles. First, many of Jesus' healings came as a response to faith. Those in need came to Jesus because they believed he could help.

The miracles of Jesus

Miracle	Scripture	Where performed	What it shows
Power over nature			
Turns water to wine	John 2:1-11	Cana	Jesus is God's Son
First catch of fish	Luke 5:1-11	Sea of Galilee	Shows Peter that Jesus is Lord
Stills the storm	Matthew 8:23-27 Mark 4:35-41 Luke 8:22-25	Sea of Galilee	Teach disciples to trust Jesus
Feeds 5,000	Matthew 14:15-21 Mark 6:35-44 Luke 9:12-17 John 6:5-15	near Bethsaida	Jesus cares about people in need
Walks on sea	Matthew 14:22-33 Mark 6:45-52 John 6:16-21	Sea of Galilee	Shows disciples Jesus' power
Feeds 4,000	Matthew 15:32-39 Mark 8:1-9	near Bethsaida	Jesus cares about the hungry
Money from fish	Matthew 17:24-27	Capernaum	Pay Peter's tax
Withers fig tree	Matthew 21:17-22 Mark 11:12-14; 20-25	Jerusalem	To teach faith
Second catch of fish	John 21:1-14	Sea of Tiberias	Reveal Jesus to disciples
Power over sickness			
Heals nobleman's son	John 4:46-54	Cana	Faith
Cures man with harmful skin disease	Matthew 8:1-4 Mark 1:40-45 Luke 5:12-15	Galilean city	Faith, caring
Heals soldier's servant	Matthew 8:5-13 Luke 7:1-10	Capernaum	Faith
Heals Peter's mother-in-law	Matthew 8:14-17 Mark 1:29-31 Luke 4:38-39	Capernaum	Friendship
Heals paralyzed man	Matthew 9:1-8 Mark 2:1-12 Luke 5:17-26	Capernaum	Jesus has power and can forgive sins
Cures woman of bleeding	Matthew 9:20-22 Mark 5:25-34 Luke 8:43-48	Capernaum	Faith
Gives blind their sight	Matthew 9:27-31	Capernaum	Faith

Miracle	Scripture	Where performed	What it shows
Heals crippled hand	Matthew 12:9-14 Mark 3:1-6 Luke 6:6-11	Galilee	God cares for people more than for religion
Heals non-Jewish girl	Matthew 15:21-28 Mark 7:24-30	Tyre	God loves all peoples
Heals deaf man who cannot talk	Mark 7:31-37	Decapolis	Bring friends to Jesus
Heals a man at a pool	John 5:1-18	Bethesda	Faith
Gives back sight	Mark 8:22-26	Bethesda	Bring friends to Jesus
Gives sight to man born blind	John 9:1-41	Jerusalem	God's power
Heals man with dropsy	Luke 14:1-6	Jerusalem	God loves people more than religion
Heals ten of harmful skin disease	Luke 17:11-19	Galilee	Need to be grateful
Replaces ear of high priest's servant	Luke 22:49-51 John 18:10-11	Garden of Gethsemane	Jesus' deep love for enemies
Power over evil spirits			
Heals man who could not talk because of demon	Matthew 9:32-34	Capernaum	Jesus' power is from God
Sends evil spirit from man	Mark 1:23-27 Luke 4:33-36	Capernaum	Jesus has power over the Devil
Heals man who was blind and could not talk	Matthew 12:22 Luke 11:14	Galilee	Jesus' power is from God
Heals child with demon	Matthew 17:14-20 Mark 9:14-29	Mt. Tabor	Faith is greater than Satan
Heals woman crippled for 18 years	Luke 13:10-17	Jerusalem	God loves people, not religion
Power over death			
Raises Jairus' daughter	Matthew 9:18-26 Mark 5:35-43 Luke 8:41-42, 49-56	Capernaum	Faith
Raises widow's only son	Luke 7:11-16	Nain	Caring
Raises Lazarus	John 11:1-45	Bethany	Jesus has power over death

Second, Jesus' healings are the clearest expression of God's love in the Gospels. Never did Christ curse a person with illness, not even those who opposed and hated him. Third, several such miracles reveal God's priorities. Several times Jesus healed on the Sabbath, in spite of severe criticism (Matthew 12:9-14; Luke 13:10-17; 14:1-6). The "religious" attacked Jesus for doing "work" on the Sabbath. Christ responded by saying that it is never against the divine law to do good on the Sabbath (Matthew 12:12).

Medicine or God?

Knowing that Jesus can heal, some have argued that going to doctors demonstrates a lack of faith. The Old Testament does criticize King Asa, but for seeking help only from physicians and ignoring God (2 Chronicles 16:12). In biblical times balms and ointments were used medicinally. The kind of oil specified in James 5:14 and the Greek word translated "pour oil" make it clear that James is telling the sick to call church elders to pray and to have medical treatment.

Jesus' power over evil spirits

The Gospels tell many stories of demons and make it clear that these evil, spiritual beings are real. Gospel references show they oppressed humans often with sickness or madness (Matthew 8:16-17; 9:32; 12:22-28;

Mark 1:32; 5:1-20; Luke 4:33-35; 8:27-39; 9:37-42). Many people believe that the demons of the New Testament were angels who followed Satan when he first chose to sin.

Demons, like Satan, are antagonistic to human beings and dedicated to doing them harm. Many have suggested that the high level of demonic activity reported in the Gospels suggests that Satan was marshalling forces to oppose Jesus.

Christians have expressed concern about demon-possession today. Surely evil spirits are real. Thus, Christians should avoid any involvement in the occult. When a person becomes a Christian, Jesus becomes part of his or her life. Jesus, who cast out demons in New Testament times, can guard us against their influence today. "The one who is in you is greater than the one who is in the world [Satan]" (1 John 4:4).

Jesus' power over death

The New Testament tells of three persons Jesus restored to life. Two must have just died (Jairus' daughter, Matthew 9:18-26; the widow's son, Luke 7:11-16). A third, Lazarus, had been buried for four days (John 11:1-45). In biblical Palestine bodies were wrapped in linen and spices and buried almost immediately, for in that hot climate decay came quickly.

The persons Jesus recalled to life were not resurrected to eternal life at that time but were recalled to earthly life. That is, they were brought back to biological life but were destined to die again. Yet, by his exercise of power over physical death, Jesus authenticated his claim to be able to recall the dead to endless life at history's end. "I am the resurrection and the life," Jesus told the sisters of Lazarus. "He who believes in me will have [eternal] life even if he dies [physically]" (John 11:25).

Resurrection

The ultimate miracle and ultimate proof of Jesus' claims to be the Son of God would come only after Christ's death on the cross. After three days in a tomb, Jesus was resur-

This is the tomb in which many believe Lazarus lay when Jesus raised him from death.

rected, recalled by the Father to eternal life. As the Bible says, Jesus "was appointed to be God's Son with great power by rising from death" (Romans 1:4).

Did miracles provoke faith?

The Bible uses many different words to describe the reactions of those who wit-

Jesus' compassion often reached out tenderly to heal handicapped people, such as this blind woman.

nessed Jesus' miracles. One word usually found in miracle stories is *thaumazo*, which indicates utter astonishment. Other Greek words suggest amazement mixed with fright (see Mark 1:27; 10:24,32). In general, the miracles confirmed and deepened the faith of those who already believed in Jesus (John 2:11). But those unwilling to believe Jesus' words and his enemies were frightened by the miracles while remaining unconvinced (John 9:33-34).

Insight: Some dismiss the Bible's report of miracles, arguing that in ancient times people were superstitious and easily tricked. The very words the Bible uses disprove this argument. Jesus' miracles were so amazing and awe-inspiring that even superstitious people were stunned!

Acts tells us that converts in Ephesus burned their books of magic. The appeal of magic in that city is shown by the fact that the books burned were worth about a million and a half dollars (Acts 19:17-20).

Exorcism. The Bible gives no ritual for casting out demons. Jesus simply spoke to the demons and commanded them to leave. The only exorcism the New Testament describes is in Acts 16:16-18. There Paul spoke to the evil spirit and said, "In the name of Jesus Christ I command you to come out of her."

Modern miracles?

The Bible reports only a few periods in which many miracles were performed. The first was the Exodus period, when God used miracles to force Pharaoh to release his people. The second was in the time of Elijah and Elisha, when the aggressive introduction of Baal worship by King Ahab and his wife Jezebel created a spiritual crisis. The third period was that of the Gospels and early Acts, when miracles authenticated the message of Jesus and the preaching of the early church about him.

Throughout history most believers have lived without experiencing or witnessing miracles of the sort described in the Gospels. But an absence of obvious miracles does not mean God is inactive. In fact, God has been at work through "natural" events to bless his people and to carry out his purposes. Christians who experience God's answers to prayer and his work within their own lives are well aware that God is at work now.

The focus of God's work now is not external in the physical universe but internal within the hearts of his people. As the Bible says, "With God working in us, God can do much, much more than anything we can ask or think of" (Ephesians 3:20).

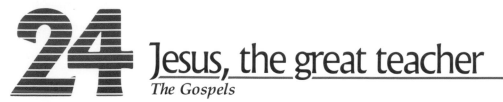

24 Jesus, the great teacher
The Gospels

Jesus' ministry on earth was marked by teaching as well as healing. Many of Christ's teachings were public, presented to eagerly listening crowds.

Jesus often illustrated his sermons by stories and parables. Frequently, he used everyday examples to make his message clear. But some parables are difficult and were not intended to be understood by those who did not believe in him (Matthew 13:11-14).

A survey of Jesus' teachings shows us how important his words are to you and me as we seek to please God with our daily lives.

MASTERY KEYS to Jesus, the great teacher

- What are some of the ordinary practices or objects Jesus used to illuminate spiritual truths?
- What are five subjects Jesus dealt with in his public teaching, and what did he say about each?
- What is the subject of Jesus' parables that are purposely hard to understand?

Jesus' teaching ministry

Jesus' teaching differed in several important ways from what we think of as teaching today. Jesus did not teach in a building or hold formal classes. Instead, Christ simply talked to crowds that gathered around him as he traveled about the land. Christ's classroom was the hillside or a boat from which he instructed a crowd on shore or a house surrounded with eager men and women who wanted to hear what was going on inside. In general, Jesus did not even try to communicate new information. The Jewish people were already familiar with the Old Testament. What Jesus did was to put familiar truths in new perspective and to show the missed meaning of what his hearers already

The Good Samaritan Inn shown above is a reminder of one of Jesus' most memorable teachings.

This narrow road led between Jericho and Jerusalem and was known as a dangerous road to travel. It was on such a road that the story of the Good Samaritan was pictured.

knew. To illuminate fresh meaning, Jesus often told stories or used illustrations from nature and ordinary life.

A few examples help us understand this teaching strategy.

Matthew 13:1-8, 18-23. In Jesus' day farmers planted grain by "broadcasting." A man took a handful of seed and with a sweeping motion released just enough to evenly cover the ground. But not every seed fell on good ground. Some fell on rocky or weedy places. Jesus used this familiar scene to illustrate an important truth. God, too, "broadcasts" his word, seeding the community with his message. But human hearts are like soil. How the individual responds to God's word will determine whether or not it produces fruit. Thus, every hearer is ac-

countable for his own response to God's word.

Matthew 7:24-28. In Palestine most villages in Jesus' day were built on rocky hillsides. In desert lands rainwater does not sink into the ground. Instead, it rushes with terrible force along watercourses such as the sandy track shown in the picture above. So Jesus told a story about two men. One, who was wise, selected a rocky area on which to build his house. The other, who was foolish, built on the sand, which is found along a watercourse. When the rains came, the house of the foolish man was destroyed by the rushing water while the house of the wise man stood firm. Jesus then told his listeners that his own words were a safe, rocklike foundation on which a person might build his or her life.

But, to build there, a person must do what Jesus said, not just listen. A person who listens and learns without obeying is like the foolish man who built his house where it was sure to be destroyed.

Insight: The Bible often presents obedience to God's word as essential evidence of a true faith in God and love for God (see John 14:23-25; James 1:22-25).

Luke 10:25-37. An expert in Old Testament law tried to limit his obligation to "love your neighbor" by asking who "neighbor" included. Jesus responded by telling the story of a Jewish man who was attacked and injured by robbers when he traveled the narrow road between Jerusalem and Jericho. Two fellow Jews hurried by him, probably worried that the robbers were still near. In those days the Jews despised Samaritans, whom they viewed as a half-breed people who distorted the true faith. But a Samaritan stopped and helped the injured Jew! When Jesus asked who was a neighbor to the injured man, the expert in the Old Testament had to say the Samaritan, for being a neighbor means showing love in a practical way. Then Jesus told his listeners to go and do as the Samaritan had done.

Insight: Most Jews in Jesus' day thought of a "neighbor" as a near relation or at least a fellow Jew. Jesus expanded the definition of "neighbor" in God's law (Leviticus 19:18). The neighbor is no longer just one of "your people," but anyone in need—even an enemy!

Luke 15:8-10. When a woman married in New Testament times, she was given a dowry by her father. The dowry was usually money, and often coins were strung together on a string. This dowry money was very precious to women of Jesus' day. So when Jesus told the story of the woman with ten coins, who lost one, every listener understood why the lost coin was important to the woman, even though it was worth only 18 cents!

She searched for that coin, and when she found it, she ran to her neighbors to share her excitement and relief.

Each individual person, Jesus said, is as important to God as that dowry coin was to the woman who lost and then found it. Heaven itself is filled with excitement and relief when just one person who was lost is found and restored to the Lord.

Jesus' sermons

Much of Jesus' teaching was conveyed through brief stories. At times Jesus also gave longer sermons. One of these is recorded in Matthew 5–7. This sermon, delivered on a mountainside, began with the beatitudes. Then Jesus continued.

Matthew 5:17-20: Fulfilling the law. Jesus' enemies accused him of being against Old Testament law. Jesus said he came to "fulfill" the law. To the Jews "fulfill the law" meant "to explain the law's true meaning." Jesus aroused opposition because his explanation disagreed with that of the Pharisees of his time.

Matthew 5:21-48: "It was said long ago." Old Testament law condemns certain actions. Jesus explained the law's true meaning by showing that the motives that lead to wrong acts are God's concern too. Murder begins with anger, and adultery with lust. To truly be like God a person must *be* good as well as do good! This kind of righteousness was far more than expected or required by the Pharisees (see 5:20).

Matthew 6:1-18: "The hypocrites." Many wonderful ideals were promoted in first century Judaism, such as praying regularly and giving to the poor. But Jesus attacked those who practiced their religion publicly just so others would think they were spiritual. As these were practices of many religious leaders, Jesus' criticism increased their hostility.

Matthew 6:19-24: Wealth. First century Jews thought that a person's wealth was a measure of his spirituality, and showed God was pleased with him. Jesus taught that too many who are rich serve money rather than God.

Stories Jesus told

Parable	Passage	Subject	Lesson
New winebags	Matthew 9:16-17	Jesus' message	Jesus has a new message from God
Farmer and the seed	Matthew 13:1-8 Mark 4:3-8 Luke 8:5-8	God's word	We must hear and obey God's word
Weeds	Matthew 13:24-30	God's people	The good and bad will be separated
Mustard seed	Matthew 13:31-32 Mark 4:30-32 Luke 13:18-19	God's people	Small beginnings can lead to big things
Yeast	Matthew 13:33 Luke 13:20-21	God's people	Small beginnings can lead to big things
Hidden treasure	Matthew 13:44	God's people	Choose what is truly valuable in life
Very valuable pearl	Matthew 13:45-46	God's people	Choose what is truly valuable in life
Fishing net	Matthew 13:47-50	God's people	The good and bad will be separated
Lost sheep	Matthew 18:12-14 Luke 15:3-7	God's love	God loves each person deeply
Servant who would not forgive	Matthew 18:23-25	God's people	We forgive because God forgave us
Workers in a vineyard	Matthew 20:1-16	Service	God rewards us generously
Two sons	Matthew 21:28-32	God's love	God welcomes the sinner who comes to him
Evil renters	Matthew 21:33-46 Mark 12:1-12	Punishment	People who hate God's Son will be punished
Wedding dinner	Matthew 22:1-14	Punishment	People who do not accept God's invitation will be punished
Ten virgins	Matthew 25:1-13	Jesus' return	We must be ready when he comes back
Talents	Matthew 25:14-30	Service	We must use our abilities to serve God
Wise and evil servants	Matthew 24:45-51 Luke 12:42-48	Service	We are to serve God and others as we wait for Jesus to return
Two men who owed money	Luke 7:41-43	God's people	We love God more when we realize we are sinners
Good Samaritan	Luke 10:30-37	Service	Do good to all in need
Friend at midnight	Luke 11:5-8	God's love	God is always willing to help
Unimportant seat at party	Luke 14:7-11	Humility	Don't be proud: let God reward
Lost coin	Luke 15:8-10	God's love	Each one is important to God
Son who left home	Luke 15:11-32	God's love	God forgives all who change their hearts and minds and return to him
Clever manager	Luke 16:1-10	God's people	We are to use money to do good and prepare for the future
Rich man and Lazarus	Luke 16:19-31	Punishment	People who love money more than God are foolish
Unworthy servants	Luke 17:7-10	Service	Serve God because we are thankful
Unfair judge	Luke 18:1-8	God's love	God will answer our prayers if we ask him
Pharisee and tax collector	Luke 18:9-14	God's love	Anyone who changes his heart and life can be forgiven
Bags of money	Luke 19:11-27	Service	Use our talents to serve God

Matthew 6:25-34: "Your heavenly Father." The Jews thought of God as father of their nation, as its sense of origination. Jesus now called individuals to think of God as their own Father, and trust him to care for them as they would their own children.

Matthew 7:1-6. Judging others. Jesus warned those who were always judging to examine themselves for faults, not others. Here the phrase "throw your pearls to pigs" means, do not attempt to share the Gospel with unbelievers who do not want it and would despise it.

Matthew 7:7-14: Prayer. The stunning notion that God is a father to individuals brings great confidence in prayer. It also means we can expect God to answer prayer, not because we are good, but because he is gracious and loves us.

Matthew 7:15-23: Evidence. Religious acts or leadership is not evidence of relationship with God. What counts is an obedient life.

Matthew 7:24-27: Obedience and authority. The Jews expected to obey the Old Testament laws. Now Jesus said that they must obey him.

In all he said, Jesus claimed to have a better understanding of God's word than the recognized religious leaders. Because many of the things he taught were different, people had to decide to accept or reject his authority. For hundreds of years rabbi's had studied Old Testament law and written their interpretation. Usually any teacher of the law quoted some long-dead teachers to support his preaching. Jesus' listeners were astonished because he "taught them as one who had authority, not as the teachers of the law" (Mark 1:22).

Jesus' obscure parables

Some of Jesus' parables were spoken in order to withhold the truth from insincere people, "For these people have become stubborn. They do not hear with their ears. And they have closed their eyes" (Matthew 13:11-15). In each Gospel most of the obscure parables are about the kingdom of heaven.

What is the "kingdom of heaven"? The Jewish people expected the Messiah to set up immediately an earthly kingdom and rule the whole world. But Jesus came to suffer and die, and he immediately established a spiritual kingdom. Christ used parables to describe this spiritual expression of his kingdom, which those who rejected a servant Savior would be unwilling to hear.

Subjects about which Jesus taught

Jesus touched on all the Bible's basic themes. He spoke of God's love, of himself, of eternal life, of the future, of prayer and of the role of individuals in God's plans. Here are a few of the things Jesus said about these topics which touch each of us today.

God's love. Jesus taught that God should be seen as father. No rabbi has suggested such an intimate, personal relationship although God was seen as father (in the sense of "founder") of the nation. As the individual's father, God values each person more than the flowers or birds for whom he provides (Matthew 6:25-34). But the ultimate proof of God's love is that God gave his Son "that whoever believes in him may not be lost, but have eternal life" (John 3:16).

Jesus himself. Jesus used many images to teach about himself. Bread was the basic food of Palestine, so he called himself the bread of life (John 6). All knew the care shepherds took to protect their sheep. Jesus called himself the good shepherd, who was willing to lay down his life for his sheep (John 10). Grapes were one of the land's most important crops. Jesus pictured himself as the true vine, the source of that vital life which would enable branches to bear fruit (John 15). But Jesus also spoke of himself in blunt, plain terms. He claimed to be the giver of eternal life (John 5); indeed Jesus claimed to be the Old Testament's God (John 8:48-59; 17:20-24).

Eternal life. Jesus taught that no one's existence ends at death (Luke 16:19f). Those who believe in him will be raised to eternal life (John 3; 5).

Oil lamps were a common form of light in Bible times. Jesus compared his followers to a light in a dark world.

The future. Jesus warned that wars and suffering would occur on earth before he comes back. But Christ clearly promised that he would return (Matthew 24; Mark 13).

Prayer. Christ made many promises about the believer's access to God the Father and God's eagerness to answer prayers offered in Jesus' name (Matthew 6:5-15; John 16:23-24). To pray "in Jesus' name" means to rely fully on Jesus, and to seek what he has taught us is right and good. The Bible's most familiar prayer is a model that Jesus taught his disciples to follow. This familiar "Lord's prayer" is explained on the chart below.

Individuals. Each person is not only important to God but has a significant role to play in his present kingdom. Jesus called his followers to be lights in the world (Matthew 5:14-16; Luke 8:16-18). In New Testament times lamps were made in the form of shallow cups. Olive oil was put in the lamps, and a bit of flax was used as a wick. Even such dim lamps could always be seen in a dark house. The good lives of Jesus' people will be visible in our dark world and so will glorify God.

Jesus also pictured believers as servants whose master was away (Matthew 25:14-30). Each servant was given resources to use for his master's benefit. While our abilities vary, we each have personal resources we are to use to serve and glorify God.

The stories that emphasize faithful service while Jesus is away always stress the fact that Christ's return will be unexpected (Matthew 24:36; 25:13). Believers are never to think, "my master is staying away a long time" (NIV) and stray from the path of obedience. We do not know when Jesus will come back, but we do know that he might return at any moment.

25 Jesus' disciples

The Gospels

Many of those who heard Jesus teach and saw his healings were drawn to him. Jesus chose twelve men to become his disciples, the future leaders of his church.

MASTERY KEYS to Jesus' disciples:

- What were some of the admirable personality traits of Jesus' first disciples?
- How were disciples trained in Judaism in Jesus' day?
- What are three qualities of disciples Jesus seeks in his followers today?

"Disciple" in the New Testament

The Bible uses this word in several ways. It identifies the twelve special men Jesus chose to be with him, but it is also used of people who are adherents of a movement. In this sense there were disciples of the Pharisees and of John the Baptist—persons who followed their teachings. Also, many people who are called disciples of Jesus thought of themselves as his followers but were not true believers. The Bible says many such disciples "left him. They stopped following him" when his teaching became more difficult (John 6).

This is a typical fishing boat often seen on the Sea of Galilee.

Calling on men to use the natural talents God had given them, Jesus called Simon Peter and his brother, Andrew, who were professional fishermen, to become fishers of men.

Training disciples

In New Testament times persons were not trained for spiritual leadership in schools or seminaries. Instead, students came to live with acknowledged rabbis (experts in Scripture). The student would listen to the rabbi's words and observe his way of life. The student's goal was to learn all that his teacher knew and, also, to become like his teacher in personal holiness. The student was committed to serve his rabbi in any way possible. In return, the rabbi fed and housed his students, pleased that they would pass on his understanding of Scripture to others.

While even the most famous rabbis were expected to have a trade, the cost of providing for disciples was usually met by admirers who contributed money. A number of women served Jesus in this way (Matthew 27:55).

When the Bible tells us that Jesus selected twelve men "to be with him" (Mark 3:14), it reflects their entrance into this well-established rabbi-disciple relationship. Only by being with Christ always, seeing all he did and hearing all that he taught, could the twelve be prepared for leadership in Jesus' church.

After the church was established, the discipleship method of training leaders was altered from the rabbi-disciple relationship to an older brother-younger brother relationship. Why? Jesus said that no hierarchy of leaders should exist in the church, but all should be brothers (Matthew 23:8-12). After the Twelve died, leaders were to be selected for their exemplary Christian lives and gifts, not formal training (1 Timothy 3; Titus 1).

The twelve disciples

The Twelve were all ordinary men. Not one had special theological training or was a rabbi. All were men who had worked at their trade and been successful. Many of the great movements in church history have been launched by just such ordinary Christian men and women.

The disciples were Simon (Peter), Andrew, James, John, Philip, Bartholomew, Matthew, Thomas, James ("the younger"), Thaddaeus, Simon the Zealot and Judas. The Gospels reveal these facts about each of these men.

Simon Peter

Simon was a successful fisherman, a leader who was willing to risk, although he was often impulsive. He is named first on each list of the disciples. Although he denied Jesus the night before the crucifixion, Peter was the first to preach the Gospel after Jesus was raised from the dead, the first to perform a miracle and the first to preach to Gentiles. Peter's affirmation of faith, that Jesus "is the Christ, the Son of the living God," identified the foundation on which Jesus' church rests—the truth that he is God's son. Peter is mentioned more often than any other disciple. See Luke 5:1-11; Matthew 16:13-26; 26:31-35,69-75; John 21:15-19; Acts 1:15-26.

Andrew

Andrew was a fisherman like his brother Peter. He became a disciple of John the Baptist and heard John identify Jesus as the Lamb of God. He brought Peter to Jesus, and both followed Christ faithfully. See Matthew 4:18; Mark 1:16-18; 13:3; John 1:40; 6:8.

James

James was also a fisherman. He and his brother John were partners of Peter. These three formed the inner circle of disciples. They were also closest to Jesus when he wept in Gethsemane. James and John were hot tempered and were nicknamed "sons of thunder." This nature is illustrated by their suggestion that Jesus call fire down on a Samaritan village which would not welcome him. James, the disciple, was put to death by King Herod not long after Jesus' resurrection. The James who led the Jerusalem church (Acts) was not this man, but the Lord's brother. See Matthew 4:21; 17:1; Mark 5:37; 9:2; 10:35; Mark 13:3; 14:33; Luke 5:10; 8:51; 9:28; Acts 1:13; 12:2.

John

John wrote a Gospel and three New Testament letters. His theme of love illustrates how Christ transforms even the hot-tempered. When Jesus was crucified, he entrusted his mother to John's care. John outlived all the other disciples and lived to see the church spread throughout the Roman

There were many fruit-bearing trees in the East. This is one of the oft-mentioned olive trees in the Bible. Jesus condemned a fruit tree once when its blooms advertized that it had fruit to share, but it was barren.

world. His book of Revelation is the last book in the New Testament. John is called "the beloved disciple" because of his close relationship with Jesus. Yet, Revelation tells us that when he saw Christ in his full glory John "fell at his feet as though dead." See Matthew 4:21; 17:1; Mark 5:37; 9:2; 10:35,41; 13:3; 14:33; Luke 5:10; 8:51; 9:28; Acts 1:13; 12:2.

Philip

Philip was a personal worker who introduced individuals such as Nathanael to Jesus. He is mentioned in John 1:43-48; 6:5-7; 12:21-22; 14:8-9; Acts 1:13.

Tax collectors were very unpopular because they were often dishonest. Jews, working for the Roman government, collected taxes from their fellow Jews, but they often collected much more than the Romans required and pocketed the difference.

Nathanael

When introduced to Jesus by Philip, he was the first to acknowledge Christ as the son of God. Nathanael (who was surnamed Bartholomew) realized from a remark that Jesus made that Christ was no mere man. This quick belief is a model for all who did not have the chance to meet Jesus, yet who have believed on him. See John 1:45-49; 21:2; Acts 1:13.

Matthew

Matthew is also called Levi in the New Testament. He was a tax collector. In Jesus' day rulers sold the right to collect taxes. Tax men made their profit by assessing more tax than was due. Jews who collected taxes were viewed as traitors, who took sides with the Roman overlords against their own people. Thus, tax collectors are often linked in the Gospels with "sinners." This transformed sinner became a disciple and wrote the first book of the New Testament. See Matthew 9:9; 10:3; Mark 2:14; 3:18; Luke 5:27-29; Luke 6:15; Acts 1:13.

Thomas

He is often called "Doubting Thomas" because he could not believe the report of Jesus' resurrection. He had to touch Jesus' wounds before he would believe. Yet, when Jesus appeared to him, Thomas immediately fell to the ground and confessed, "My Lord and my God." Tradition says Thomas went to India and established a church, which still exists there today. See John 11:16; 14:5; 20:23-28; Acts 1:13.

James (the Less), Thaddaeus, Simon

Little is known of these three disciples. James is often confused with other men named James in the New Testament. He is called "the Less" because he was younger than the better known James. The other name of Thaddaeus was Judas, often identified as "not Iscariot." Simon is called "the Zealot." The Zealot movement was one which urged turning the Romans out of the Holy Land by armed revolt. After Jesus' resurrection, each of these disciples, then an apostle, went out to preach the Gospel. See Matthew 27:56; Mark 15:40; Mark 16:1; Luke 24:10; John 14:22.

Judas Iscariot

Judas was the treasurer of the little group and often helped himself to their funds. Be-

Today travel improvements allow missionaries to travel to countries worldwide to share the Good News of Jesus.

lievers have puzzled over Judas' betrayal of Jesus. Did he perhaps think that Jesus would escape, as he had so often in the past, and that Judas would then laugh at having fooled the priests to whom he sold Christ? Judas' history as a thief suggests he simply sold Jesus because he loved money more than the Lord. His later sorrow was not true repentance, for he did not turn to God but committed suicide. See Matthew 26:14-27; 27:3-5; Mark 14:10,43; Luke 22:3, 47-48; John 6:71; 12:4; John 13:2, 26-29; 18:2-5; Acts 1:16-25.

Discipleship today
John 1:43-49

The New Testament letters do not mention the word "disciple." Terms like "saint" and "brother" describe the committed believer. Perhaps one reason is that "disciple" in Judaism was associated with a process of training for spiritual leadership that the church never practiced. Instead of learning from an exalted "rabbi," Christians come to-

gether in local assemblies of the body of Christ. There each person uses a spiritual gift to minister to others.

Spiritual gifts are best understood as special enablement by the Holy Spirit to make a distinctive contribution to the spiritual growth of others. According to 1 Corinthians 12 each believer is given at least one of these gifts "for the common good." As Christians share, pray and encourage each other, these gifts come into play, and the Holy Spirit works within all to promote spiritual growth (Matthew 23:8-12; 1 Corinthians 12; Ephesians 4:11-16).

At the same time there does remain a valid use of the term disciple. The original disciples were persons who acknowledged Jesus as the Son of God and committed themselves to follow him. To become a disciple of Jesus today, we must share that original faith and express our faith in a personal obedience to Jesus as Lord.

The disciple's mission

Matthew 9:35 –10:42; Luke 9:1-6

Jesus traveled the rocky land of Palestine, going to its towns and villages. Wherever Jesus went, he taught and healed. Everywhere Jesus found hopeless, helpless people. He told his disciples to pray that God, the Lord of the harvest, would send workers to help with the harvest. Then Jesus sent his followers out to the towns he had no time to reach, to preach and to heal in his name.

Today there are many in the world like the lost and helpless of Jesus' time. Some live in our neighborhoods and work by our sides. Others live in distant corners of the world. Jesus' disciples, who share his love and concern for others, reach out to such persons with practical help and, most importantly, with the Good News about Jesus.

Insight: Jesus defined discipleship as servanthood. He said, "If one of you wants to become great, then he must serve the rest of you like a servant. If one of you wants to become first, then he must serve the rest of you like a slave. So it is with the Son of Man. The Son of Man did not come for other people to serve him. He came to serve others. The Son of Man came to give his life to save many people" (Matthew 20:26-28).

The disciple's way of life

Luke 12,17

Followers of Jesus are called to live distinctive lives. Two chapters in Luke give us special insight into the lifestyle appropriate for Christ's disciples.

Disciples evangelize: Luke 12:1-12. We are not to fear what others might say or think but must seek to please God. We are to "stand before others" and confess that we belong to Jesus. The Holy Spirit has taught us what to say when we speak up to share our faith.

Disciples rely on God: Luke 12:13-34. The average person worries about money, and many desire to be rich. Jesus told his followers not to be concerned even about necessities. God, who clothes the flowers and feeds the birds, knows our needs. Because we are more precious to him than they, he will meet our needs. Trusting in God to supply needs releases the believer to put God first. And reliance on God is demonstrated by seeking always to please the Lord, trusting him to meet our needs as we do his will.

Disciples serve others: Luke 12:35-48. In the New Testament "slave" (Greek *doulos*) emphasizes the surrender of our will to God that he might direct us. "Servant" (*diakonos*) typically emphasizes doing good to benefit others. Our Lord's will is that we should actively seek the good of others as an expression of our commitment to him.

Disciples live together in harmony: Luke 17:1-10. Even Jesus' disciples will sin against and hurt one another. These hurts can drive wedges between people and disrupt the fellowship and harmony which are so vital. Jesus' solution is confrontation and forgiveness. We express our hurt to the one who sinned against us and freely forgive that person.

This seemed hard to the disciples, who begged for more faith. Jesus' answer makes an important point. Servants are expected to obey their masters. The disciples did not need more faith to confront and forgive. They simply needed to remember that Jesus is Lord and to obey this command which he has uttered.

Disciples eagerly expect Jesus' return: Luke 17:20-37. Jesus has promised that he will return. While most persons will be caught up in their own affairs, immersed in everyday activities, Jesus' disciples will be on the watch. Each day we need to be about the things that will please him, aware that he may appear at any moment.

26 Jesus and his enemies
The Gospels

Some who heard Jesus responded eagerly to him. But most held back, unable to make up their minds. Still others hated Jesus and became his active enemies. It was these enemies who finally convinced the Roman governor to permit Jesus' execution.

MASTERY KEYS to Jesus' enemies:

- What groups became Jesus' enemies, and what were their motives?
- In what ways did Jesus' enemies try to discredit or destroy him?
- How did Jesus deal with his enemies and with the charges they made against him?

Open-air markets, prominent in Bible times, are still part of the Eastern culture today.

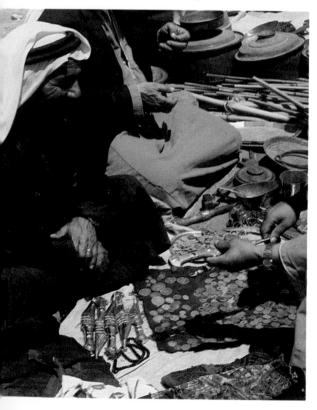

Jesus' anger
John 2:12-19

Jesus, so patient and sensitive with the needy, was openly hostile toward those who used religion to prey on others. One of the clearest instances of this hostility is seen in an event that took place at the great Jerusalem Temple.

God's people were commanded in the Old Testament to attend three major annual celebrations there. Also, individuals were told to have a priest make animal sacrifices for them as offerings or for forgiveness of sins. Each sacrificial animal had to be pronounced ritually clean (unblemished) before it could be sacrificed.

Josephus, the first century Jewish historian, tells us that the family of Annas, the high priest, controlled all products used in worship through four "booths [buildings, enterprises] of the sons of Annas." Legendary for greed, this priestly family defrauded Jewish worshipers and gained vast wealth. Another source of family income was the Temple tax, which could not be paid in Roman or Greek coins, which often carried the picture of a pagan deity. The acceptable Temple shekel was also sold to the worshipers at exorbitant prices. Thus, money changers sponsored by the priestly families were also found in the Temple court.

These practices made Jesus furious. He took a whip and physically drove the merchants from the Temple. God's house, which had been dedicated to prayer, had been turned into a den of robbers! Christ's action made the guilty priests implacable enemies.

Grain crops such as wheat and barley were a primary food source in the East. Roads often were built between two grain fields.

Insight: Many of Jesus' enemies were not motivated by religious convictions but by greed and by a desire for worldly power.

The Pharisees
Matthew 12:1-14

In Jesus' day there were some 6,000 Pharisees in the Holy Land. These were men who dedicated themselves to keep every detail of God's Law, and who were highly respected by their fellow Jews for this commitment.

Not all Pharisees were legalists. Jewish writers distinguished between the "ostentatious Pharisee" (who cared only that people thought him religious), the "bleeding Pharisee" (who, to avoid looking at a woman, would run into a wall and bloody his nose), the Pharisee who was pious out of fear and the "genuine Pharisee," who did God's will out of love for the Lord. We should not suppose that the Pharisees who opposed Jesus represent all who were members of this highly dedicated sect.

Even so, Jesus' teaching did conflict with the Pharisees' approach to the law. One Sabbath Jesus' disciples plucked some grain to eat as they walked beside a field. (Old Testa-

Various types of priests, identifiable by their clothing, served in the Temple.

ment law permitted travelers to do this but not to take more than a handful.) When the Pharisees saw this, they were outraged. Jesus' followers were breaking the Sabbath law against "work"! When Jesus went into their synagogue to worship, he found a man with a crippled hand. The Pharisees challenged Christ directly by asking if it were lawful to heal on the Sabbath. Their hardheartedness angered Jesus, who told them that God's law permits doing good on any Sabbath. And then Jesus healed the crippled man.

By Jesus' placing human needs above the legalistic quibbling over interpretation of the law, he revealed the hypocrisy of many Pharisees.

They had become so concerned with details that they ignored the love which the law was intended to encourage.

"Jewish law"
Matthew 7:1-23

To understand the Pharisees' conflict with Jesus, we need to understand their beliefs. The Pharisees believed that when God gave the Old Testament's written law, he also gave Moses an oral law which interpreted it. This oral law, which had been passed on from teacher to teacher, held the same authority as Scripture for the Pharisee.

Some examples of oral Sabbath law illustrate its nature. It was all right to spit on a

stone on the Sabbath. But it was wrong to spit on soft ground, for you might move the dirt, and this would be plowing. A person could travel only a certain distance away from home on the Sabbath. But if someone left a little food or clothing one "Sabbath day's journey" from his house, those possessions made that place "home." So he could go on another "Sabbath day's journey" further.

We see similar treatment of the law today. Since 1987 was a "sabbatical year" in modern Israel, Old Testament law required that the land not be cultivated but be given its own seventh year (Sabbath) rest. But Israel's rabbinic court, its highest religious authority, ruled that Jews could lease their land to non-Jews for cultivation because of the impact resting the land would have on the nation's economy.

There were at least seven different types of Pharisees in the times of Jesus. Each group observed special rituals that distinguished it from other groups.

Such interpretations in Jesus' time led to a focus on the trivial and to ignoring the true message of Old Testament law. Jesus told the Pharisees, "You have stopped following the commands of God. Now you only follow the teachings of men" (Mark 7:8). For many of the Pharisees, a failure to grasp the love that underlay all of Scripture's law led to major flaws in their movement.

Not all Pharisees were hypocrites. But Jesus identified these faults in the movement.

- Pride   Matthew 23:1-12
- Hypocrisy   Matthew 23:13-15
- Spiritual blindness   Matthew 23:16-22
- Lack of mercy   Matthew 23:23-24
- Wickedness   Matthew 23:25-36

The Sadducees
Matthew 22:23-33; Luke 20:20-26

Josephus, the first century Jewish historian, is our best source of information about this group. The Sadducees were an aristocratic party, committed to keeping peace with Rome and protecting their wealth. They were closely linked to the priests and were influential in the Sanhedrin, the ruling Jewish council. Unlike the Pharisees, the Sadducees were not popular with the people.

The Pharisees were the religious conservatives of Jesus' day, while the Sadducees were the liberals. They accepted only the five books of Moses as Scripture and did not believe in angels or in life after death. The high priestly family, headed by Annas, controlled this party and the Sanhedrin, the ruling Jewish council. Annas' influence was so great he placed five sons, a son-in-law (Caiaphas) and a grandson as high priest during his lifetime.

The Sadducees rejected the Pharisees' view that oral law had the same authority as the written word. They gave priority to the five books of Moses. They also reserved the right to interpret Moses' writing and ridiculed the Pharisees' reliance on tradition. Yet, the Sadducees were very concerned that religious rituals be conducted correctly.

This second-century synagogue near Capernaum was built over the ruins of a first-century synagogue in which Jesus may have taught.

These stairs lead to the House of Caiaphas. Jesus may have climbed these steps the night before his crucifixion.

The Sadducees believed in free will and insisted that each person was totally responsible for his choices. But the good or ill those choices earned would be worked out in this life. They believed the soul perishes with the body and that there is no resurrection.

Once when the Sadducees tried to trap Jesus with a trick question, Jesus said publicly to these spiritual leaders, "You don't understand because you don't what the Scriptures say. And you don't know about the power of God" (Matthew 22:29).

The Sadducees were not troubled by Jesus at first. However, when he became popular, they became worried.

Enemy strategies
Matthew 12:22-37; 22:15-22; John 8:12-59

The Pharisees and Sadducees were usually enemies, but they united to undermine Jesus. At first they attacked his practice of healing on the Sabbath as lawbreaking. But Jesus not only proved them wrong, he exposed their hardheartedness.

Later the two groups attempted to trap Jesus into taking unpopular positions. When one of them asked "Is it right to pay Caesar taxes?" he seemed to have set a perfect trap. If Jesus said "No," he could be accused as a rebel to the Romans. If Jesus said "Yes," the people, who hated their Roman masters, might turn against him. But Jesus answered that coins bearing Caesar's likeness might be given to Caesar, but one must be careful to give God what is his.

Stories about Jesus and his enemies

Jesus clears the Temple	Mark 11:15-19	Jesus tells a story about his enemies	Matthew 21:33-43
Jesus heals on the Sabbath	Matthew 12:9-14	Jesus avoids the Pharisees' trap	Matthew 22:15-22
Jesus rejects human rules for living	Mark 7:1-23	Jesus avoids the Sadducees' trap	Matthew 22:23-33
Jesus is accused of being Satan's friend	Matthew 12:22-27; Mark 3:20-30; Luke 11:14-28; John 8:12-59	Jesus judges his enemies' sins	Matthew 23:1-36

This picture is a reenactment of Jesus' death on the cross.

The enemies also began a whispering campaign, suggesting that Satan was the source of Jesus' power over demons. Christ openly confronted them. Only those who have no personal relationship with God could possibly hate Jesus, for Jesus came from God. Attacks on Jesus prove that the attackers, not Christ, follow the devil's evil paths.

Intent to kill
John 18–19

In John's Gospel "the Jews" does not mean the Jewish people. The phrase refers to those leaders who hated Christ.

Although these men controlled the Jewish Council, which administered local law, they had no power of execution. For this reason they were forced to appeal to the Roman governor to order Jesus killed. Pontius Pilate did not want to execute Jesus, who, he believed, was innocent. But when the Jews threatened to accuse Pilate in Rome of refusing to deal with a person who called himself "king of the Jews," Pilate gave in. The emperor might not understand a spiritual kingdom and might take the title as a sign of political rebellion.

In effect, the Jewish leadership proved so determined to have Jesus killed that they were willing to lie in order to commit judicial murder! Their hatred of Christ clearly reveals the emptiness of all their claims of spirituality and godliness.

27 Dead, but alive!
The Gospels

Jesus had traveled and taught in Judea and Galilee for over three years. Then one of Christ's own disciples betrayed him. Jesus was given an illegal nighttime trial and finally was condemned to crucifixion by an unwilling Roman governor. But three days after he was buried, Jesus was raised from the dead. That resurrection is one of the best attested of all ancient events.

MASTERY KEYS to Jesus' death and resurrection:

- What was the sequence of the most important events of Jesus' last week on earth before his crucifixion?
- What kinds of evidence provide solid proof that Jesus' resurrection actually took place?

Jesus' last week

Each Gospel devotes a major number of its pages to the description of Jesus' last week on earth. Most believe the events described in the four Gospels (see chart, page 161) took place in A.D. 30. The week began on a Sunday when Jesus entered Jerusalem riding on a donkey, cheered as "Son of David" by the crowd. This was one of the titles of the Old Testament's promised Messiah, and it crystallized the fears of Jesus' enemies. If the people were ready to acknowledge Jesus as the Messiah, they would surely be swept out of their places of spiritual leadership. What followed was a concentrated effort to have Jesus killed.

Jesus was crucified on Passover about A.D. 30. He was buried in a cemetery much like this one located in the Kidron Valley outside the city of Jerusalem. But he arose! He was victorious over sin and death.

Jesus' last week on earth

		Matthew	Mark	Luke	John
Jesus enters Jerusalem on donkey	Sunday	21:1-17	11:1-11	19:29-44	
Jesus drives sellers from the Temple	Monday	21:12-13	11:15-18	19:45-46	
Jesus teaches in the Temple	Tuesday	22:23–24:14	11:27–12:12	20:41-44	
Judas agrees to betray Jesus	Wednesday	26:14-16	14:10-11	22:3-6	
Jesus shares last supper with his disciples	Thursday	26:17-25	14:12-26	22:7-30	13:1-30
Jesus gives last teaching to his disciples	Thursday night				14—16
Jesus prays in Gethsemane garden	Thursday night	26:30-46	14:26-42	22:39-46	18:1
Jesus arrested and tried by Sanhedrin	Friday (before dawn)	26:47–27:1	14:43–15:1	22:47-71	18:2-27
Jesus judged to die by Pilate	Friday (morning)	27:11-26	15:1-5	23:1-25	18:28–19:16
Jesus is killed on a cross	Friday	27:31-56	15:20-46	23:26-49	19:17-30
Jesus is buried	Friday to Sunday	27:57-66	15:42-47	23:50-56	19:31-42
Jesus' tomb found empty	Sunday	28:1-10	16:1-8	24:1-12	20:1-10
Jesus seen by Mary	Sunday		16:9-11		20:11-18
Jesus seen on Emmaus Road by two believers	Sunday		16:12-13	24:13-35	
Jesus comes to his disciples	Sunday		16:14	24:36-43	20:19-25

Jesus seen by many in the next 40 days!

We can best understand each event if we walk with Jesus through that last week.

Jesus enters Jerusalem
Matthew 21:1-11

On Sunday, the first day of the week, Jesus entered Jerusalem riding on a young donkey. This fulfilled a prophecy of Zechariah, who had written five hundred years before, that the king God promised his people would enter Zion (another name for Jerusalem) in just this way (Zechariah 9:9). That Jesus rode a donkey is significant. When kings went to war, they rode horses. A king entering a city in peace rode a donkey. Jesus' mount demonstrated that he came to his people in peace, bringing peace (see Zechariah 9:9-10). The cry, "Praise to the Son of David" (Matthew 21:9) tells us that the crowds acclaimed Jesus as king. The Old Testament predicts that Israel's Messianic King will be a descendant of David, so this shout was tantamount to recognition of Jesus as the Messiah. At this time Jesus was well known to all, for his

In Bible times, palm branches were put on the path of someone being honored. A great crowd honored Jesus with palm branches when he made his triumphal entry into Jerusalem.

teaching and healing and his confrontations with spiritual leaders had been a major topic of conversation for everyone for nearly three years. Yet in just a few more days, some would be calling for his execution, and those same crowds would be silent at Jesus' crucifixion.

Insight: Crowds are often carried away by the emotion of the moment. Emotionalism should not be mistaken for commitment.

Judas' betrayal
Matthew 26:14-16

Judas took the initiative and went to Christ's enemies with an offer to betray him. He was paid 30 pieces of silver, which then was worth only about $4.80! Judas' promise to betray Jesus implies more than leading Temple guards to Christ when he was away from the crowds. Under Roman law a person had to be charged with a crime by witnesses who would sign papers and give testimony.

Jesus and his disciples shared wine and unleavened bread at the Last Supper.

Judas intended to speak against Jesus in court! Judas had joined his Lord's enemies.

When it was too late, Judas felt remorse. He tried to return the money, but the priests wouldn't take it back. So, Judas hanged himself, and his body fell down a cliff (Matthew 27:1-5; Acts 1:18).

The "Last Supper" and the "Lord's Supper"
Matthew 26:17-37; John 13–16

On Thursday evening Jesus and his disciples ate a Passover meal together in Jerusalem. They ate in an upper room, not far from the home of the Jewish high priest (see map, page 164). The Passover meal commemorated God's deliverance of the Jewish forefathers from Egypt. It specifically reminded Israel of how God spared Jewish children when the oldest son in each Egyptian household was struck dead. The blood of a lamb was sprinkled on each Israelite's doorway, and death passed over them.

After this commemorative meal, Judas went to complete plans for the betrayal. Alone with his own, Jesus told them that his own blood would soon be poured out for the forgiveness of sins.

Today Christians remember Jesus' death by celebrating communion, which is also called the Lord's Supper. The cup of juice reminds us of the blood Jesus shed on the cross, and the broken bread recalls his suffering body. Each remembrance reminds us that because Jesus died for our sins, we are forgiven and renewed.

Jesus spoke for some time that night. His Last Supper discourse, found in John 13–16, touches on most truths that are developed in the New Testament epistles. These chapters have been called the "seedbed" of New Testament faith.

Insight: The Lord's Supper is a vital reminder for Christians of personal relationship with Jesus. There are several important purposes of the Lord's Supper: (1) Fellowship (1 Corinthians 10:15-17), (2) Reminder (1

The Garden of Gethsemane, where Jesus was betrayed by Judas and arrested by Roman soldiers, is still a beautiful garden today containing some of the original olive trees under which Jesus and his followers may have rested.

Corinthians 11:24), (3) Proclamation (1 Corinthians 11:26). We are to observe it regularly until he comes (1 Corinthians 11:23-26).

Jesus' prayer at Gethsemane
Matthew 26:30-46

It was late at night when Jesus and the eleven disciples left the upstairs room. They went down stone steps into the Kidron Valley and traveled along it until they came to a path leading to an olive garden named Gethsemane.

The Bible describes Jesus' anguish there and records his prayer: "My Father, if it is possible, do not give me this cup of suffering. But do what you want, not what I want." Some have suggested that the "cup" was not the physical suffering but that the anguish of bearing our sins was what so deeply troubled God's sinless Son (see 2 Corinthians 5:21). It was God's plan that the Son should die for us. In his humanity Christ felt the pain. But he willingly submitted to the Father's will.

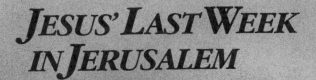

JESUS' LAST WEEK IN JERUSALEM

(4) (6)

Fortress
Antonia

Mount of Olives ▸

(2) Gethsemane ▸

(7)

Gordon's Calvary
& Garden Tomb

Temple

Golden Gate

Court of
the Gentiles

Herod
Family
Palace

(5)

Herod's
Palace

*UPPER
CITY*

(3)

Home of
Caiaphas

Mt. Zion

Kidron Valley

Upper
Room

(1)

*LOWER
CITY*

*HILL
OPHEL*

Hinnom
Valley

Insight: Hebrews says that "He prayed with loud cries and tears to the One who could save him from death. And his prayer was heard because he left it all up to God" (Hebrews 5:7). Death was not the end for Jesus: he was raised to life again!

An illegal trial
Matthew 26:47–27:1

After praying, Jesus was seized by a mob led by Judas, as his frightened disciples fled. The mob led Jesus back through the Kidron Valley to the home of the high priest. The Sanhedrin, the Jewish council, which had civil as well as religious authority, was assembled there.

At that trial the high priest asked Jesus if he was the "Son of God." Every person there understood this would involve a claim to actually be God. Jesus answered, "Yes, I am." The Sanhedrin refused to believe that Jesus could be their God come as a human being and, so, decided Jesus was guilty of blasphemy and must die.

Yet that night the council members broke the law they were dedicated to uphold. The trial of Jesus by the Sanhedrin was illegal according to Jewish law. That law stated the Sanhedrin could not meet at night, and that at least a day must pass before a person who was tried and found guilty could be sentenced.

Three different religious groups questioned Jesus that night. One met at the house of Annas, a former high priest and the father-in-law of the current high priest, Caiaphas (John 18:12-14). Another met at the house of Caiaphas (Matthew 26:57-68). Finally, the Sanhedrin questioned Jesus and determined that he must be put to death (Matthew 27:1-2).

The influence of Annas, who served as high priest, was so great that he placed five sons, a son-in-law (Caiaphas) and a grandson in the high priesthood during his lifetime. His powerful influence was now directed against Jesus, seeking Christ's death.

Pontius Pilate
Matthew 27:2-26

Pilate was the Roman governor, and only he could order execution. Jesus was brought to Pilate in the Fortress Antonia (see map page 164 , #4) very early the next morning. Since Jesus was from Galilee, Pilate sent him to Herod Antipas (map, #5), who returned him to Pilate.

Jesus was beaten and mocked by the Roman soldiers near this stone pavement that remains in Jerusalem today.

Jesus on the Cross

Jesus was offered drugged drink	Matthew 27:34
Jesus is crucified	Matthew 27:35
Jesus cries, "Father, forgive them"	Luke 23:34
Soldiers gamble for Jesus' clothes	Matthew 27:35
Jesus is insulted by his enemies	Matthew 27:39-44
Jesus is told cruel things by the thieves	Matthew 27:44
Jesus is believed in by one of the thieves	Luke 23:39-43
Jesus says, "Today you will be with me in paradise"	Luke 23:43
Jesus says to Mary, "Behold your son"	John 19:26-27

Darkness falls over the whole land
Matthew 27:45; Mark 15:33; Luke 23:44

Jesus says, "My God, my God, why have you left me alone?"	Matthew 27:46-47 Mark 15:33
Jesus says, "I am thirsty"	John 19:28
Jesus says, "It is finished"	John 19:30
Jesus cries, "Father, I give you my spirit"	Luke 23:46
Jesus dies	Matthew 27:50 Mark 15:37

Insight: In Rome the Emperor Tiberius had just executed the captain of his Praetorian Guard, Suetonius, for plotting to replace him. Many of Suetonius' political associates had been murdered. Many Bible scholars believe that Pilate received his appointment through Suetonius. In view of the political upheaval in Rome, Pilate would be especially frightened when the Jewish leaders threatened to accuse him of failing to support the Emperor by permitting a rival "king" to live.

Crucifixion

Death by crucifixion was so cruel that Roman law limited it to slaves, though sometimes in the provinces governors used it on criminals who were citizens to preserve law and order. A person's arms were nailed to a crossbar near the top of a tall pole. Death came as lungs were crushed and filled with blood. A person who was crucified often lived for several days. Jesus was crucified on a public execution ground established on a hill called Golgotha ("Skull hill") beside a well-traveled major highway. A chart on page 166 gives the sequence of the events reported in the different Gospels.

Jesus' burial
Matthew 27:57-66

A number of first century tombs like the one Jesus must have been buried in have been located around Jerusalem. These were dug in soft rock and usually featured several chambers in which bodies would be placed. The Bible says that Jesus was placed in a new tomb near the execution ground. Two sites have been suggested as the place of Jesus' burial. One is under the Church of the Sepulcher. The other is known as the "Garden Tomb" (see photo on page 167). The characteristics of the Garden Tomb fit the description of events as reported in the Gospels.

Jesus' empty tomb

On the morning of the third day, Sunday, there was an earthquake. The stone was rolled away, and the soldiers became unconscious. A series of visitors to the tomb were stunned to find that it held nothing but the empty grave cloths in which Christ's body had been wrapped. Only after the disciples saw Jesus alive did they recall his promise to rise from the dead. The enemies of Jesus never challenged the fact of the empty tomb. They never questioned the fact of his death. They did, however, spread a rumor that Christ's body had been stolen by friends.

Resurrection evidence

The New Testament was written by men who were eyewitnesses to the resurrection.

The Son of God was buried in this tomb, or one like it, and a giant stone was rolled into place to cover the entrance. The tomb in which Jesus was buried belonged to Joseph of Arimathea.

They were so convinced that Jesus lived that they were willing to be beaten or even executed to spread the Gospel. How foolish to imagine that so many persons would be willing to suffer for something they knew was a lie! (See A. J. Hoover's *The Case for Christian Theism*, Baker, 1976.)

These witnesses to the resurrection were committed to spreading the Good News about Jesus. Within a few years thousands all over the world had turned to Christ as Savior.

Michael Green in *Man Alive* (Intervarsity Press) makes this important point well. "Christianity does not hold the resurrection to be one among many tenets of belief. Without faith in the resurrection there would be no Christianity at all. (See 1 Corinthians 15:12-17.) Christ's church would never have begun; the Jesus movement would have fiz-

zled out like a drenched fire with his execution." The Jesus movement did not fizzle out. Instead, it spread like wildfire.

Early apostolic sermons, recorded in Acts, all focus on the resurrection of Jesus as proof of his claims and the basis of the believer's assurance of forgiveness.

Perhaps most compelling, however, is the evidence of changed lives. The first disciples of Jesus demonstrated a commitment to the risen Christ that far surpassed their commitment to him while he lived on earth. And there is more. Since the first century, literally millions have experienced Jesus' forgiving touch. Only the power of a living Christ could possibly turn so many to loving, righteous paths. The ultimate evidence for the resurrection is ours when we turn to Jesus and experience a personal spiritual renewal.

Christ's church established

Acts 1,2

Forty days after Christ's resurrection, he returned to the Father. Jesus told his disciples to wait in Jerusalem for the gift of the Holy Spirit, who would give them power to carry out their mission. When the Spirit did come, Peter preached the first sermon. This occurred on the Jewish feast day of Pentecost, a date that is considered the birthday of Jesus' church.

MASTERY KEYS to the beginning of the church:

- What is the nature of the book of Acts and its role in the New Testament?

- What made the events of Pentecost so special?

The book of Acts

The book of Acts was written about A.D. 62 by Luke, Paul's missionary companion and friend, the doctor who also wrote the Gospel of Luke. Several clues indicate that Luke wrote Acts as well as his Gospel. The author begins to use "we" in Acts 16, just after Luke joined the missionary party. The

The Mount of Olives is seen through these arches. Jesus ascended into heaven from the highest point on the horizon.

beautiful literary Greek of the two books suggests one author. Both books are dedicated to Theophilus, a new convert (Luke 1:4). "Most excellent" was a title of high rank in the Roman bureaucracy. Acts is one of the books of narrative history in the New Testament. It focuses on the efforts of two men—Peter and Paul.

The book of Acts can be viewed as describing ever-widening circles of evangelism Acts 1:8).

Outline

I. The Jerusalem church   1:6–6:7
II. Expansion in the Holy Land 6:8–9:31
III. The first Gentile converts   9:32–12:24
IV. Era of Gentile missions   12:25–16:5
V. The Gentile church   16:6–19:20
VI. Paul's imprisonment   19:21–28:31

A theme that is often emphasized in the book of Acts is the unique ministry of the Holy Spirit. Acts *describes* what happened; the epistles *explain* what happened. Acts' descriptions of what the Holy Spirit did in the first decades of the New Testament church and the epistles, which contain the teaching of the apostles, combine to give us insight into the nature and workings of the Holy Spirit.

Apostles
Acts 1

The term "apostle" indicates a person sent on a mission as a personal representative of another. The apostles were personal representatives of the Lord, given the mission of founding the church and of revealing the truth by which Christians live (Ephesians 2:20). Since the original apostles died, no one has had that unique commission from God.

Acts 1:6-8 explains their foundation-laying ministry clearly. Christ's last recorded words to his followers were to "be my witnesses in Jerusalem, and in all Judea and Samaria, and to the ends of the earth."

The apostles were Jesus' original disciples plus Judas's replacement (1:23-26), plus the Apostle Paul. These persons held special authority in the early church. Yet the word "apostle" is also used in a weaker sense and used of other persons (see Acts 14:14; Romans 16:7). It's likely that our word "missionary" best expresses the other meaning of "apostle."

Insight: In this sense each Christian is called to an apostolic ministry. As Paul writes, "we are Christ's ambassadors, as though God were making his appeal through us. We implore you on Christ's behalf: Be reconciled to God" (2 Corinthians 5:20, NIV).

Jesus' present ministry
Acts 1

Acts reports Jesus' ascension into heaven from the Mount of Olives (see map, page 164). It also records the promise conveyed by angels that Jesus will return in visible form (1 Thessalonians 4:17). Other New Testament passages give us an insight into what Jesus is doing now between his first and second comings.

Jesus said when away he would (1) prepare a place for his followers (John 14:1-3). The book of Hebrews tells us (2) that Jesus now provides immediate access for us to the throne of grace, so that we can come to God in any time of need (Hebrews 4:14-16). John's first letter (3) shows that Jesus speaks in our defense when we fall into sin, pleading his own blood as the basis of continuing forgiveness (1 John 2:1-2). Colossians tells us (4) that the universe itself is being held together only by an exercise of Jesus power (1:17). As head of his church, (5) Jesus' words guide and direct believers by communicating his will to us (Ephesians 1:20-22). As the vine (6) Jesus actively nourishes believers who keep his word, thus enabling us to bear spiritual fruit (John 15:1-11).

When we understand the fact that Jesus is actively at work today as our risen Lord, we realize that the book of Acts is not so much a report of what the apostles did as it is a revelation of what Jesus accomplished through the Holy Spirit in their lives.

This stained glass pictures Jesus' ascension into heaven after he had been raised from death.

Jesus' return
Acts 1

Acts simply states that "this same Jesus, who has been taken up from you into heaven, will come back in the same way you have seen him go into heaven" (1:11). Many passages deal with Jesus' second coming. It is important to remember that as Jesus' first coming spanned some 33 years, so the many events associated with the second coming may span a number of years. Considering this span of years, we should not expect to fit the many prophecies into some neat chart showing the second coming, step by step. However, two main points are clear: the second coming means blessing and judgment. When Jesus comes it will be to resurrect his

saints and to call living and dead believers home to be with him (1 Thessalonians 4:13-18). And, to those who do not know God or obey the Gospel, "the [Lord Jesus] will come from heaven with burning fire . . . those people will be punished with a destruction that continues forever" (2 Thessalonians 1:5-10).

Insight: For other descriptions of the second coming see Matthew 24:36–25; Mark 13; 2 Thessalonians 2; Revelation 19–20.

The Holy Spirit
Acts 1

Jesus told his apostles to wait for the Holy Spirit who would bring them power (1:8). Who is the Holy Spirit?

The Holy Spirit is one of the three Persons of the Godhead, just as fully God as the Father and the Son. Other biblical names for the Spirit are the Spirit of God, the Spirit of Christ and the Comforter. Jesus promised that the Holy Spirit would be with his followers "forever" (John 14:15-17). This is a vital relationship, for the Spirit is the living link between the individual and Christ. The Spirit teaches us (John 14:25-27), aids our prayers (Romans 8:26-27) and strengthens us (Romans 8:2-11). In most references to the Spirit, the adjective "holy" is included. This is not only because the Spirit himself is holy, but because he is the source of our holiness and moral transformation (Galatians 5:22-23). The Bible speaks of our bodies as temples of the Holy Spirit and urges us to live so that we reflect his holy character.

Insight: Knowing the Spirit is within us is a powerful motive for holy living.

Pentecost
Acts 2

The Day of Pentecost came 50 days after Passover on the Jewish religious calendar. It was a joyful harvest festival, during which the first of the new crop was offered to God.

The meaning of the events reported in Acts has been much debated. Particularly, are the "tongues" in which the disciples spoke an evidence of "baptism of the Spirit," and are they for today? Looking at the text, we note that there were three visible signs of the coming of the Holy Spirit: (1) the sound like a rushing wind, (2) something like visible flames over the disciples, and (3) the disciples speaking in different languages, which were understood by visitors from foreign countries. Peter pointed to these miraculous signs as evidence that a prediction of the prophet Joel, that God would give all believers his Holy Spirit, was now fulfilled (Joel 2:28).

If we compare Pentecost with other mentions of "tongues" in the New Testament, we note that in Acts they involve speaking in foreign languages. In 1 Corinthians 14:2-4 tongues (*glossolalia*) involve speaking to God or oneself in an unlearned language. And the same epistle defines baptism of the Spirit as the work by which the Holy Spirit joins the believer to Christ's body. And the epistle says this experience is for us "all" (1 Corinthians 12:13).

While the Bible does not identify speaking in tongues as "the" evidence of possession of the Holy Spirit, neither does it question the validity of speaking in tongues as a spiritual gift in the early church (1 Corinthians 14:5).

The church

The word "church" is the translation of the Greek work *ekklesia*, meaning a "called-out assembly." It is an appropriate word, for those who respond to Christ's Gospel are "called out" of the crowds of unbelievers to form a new community, held together by shared loyalty to and love for Jesus Christ.

The New Testament uses three word pictures to help us understand the nature of Jesus' church: (1) The church is a body (Romans 12; 1 Corinthians 12; Ephesians 4). Where this image is found, the New Testament emphasizes God-given spiritual gifts which enable each believer to help others and the need of each believer for close re-

lationships with other Christians who will help him or her grow in the Lord. (2) The church is a family (Ephesians 3:14-18). The family image is rooted in the fact that we Christians have God as our Father. Because we have a common Father, we must be each other's brothers and sisters. Where this image is found in the Bible, the text emphasizes close, caring "family" relationships which are to be developed by God's children. (3) The church is a holy temple (Ephesians 2:21-22; 1 Peter 2:5). This image of a temple reflects the relationship of the church to God. We are to be holy, to worship the Lord and seek to glorify him in everything we do.

It is important when reading the Bible to remember that the "church" of Jesus is people, not buildings or organizations. Christians, united in Jesus' living body, are the church. We live together as the church by serving and loving each other and worshiping God together.

Sabbath to Sunday

Christian worship takes place on Sunday. The Jewish Sabbath is on Saturday. The Sabbath was given to Israel by God as a day of rest. It commemorated God's work of Creation. Sunday is called the "Lord's Day" because Jesus was raised on the first day of the week. By meeting on Sunday, Christians celebrate Jesus' resurrection.

Early Christian preaching
Acts 2

The book of Acts summarizes several evangelistic sermons given by the apostles Peter and Paul. The first of these sermons in Acts 2 contains every major element of the Gospel message.

Each of these elements is as basic to the Christian Gospel today as in the first century. Jesus lived a human life, died on the cross and was raised again and exalted to God's right hand, where he lives today to be trusted as Savior and worshiped as Lord.

Insight: Paul warns against "something different than Good News" (Galatians 1:6–7). No element of this Gospel can be changed without perverting the Christian message.

Responding to the Gospel
Acts 2

Acts describes many of those who heard that first sermon as "sick at heart." When they asked Peter what they could do, Peter told them "change your hearts and lives and be baptized."

The word repentance means a "change of heart and mind." However these Jewish listeners may have viewed Jesus before, they now had to change their minds about him and acknowledge him as Lord and Savior. Water baptism is a beautiful picture of the death, burial and resurrection of Christ. Those who did repent of their sins and were baptized were promised both the forgiveness of sins and the gift of the Holy Spirit. The Bible tells us that some 3,000 were converted that first Pentecost.

Belief or faith

Later in Acts Paul tells a jailor, "Believe in the Lord Jesus Christ and you will be saved" (Acts 16:31). What is the relationship of this promise to Peter's call for repentance and baptism?

In Scripture "faith" is not belief about a set of facts but rather an active trust in a person. The kind of trust in Jesus that the Bible describes by the word "faith" or "belief" is an active response to God, demonstrated by obedience to his word. Those who heard Peter's message and repented and were baptized showed the only kind of faith which can save. The clearest single explanation of faith is found in Romans 4, which notes that when Abraham was told he and Sarah would have a son despite their advanced age, "he never doubted that God would keep his promise . . . Abraham felt sure that God was able to do the thing that God promised" (4:20-21). Hebrews 11 contains a list of great things accomplished by faith.

A loving community
Acts 2:42-47

The first Christians formed a loving community. Love for God was expressed by devotion to the apostles' teaching, by sharing communion (the "breaking of bread"), by prayer and by praise. Love for one another was expressed by being together, sharing meals, and by a willingness to sell possessions to meet others' needs. This last aspect of community life does not indicate a "Christian communism." Each person still had a right to his or her own possessions (see Acts 5:4). Instead this comment demonstrates that the early Christians valued one another more than they valued possessions. The love this community of faith demonstrated so powerfully was compelling evidence of Christ's presence and a vital element in New Testament evangelism (see John 13:34–35).

Expansion!

Acts 3—12; James; 1,2 Peter

Excitement gripped Jerusalem as thousands turned to Christ. The Jewish leaders, shocked by these events, responded by persecuting the apostles and then ordinary Christians. But the Gospel message spread beyond Judea and beyond Judaism! During these years two leaders were prominent: Peter, who led in outreach, and James, the younger brother of Jesus. Although James is not mentioned in these chapters of Acts, he wrote the earliest of our New Testament epistles.

MASTERY KEYS to the expansion of the church:

- What challenges did the early church face and how was each met?
- What patterns of church life might serve as models for our own congregations, and how might they be implemented?
- What are three things the book of James teaches us about a life of faith?
- What is the main emphasis in each of Peter's two New Testament epistles?

"Unschooled, ordinary men"
Acts 3; 4

Peter healed a man crippled from birth. He used the opportunity to preach the Gospel to the amazed observers outside the gate of the Jerusalem Temple. The leaders who had manipulated Jesus' crucifixion were so upset that they had Peter and John arrested. Instead of being afraid, the two apostles preached Christ to the very men who had arranged his murder! The members of the Sanhedrin (the Jewish court) were amazed that these were "unschooled, ordinary men."

Insight: God still empowers and uses ordinary people to share the Good News of Jesus.

The challenge of opposition
Acts 4:23-31

Peter and John were officially ordered to stop preaching about Christ. They immediately went to the church and reported what had been said so all could pray about the situation. In that prayer the Christians (1) affirmed God's sovereignty over all earthly powers, (2) asked for "great boldness" to speak God's word and (3) asked God to work wonders through Jesus' name. God responded to their prayer by filling them with the Holy Spirit. Here and elsewhere the term "filling" indicates endowing with power either for ministry or holy living (see Ephesians 3:19; 5:18).

Sin in the church
Acts 5:1-11

The sudden deaths of Ananias and Sapphira for lying to the Holy Spirit raised

The Mamertine Prison in the city of Rome is where the Apostle Paul was imprisoned.

the issue of holiness. God's judgment of this pair set a standard for the church and showed everyone that sin is not to be tolerated in Christ's church. First Corinthians 5 makes Christians responsible for disciplining other believers who make a habitual practice of sin. Such persons are to be "put out" of the church. This is not intended as punishment but as part of a process that may bring repentance (see 2 Corinthians 2:5-11).

Holy. Hebrew and Greek words for "holy" mean "consecrated to God." In Old Testament times holy things were separated from daily life. God's people were isolated, too, as a separate nation. But God's New Testament people were scattered to every country in the world. We show holiness not by keeping away from others, but by keeping away from sin, and by our dedication to love and good deeds.

The challenge of authentication
Acts 5:12-16

The Bible makes it clear that in the early days of the church, the apostles did perform "many miraculous signs and wonders." The Bible reports several periods of miracles (the Exodus, the time of Elijah and Elisha and the time of Jesus and the early days of the church). Calling such miracles "signs and wonders" makes their purpose clear. Each term indicates that the miracles were intended to demonstrate to observers that the person who performed it did actually speak for God.

What about miracles today? While God surely is able to perform them, many have pointed out that today we have a completed Bible. We do not need miracles to authenticate the message of a speaker or teacher. Now we can look to see if what is taught is in harmony with the word of God.

The challenge of governmental restriction
Acts 5:17-42

The Sanhedrin had civil as well as religious authority in Judea. This group, angry because "you have filled Jerusalem with your

teaching and are determined to make us guilty of this man's blood," used its power to arrest the apostles. These government officials then had the apostles beaten and ordered them not to preach about Jesus any longer.

It is important to understand Peter's response. He openly said to them, "We must obey God not men!" After the apostles were released, "they did not stop teaching people. Everyday in the Temple and in people's homes they continued to tell the Good News—that Jesus is the Christ."

Romans 13 teaches that human governments are ordained by God to maintain public order and punish evildoers. In most circumstances Christians should obey their government's laws. The apostles' action here identifies the one exception to this rule. When man's law directly conflicts with God's express will, we obey God.

Insight: First Peter 2:13-22 deals with this problem and emphasizes that submission is the pathway the Christian is normally to follow. "So when you do good, you stop foolish people from saying stupid things about you."

The challenge of divisions
Acts 6:1-7

Greek-speaking Jewish Christians complained that the widows of Aramaic-speaking Jewish Christians were given favorable treatment when food was distributed to those in need. The Twelve gathered all the believers together and told them to choose seven men, "full of wisdom and full of the Spirit" to supervise the distribution. Every one of the seven selected by the congregation carried a Greek name.

The term by which the seven are known is "deacon." The noun *diakonos* means "servant" or "minister" and is used 37 times in the New Testament. As here, the ministry of deacons in the New Testament era focused on meeting material needs. While only men are named in Acts 6, Romans 16:1 speaks of "our sister Phoebe," who is identified as "a servant" (literally, a deaconess) of the church in Cenchrea. It is important to note that Acts 6 emphasizes spiritual qualifications for this ministry: deacons are to be "full of wisdom and full of the Spirit."

Insight: Meeting the material needs of others can also be a spiritual ministry.

The challenge of martyrdom
Acts 7–8:4

Stephen, one of the church's first seven deacons, was also a powerful preacher. When members of a particular Jerusalem synagogue could not debate him successfully, they produced false witnesses to testify that Stephen had spoken against "the Law of Moses." Stephen's speech before the Sanhedrin so enraged his listeners that they dragged him outside the city and stoned him to death.

With the death of Stephen, "the Jews began trying to hurt the church in Jerusalem." While ordinary believers were forced to flee the city, "everywhere they were scattered, they told people the Good News." Historically, severe persecution has always tended to strengthen the church, so much so that it has been said "the blood of its martyrs is the seed of the church."

Insight: We should not fear persecution. The suffering we experience will ultimately promote the spread of the Gospel.

James: the book of faith at work

The James who wrote this New Testament book about A.D. 46 or 47 was a younger brother of Jesus. At first he had not believed Jesus was the Savior (John 7:2-5). After the resurrection James did become a Christian and a leader of the Jerusalem church.

Tradition tells us that James was nicknamed "camel knees" because he spent so much time in prayer that his knees became as rough and hard as those of a camel. This

Christian tradition identifies this gate, midway along the east face of Jerusalem's walls, as the site of Stephen's martyrdom. It is known as St. Stephen's Gate.

James is mentioned in Acts 12:17; 15:13; 21:18; 1 Corinthians 15:7; Galatians 1:19; 2:9.

Some people become confused in comparing the discussions of faith by the apostles Paul and James, thinking the two inspired writers disagreed. In reality, however, it was not disagreement but rather a difference in emphasis.

James' letter of instruction was written for the young Jerusalem church and actually refers to "faith" more often than Paul's letter to the Galatians. But while Paul wrote there of the *object* of faith (that is, what one must believe), James is concerned with the *expression* of faith (that is, how a person with faith will live). There is no conflict between Paul and James, for when James says that "faith without works is dead," he means that a person who claims to follow Jesus without any evidence of it in his life has a "dead," rather than real, faith. As James points out, even demons believe intellectually that God exists. Any "faith" which exists apart from an active obedience to God is not what the Bible means by faith in the Lord.

In his letter, then, James urges each reader to put his faith to work to deal with situations that challenge all Christians.

Outline of James

The challenge of expansion
Acts 8:4-25

One person who left Jerusalem during the first persecution of the church was an-

Peter stayed in this home in Joppa with Simon the tanner.

other deacon, Philip. He went to Samaria and "preached about the Christ." Peter and John came to see what was happening, for the Samaritans were not true Jews. The Bible says that when Peter and John prayed for the believing Samaritans and placed hands on them, "they received the Holy Spirit." This is the only such report in the New Testament. Why did it happen only here? The Samaritans practiced a rival religion that they claimed was the true Old Testament faith. They rejected Jerusalem as the site of God's Temple, and held that it should be on Mount Gerizim. By giving the Holy Spirit through the apostles, God established their authority, and he also affirmed the unity of the church.

Saul's conversion
Acts 9

Saul had been given legal papers authorizing him to imprison any Jew in Damascus who was a follower of Jesus. How could the Jewish authorities in Jerusalem write a legal order that would be valid in a different country? In the Roman empire a person was considered subject to the laws of his homeland wherever he lived. Thus, an order from the Jerusalem Sanhedrin concerning Jews had legal standing in any city in the empire.

Saul seems an unlikely candidate for the future leader of the Christian missionary movement. Later he described himself as self-righteous, legalistic and a zealous persecutor of the church (Philippians 3:3-10). Paul's conversion led to a total transformation of his character and his goals, described in this same passage. Often in church history the most bitter enemies of Christ have become dedicated ministers of the Gospel after their conversion.

The challenge of Gentile converts
Acts 10–11

The Old Testament made a sharp distinction between God's covenant people and all others.

The Jews of the first century went even farther. A Jew would not eat with a Gentile or even enter his house, and the Jewish term for a Gentile (*goy*) was the word for "dog."

The Jews firmly believed that Gentiles were "unclean," a religious term identifying anything which, if touched, prevented a Jew from approaching God in worship. So the introduction of Gentile converts into the Jewish-Christian church was sure to be resisted.

So, God carefully prepared the early church to accept Gentile members. Note these steps:

(1) 10:1-7. God appeared to Cornelius, a devout Roman army officer, and told him to send for Peter.

(2) 10:9-23. Peter was given a vision in which God told him, "do not call anything impure that God has made clean." Then Peter was instructed by God to go with three men who had come from Cornelius.

(3) 10:24-48. Thus prepared, Peter entered the house of Cornelius and shared the Good News of Jesus. The Holy Spirit not only came upon the Gentile listeners but also enabled them to speak in tongues. This visible sign provided proof that even Gentiles could know Christ as Savior, and Peter permitted them to be baptized.

(4) 11:1-18. When Peter was criticized by members of the church for going to Gentiles, he reported each of these signs and argued that "God gave them the same gift that he gave to us who believed in the Lord Jesus Christ. So could I stop the work of God? No!"

Insight: Prejudices must not lead us to reject other believers just because they may be different from us.

Peter's letters
1,2 Peter

The apostle Peter, who is so prominent in this first part of Acts, continued to minister but primarily to Jewish Christians. Within a few years Paul became leader of the Christian outreach to Gentiles. Peter was martyred in the late A.D. 60's, but he left us two important epistles. Peter's first letter, written about A.D. 64, focuses on the Christian's calling of holiness and shows how often suffering is a part of our experience. Peter uses seven different Greek words for suffering in this letter. He points out that Jesus suffered during his years on earth, and we, who are his followers, should not expect to escape suffering. But Jesus has left us an example of how to respond when suffering does come. Peter's first letter gives practical advice for dealing with our most difficult experiences.

When bad things happen to good people. First Peter 3:13-18 says if you do good and suffer for it, you are blessed. Jesus did only good and suffered. God used Jesus' suffering to bring us to God. If we suffer for doing good, God will use our suffering for some good purpose, too.

Peter's second letter, written just before his death in A.D. 67 or 68, warns against false teachers and false teachings. Both are to be found in the church of any age. The letter shows how to recognize false teachers and contains encouragement to keep the second coming of Jesus in mind as a powerful motive for holy living.

We recognize false teachers by their personalities (boldness, love of money, arrogance, 2 Peter 2:10), by their ministry (appeal to human nature, promises of freedom, 2 Peter 2:17), and by their teaching (heresy, 2 Peter 2:11).

Outline of 1 Peter

Outline of 2 Peter

30 Paul, the great missionary
Acts 13—20; Galatians

Saul, the zealous Pharisee, became Paul, the Christian leader. He led the mission that penetrated the vast Roman empire with the Gospel in a single generation. The bulk of Acts reports Paul's missionary journeys.

MASTERY KEYS to the missionary era:

- What smoothed the way for the missionary movement of the church?
- What can we learn about missions strategy from the Acts?
- How did Paul's early experiences as a believer prepare him for leadership?

The first century world

Many features of the Roman world opened the way for the first missionary movement. Nearly everyone spoke *koine* (everyday) Greek in addition to their local tongue, so there was no language barrier to overcome when preaching the Gospel.

Koine. Because New Testament Greek dif-

*Lydia, the first European convert by Paul, was a seller of purple cloth. The chief source of the famous purple dye was the tiny mollusk, **murex**, found along the coast of Phoenicia. Great labor was required to extract the purple dye; so, only royalty and the wealthy could afford purple garments.*

fers from the classical Greek used by philosophers and poets, scholars once thought *koine* was a special "sacred language," invented by the apostles. The discovery a hundred years ago of thousands of papyrus documents showed the truth. The New Testament was written in the ordinary speech of the man on the street! The Gospel was for the common man, communicated in words everyone could understand. It was the everyday language of the people.

Roman legions maintained peace, making it possible to travel from place to place by ship or on good roads. In Paul's day the trading ships that carried freight from city to city were as much as 180 feet long and could take on several hundred passengers as well as over 1,000 tons of cargo.

The Romans also permitted the free exercise of native religions within the empire. Judaism was one of these legal religions. For decades Christianity was viewed as a sect of Judaism, so missionary work was protected by law!

Godfearers. Some estimate that as many as one person in ten in the Roman empire was either a Jew or had "turned Jew," as secular writers described Godfearers who worshiped Israel's God without full conversion to Judaism.

The apostle Paul

Acts 9

Paul met the risen Christ on the road to Damascus. He had been a foe of Christianity; he became its greatest exponent. What happened to Paul after his conversion? The best reconstruction of his early Christian experience suggests that he spent some time in Arabia, then returned to Damascus for nearly three years (A.D. 35-37), boldly preaching the Christ he had come there to persecute (Acts 9:23; Galatians 1:17).

In the summer of A.D. 37 Paul went up to Jerusalem. At first the believers there were afraid to associate with Paul, fearing his conversion was a trick designed to let him infiltrate their movement. Then Barnabas, a warm and loving man who later became Paul's missionary companion, took the risk and brought Paul to the apostles. In Jerusalem, Paul's vigorous defense of Christianity aroused such opposition that the other believers "took him down to [the port of] Caesarea and sent him off to Tarsus," Paul's hometown!

Paul seems to have remained in Tarsus from A.D. 37 to around A.D. 43, when Barnabas came to find him and invite him to share with the leadership of the predominantly Gentile church in Antioch. Paul's early preaching seems to have caused more hostility than converts (Acts 9:20-30). This probably accounts for his hiatus in Tarsus. Now Barnabas gives him another chance (Acts 11:10-30). Working with Barnabas, the encourager, Paul is brought back into public ministry. It was only in A.D. 48, after about five years in Antioch, that Paul and Barnabas were called by God to set out on their first missionary journey.

Paul's missionary strategy

Each Roman province had "hub" cities, which were located on land or sea trade routes. These cities were administrative and cultural centers. People from outlying districts and towns came to these hub cities to buy and sell and to learn the latest news.

Paul brought missionary teams to the hub cities of the empire. There the teams first went to Jewish synagogues to preach the Gospel. The synagogue was a good place to begin for several reasons. First, the Jewish people had a right to hear of Jesus immediately, for he was their Messiah. Second, Gentiles who were attracted to the Jewish concept of God and high moral vision were associated with many synagogues. Those who had not completely converted to Judaism by accepting circumcision but who still adhered to many of its beliefs are called "Godfearers" or "Gentiles who worship God" in Acts. Both Godfearers and Jews typically formed the core of believers of the churches Paul's team founded.

Paul's Missionary Journeys
Acts and New Testament Letters

Crucifixion of Jesus	A.D. 30
Pentecost (Acts 2)	A.D. 30
Stephen martyred (Acts 7)	early A.D. 35
Paul converted	summer A.D. 35
Paul in Damascus (Acts 9)	A.D. 35-37
Paul to Jerusalem (Acts 9)	summer A.D. 37
Paul in Tarsus	A.D. 37-43
Paul in Antioch	A.D. 43-48
Paul's first missionary journey	A.D. 48-49
Galatians written	A.D. 49
Jerusalem Council (Acts 15)	A.D. 49
Paul's second missionary journey	A.D. 50-52
1 Thessalonians written	A.D. 51
2 Thessalonians written	A.D. 51
Paul's third missionary journey	A.D. 53-57
1 Corinthians written	A.D. 56
2 Corinthians written	A.D. 56
Romans written	A.D. 57
Paul's visit to Jerusalem (Acts 21)	A.D. 57
Paul's arrest (Acts 21-24)	A.D. 57
Paul in prison	A.D. 57-59
Paul's sea voyage to Rome	A.D. 59-60
Paul's first Roman imprisonment	A.D. 60-62
Ephesians written	A.D. 60
Colossians written	A.D. 61
Philemon written	A.D. 61
Philippians written	A.D. 62
Paul released and traveling	A.D. 62-64
1 Timothy written	A.D. 62
Paul travels to Spain	A.D. 64-66
Titus written	A.D. 66
Paul in Greece	A.D. 67
Paul arrested and taken to Rome	A.D. 67
2 Timothy written	A.D. 67
Paul put to death in Rome	A.D. 68
City of Jerusalem destroyed	A.D. 70

Paul and his team then instructed the new Christians while continuing to evangelize. At times they stayed only a few weeks in a city; they stayed in other cities as long as three years. Sooner or later they left to go on to another city to plant more churches.

Most of the time Paul did not travel alone but with a missionary team.

Paul himself also revisited the young churches with the whole team. On this return, elders were appointed from those who had demonstrated significant spiritual growth (Acts 14:23). The Greek word for "appoint" or "choose" suggests that Paul gave official recognition to leaders that the Holy Spirit had selected (Acts 20:28).

Paul also wrote letters of instruction to strengthen the young churches. These have become books in our New Testament. Paul also sent assistants like Timothy and Titus to visit the churches and help them resolve problems. In fact, throughout the early days of the church, itinerant leaders who traveled from church to church played an important role in church growth.

All this lay ahead as Paul studied and came to understand the uniqueness of Christian faith during his years in Tarsus and his years of ministry in Antioch. Then in God's time the missionary movement literally exploded upon the ancient world.

The crisis
Acts 16, Galatians

As more and more Gentile converts were made, a crisis developed. Jewish Christians began to visit Gentile congregations and teach that Christians must adopt a Jewish lifestyle and keep Old Testament law if they were to please God. Paul saw this as a serious distortion of the Gospel message. Salvation is possible only through the work of Christ on the cross. How dare anyone say that keeping Jewish law is necessary for salvation! Paul took the matter to the other apostles in Jerusalem. In a great meeting there it was agreed that allegiance to Jesus was to be the only criteria for recognizing a person as a brother or sister Christian. Jewish Christians could

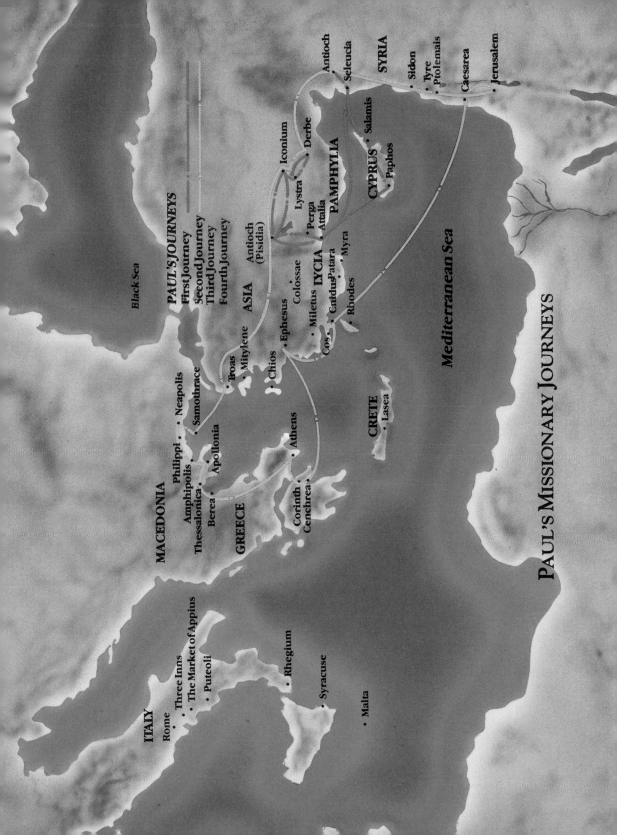

PAUL'S MISSIONARY JOURNEYS

PAUL'S JOURNEYS
First Journey
Second Journey
Third Journey
Fourth Journey

ITALY
Rome
Three Inns
The Market of Appius
Puteoli
Rhegium
Syracuse
Malta

MACEDONIA
Philippi
Neapolis
Amphipolis
Samothrace
Thessalonica
Berea
Apollonia

GREECE
Athens
Corinth
Cenchrea

CRETE
Lasea

ASIA
Troas
Mitylene
Chios
Ephesus
Miletus
Colossae
Cos
Cnidus
Rhodes

LYCIA
Patara
Myra

Iconium
Lystra
Derbe
Antioch (Pisidia)
Perga
Attalia

PAMPHYLIA

CYPRUS
Salamis
Paphos

SYRIA
Antioch
Seleucia
Sidon
Tyre
Ptolemais
Caesarea
Jerusalem

Black Sea

Mediterranean Sea

The Roman people were famous for their excellent roads, which were expensive to construct but lasted many years.

maintain their ancient ways if they wished, but Gentile believers did not have to abandon their culture. It was understood that each group would, of course, be committed to holy living as an expression of (but not as a basis of) their faith.

Galatians is an early New Testament letter in which Paul writes to mixed churches emphasizing the centrality of faith. Old Testament law can bring neither salvation nor spiritual growth. But freedom from the law is not freedom to do what we please. Christian freedom is freedom to live a godly life, relying not on our own efforts but on the Holy Spirit to transform us from within. The content of this important New Testament letter is reflected below.

Outline of Galatians

Missionary adventures
Acts 13–20

These chapters from Acts relate experiences of Paul's missionary teams in various cities of the empire (see map, page 181).

These events took place over a period of some ten years, between A.D. 48 and 57. During this short time through the efforts of Paul and other Christians like Priscilla and her husband Aquila (Acts 18:18-28), the church was planted in strategic hub cities throughout the Roman empire, which in turn fed surrounding towns and villages, thus spreading the Gospel to the Roman world.

Paul's imprisonment

Acts 21–28; Philippians

After some 10 years of work, Paul went to Jerusalem. He was almost killed in a riot outside the Jerusalem Temple but was rescued by Roman soldiers. He was arrested, and when the Roman governor seemed about to turn him over to the Jews to stand trial, Paul exercised his right as a Roman citizen and "appealed to Caesar." He must go to Rome, to be judged there in the emperor's own court.

MASTERY KEYS to Paul's imprisonment:

- How did God use Paul's Roman citizenship to protect the apostle?
- What rulers did Paul reach while imprisoned?
- What does the book of Philippians tell us about the impact of Paul's imprisonment on the spread of the Gospel?
- What key word in Philippians tells us Paul's attitude during his prison experiences?

Paul and the Jews
Acts 21

In nearly every city Paul visited, he was opposed and often persecuted by the Jewish population. Yet, now, despite the warning of prophets that imprisonment awaited, Paul turned toward Jerusalem.

The prophet Agabus warned that Paul faced imprisonment in Jerusalem. Because of this some have thought that Paul disobeyed God by going to Jerusalem. But Paul apparently took the warning as a call to prepare

A Jewish synagogue was an important meeting place in Bible times. It was used not only as a place of worship, but also as a school and a place to socialize with friends. Many of our church buildings today are being used in this good way, too.

himself, saying, "I am ready to be tied up in Jerusalem. And I am ready to die for the Lord Jesus" (21:13)!

Paul always had a great love for his own race. He wrote in Romans 9:2-3, "I have great sorrow and always feel much sadness for the Jewish people. I wish I could help my Jewish brothers, my people. I would even wish that I were cursed and cut off from Christ if that would help them." In this Paul followed Jesus' example and obeyed our Lord's teaching in Matthew 5:44 to "love your enemies. Pray for those who hurt you."

Paul's purification

In Jerusalem some Jewish Christians still kept the Mosaic law. Paul was asked to undergo a purification ritual to demonstrate that he was not against the law. Paul has been called a hypocrite for agreeing. When in gentile lands, Paul lived as the Gentiles did, and he argued strongly that Christians were not bound by the law God had given Israel. But we should see Paul's act as accommoda-

tion. Paul always sought to fit into a society in order not to offend, and in that way to keep the issue focused on Christ rather than on cultural convictions (1 Corinthians 9:22).

The Mosaic law expressed moral standards which are also taught in the New Testament. But that law also contained worship ritual and rules that were specifically for Israel before Christ came. Paul was free to keep ritual requirements or not to keep them. What he argued against in his letters was the idea that all persons must keep the full Mosaic law (and, thus, become a Jew spiritually through circumcision) in order to be a Christian.

Insight: We need to be careful not to judge how others use their Christian freedom.

Romans to the rescue
Acts 21—22

Paul was recognized for bringing non-Jews into the Temple court. In the ensuing

This detailed model depicts the fortress of Antonia.

These ruins are of the city of Caesarea, named for the famous ruler Caesar.

riot Paul was nearly killed but was rescued by Roman soldiers.

These soldiers came from the Fortress Antonia, which was built next to the Temple. Because Jerusalem was such a volatile place, extra soldiers were always on duty during the Jews' religious holidays.

The soldiers thought that Paul was a renegade who had fomented an earlier rebellion. Even so, he was arrested rather than left to be killed. The Romans were committed to the rule of law.

Paul was given permission to speak to the Jewish crowd. They listened carefully to his speech until Paul told of his call by God to go "far away to the Gentiles" (22:21). At this point the rioting began all over again, and the Roman soldiers took Paul inside the fortress.

Rights of Roman citizens
Acts 22; 25

Questioning under torture was normal in the Roman empire. When Paul was about to be whipped to make him talk, he revealed his Roman citizenship. The garrison commander was frightened, for citizens could not be examined under torture.

The Roman empire included three classes of people. Slaves were owned and had few personal rights. Citizens of subject provinces were subject to local law and were not considered citizens of Rome. Only those who held Roman citizenship could come to Roman courts, and, of course, Roman law favored citizens against noncitizens in disputes. A criminal charge could be tried only in Roman courts, and citizens were exempt from examination by torture. It was illegal even to bind a citizen until he or she was convicted by a Roman court. Even then a citizen could appeal to Rome and have his case heard in the capital city in the emperor's own court.

Roman citizenship could be inherited or purchased. Paul had been born in Tarsus, an important port in Cilicia (modern Turkey), to a father who was a citizen. When Paul's citizenship was revealed, the Roman army was compelled to protect him. When a plot to kill Paul was reported, the military commander in Jerusalem detailed 470 soldiers to escort Paul to the Roman governor in the city of Caesarea, which was on the coast 65 miles north of Jerusalem. Three thousand Roman troops were quartered in Caesarea, and the Roman governor lived there.

The Temple coffers were trumpet-shaped containers in which the people placed their gifts of money and valuables. It was into such a container that the widow placed her last mite.

Rulers Paul reached

Acts 24—26; 28

Paul was kept in Caesarea for two years. While there he had the opportunity to preach the Gospel to several key rulers:

M. Antonius Felix was Roman procurator (governor) of Judea between A.D. 52 and 59. The Roman historian Tacitus, who knew him, called Felix "a master of cruelty and lust." Felix kept Paul in Caesarea in hopes of a bribe even though he knew Paul was innocent (24:26). Paul often spoke to Felix about Jesus.

Porcius Festus was procurator in Judea between A.D. 59 and 62. Festus was a good ruler, but he died shortly after taking office. As a person unfamiliar with his new post and the people he ruled, Festus asked the advice of King Agrippa about how to dispose of Paul's case. When Festus asked Paul if he

were willing to be tried in Jerusalem, Paul exercised his right as a citizen and appealed to Caesar.

King Agrippa was a great-grandson of Herod the Great. He ruled under the Romans and controlled the temple treasury. He also appointed the Jewish high priests. The Romans often asked Agrippa's opinion on Jewish religious questions. Paul said that Agrippa believed the Old Testament prophets (26:25-27), but there is no record that Agrippa became a Christian before his death about A.D. 100.

Bernice was the sister of King Agrippa, who lived with him.

The Praetorians were a special military unit stationed in Rome as the emperor's own troops. Guards assigned to be with Paul in his rented house in Rome while he waited trial may be the members of "Caesar's household" (Philippians 4:22) that Paul reached with the Gospel while in Rome.

Malta

Acts 27—28

Malta is an island 90 miles off Sicily, 18 miles long and 8 miles wide. Tradition says that Paul founded a church on this isolated island.

The shipwreck story and the report of events on Malta indicate the power of Paul's personality as well as God's supernatural intervention. Paul was able to influence the 276 terrified men on board ship with the power of his own deep faith in God (Acts 27:21-24).

In Rome

Acts 28

In Rome Paul followed his normal pattern and first spoke to the leaders of the Jews. Some believed, but the majority resisted. Paul was in Rome awaiting trial for two years, and during this time he was free to share the Gospel with his many visitors.

Paul's prison letters

Philippians

While in Rome Paul wrote several New Testament letters. These letters, including Philippians, Colossians, Ephesians and Philemon are called the "Prison Epistles." The book of Philippians gives us the most insight into the impact of Paul's imprisonment.

There Paul said that, "what has happened to me has helped to spread the Good News" (1:12). He had reached "all the palace guards," and other Christians throughout the empire had become more courageous in speaking the word of God (1:14).

The key word in Philippians, "joy," tells of Paul's own attitude as a prisoner. He found joy in the fact that Christ was being preached (ch. 1). He found joy in the unity of Christians who adopt Jesus' own attitude of humility.

Paul found joy in the possibility that his life might be offered up as an expression of his commitment to Christ and to others (ch. 2). Paul's joy was deeply rooted in the awareness that, despite his unworthiness, Christ had called him to be a citizen of God's kingdom (ch. 3). Thus Paul called on others to rejoice with him and especially to rejoice in the Lord, who is ever near (ch. 4).

Outline of Philippians

I.	Joy in the Gospel	Chapter 1
II.	Joy in following Jesus	Chapter 2
III.	Joy in commitment	Chapter 3
IV.	Joy in the Lord	Chapter 4

After Acts

Early traditions report what happened to Paul after his first trial in Rome. Paul was kept waiting in Rome for nearly three years. Then he was acquitted of any crime and released. Paul probably then fulfilled a dream and traveled to Spain to continue planting new churches. He spent about three years there and then returned to Greece. In Greece Paul was arrested again. This time the Roman court found Paul guilty and put him to death about eleven years after Paul was first arrested in Jerusalem.

Paul the apostle

Paul had been a Christian for some thirty-three years and a missionary for about twenty years. During that time he traveled throughout most of the Roman empire, planting churches and instructing new believers. Paul wrote thirteen, or possibly fourteen, of the twenty-seven books of our New Testament.

One of the classic attacks against biblical Christianity has focused on the apostle Paul. He is cast as a harsh, unfeeling, driven man, something like a first century Lenin. Paul is said to have twisted the simple teaching of Jesus into something that the carpenter form Nazareth never intended. This caricature does not match the man we meet in New Testament letters.

We know that Paul was driven. But he was driven by love, for Jesus and for people. Paul reminds the Thessalonians, "we were gentle among you, like a mother caring for her little children. We loved you so much that we were delighted to share with you not only the gospel of God but our lives as well, because you had become so dear to us" (1 Thessalonians 2:7, 8). Paul was hardly motivated by gain. His commitment cost him dearly. "I have labored and toiled," Paul wrote, "and have often gone without sleep; I have known hunger and thirst and have often gone without food; I have been cold and naked. Besides everything else, I face daily the pressure of my concern for all the churches. Who is weak, and I do not feel weak? Who is led into sin, and I do not inwardly burn?" (1 Corinthians 11:26-28)

No, this man who gave himself so completely hardly twisted the message of Jesus. He is a product of that message—proof that Christ can take root in the hardest heart and produce a dramatic moral transformation.

Some may charge Paul with distorting Jesus' teaching. Those who meet Paul personally in his letters know better. Only a message that is true could produce a love and commitment like that shown by Paul.

Insight: What did Paul look like? A writer from the second century gives us this description: Paul was "a short man, with a bald head and crooked legs, in a healthy body, with eyebrows meeting and a nose somewhat hooked, full of friendliness."

32 Paul writes to troubled churches

1,2 Corinthians; 1,2 Thessalonians

As the apostle Paul traveled, he kept in touch with the churches he had founded and often sent them letters of instruction. Troubles in two cities generated four of these letters.

MASTERY KEYS to Paul's letters to troubled churches:

- How is the character of Corinth related to the content of Paul's letters to the church in that city?
- What misunderstandings of Jesus' second coming are reflected in Paul's letters to the Thessalonians?

Corinth

Corinth was an important trading city in Greece, with ports on two seas (see map, page 181). In Paul's day Corinth had about 600,000 people, making it larger than Denver, Colorado, or Miami, Florida.

The city had a reputation for debauchery. One street reconstructed by archaeologists had some thirty-three bars. The temple in Corinth had 1,000 sacred prostitutes, and sexual ethics in the city were so loose that "to Corinthianize" became a slang phrase throughout the empire meaning to live an immoral life.

Paul had stayed in Corinth for at least a

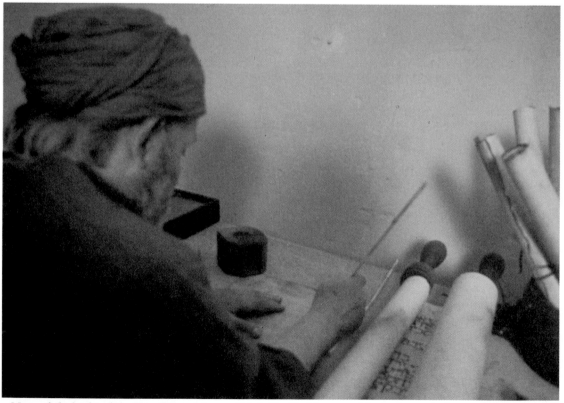

Many of the books of the New Testament were dictated by Paul to an assistant who wrote them on scrolls. Then Paul signed them.

year and a half on his missionary travels. He taught first in a Jewish synagogue and, when forced out, in a house next door to it (Acts 18:7).

Paul later wrote the book of Romans from Corinth. In the last chapter of that book he mentioned a man named Erastus (Romans 16:23). Archaeologists have uncovered a paving block on one of the roads in ancient Corinth that bears an inscription about this person, identifying him as the city treasurer.

It's not surprising then that sexuality is a major theme in Paul's first letter to the Corinthians. In chapter five Paul instructs the church to discipline a brother who was living in open immorality. And in chapter seven Paul corrects the impression that sex is wrong even in marriage and that believers should leave their spouses or live a celibate life with them.

The general unruliness of Corinth is seen in other themes in Paul's letters and in the unwillingness of the Corinthian believers, generally, to submit to apostolic instruction. Nearly every problem faced in modern society and contemporary churches is reflected in the themes discussed by Paul in these two problem-solving letters.

1 Corinthians

Five years after establishing the Corinthian church, Paul heard of problems that were destroying its unity. He responded with this first letter. The letter is organized around seven major issues. Paul's discussion of each problem area is introduced with the Greek phrase *peri de*, usually translated as "now concerning." This problem-solving structure is reflected in the following outline.

Outline of 1 Corinthians

Salutation	1:1-9
I. Division in the church	1:10–4:21
II. Discipline in the church	5:1–6:20
III. Marriage problems	7:1-40
IV. Doctrinal conflicts	8:1–11:1
V. Conflict over practices	11:2-34
VI. The nature of spirituality	12:1–14:40
VII. Doubts about resurrection	15:1-58
Parting Words	16:1-24

Division: 1 Corinthians 1–4. Like some today, the Corinthians divided over favorite Christian leaders. Paul says this factionalism shows spiritual immaturity. Human leaders, like Paul, Apollos and Peter, were simply workers in God's field. God is the one who makes things grow.

Paul's call to focus on Jesus Christ himself, the only foundation for our faith, is helpful today. Too many people identify themselves with some popular preacher and, then, are shaken when that individual falls into sin. Surely we are to respect leaders, but we place our faith in Jesus alone.

And we find a basis for unity with other Christians in our allegiance to Jesus, not in loyalty to the church we attend or loyalty to a leader we admire.

Church discipline: 1 Corinthians 5. Paul deals with a case of open immorality. He tells the church members they must "put [him] out of your group." The phrase, "give this man to Satan," suggests that physical death may result from continuing in sin (see 1 John 5:16). From this chapter and Matthew 18:15-17 we see that church discipline:

(1) is intended to be a progressive, loving attempt to bring a wayward church member back into close relationship with the Lord;

(2) is to be used when believers continue unrepentant in immoral behavior;

(3) involves an individual and loving confrontation with the person about the need to repent and then confrontation by the church leaders, if necessary, and

(4) culminates in expulsion from the fellowship if the individual will not repent.

This particular case of church discipline had the desired result. The sinning believer did repent and was restored to fellowship (see 2 Corinthians 2:5-11).

Insight: Discipline in the church is a loving act of correction, not punishment. It is God the Father's way to correct his children, as an earthly father would correct the child he loves.

Spirituality: 1 Corinthians 12–14. In the first century a person having an epileptic seizure or similar symptom was thought to be touched by god. Epilepsy itself was called the "divine disease." So in Corinth, those who spoke ecstatically in tongues were thought of as specially spiritual.

Paul shows that every Christian has a spiritual gift given by God's Spirit. These gifts are to be used to minister to Christian brothers and sisters (ch. 12). The measure of spirituality is love, not what gift a person has (ch. 13). Church meetings should emphasize understandable speech so Christians may learn and any non-Christian who comes in will be convicted of sin and converted (ch. 14).

Marriage: 1 Corinthians 7. Paul corrects the impression that sex in marriage is wrong. He also denies the popular notion that women are playthings without rights. Each spouse has marital rights (7:4), and neither is to be "deprived" of marital relations.

Some had so misunderstood Paul's stand against immorality that they were ready to divorce in order to live a more "holy" celibate life. Paul commands the married not to separate or divorce.

But the unmarried must realize that marriage rightly brings a concern for the spouse, which limits concern for the Lord's affairs. Each person should carefully consider both marriage and celibacy as his or her particular calling.

Insight: Paul extends Christian women rights they were denied in their culture. Let's not misunderstand the New Testament as being anti-women.

Doctrinal disputes: 1 Corinthians 8–11. The Corinthians' dispute over whether or not a person should eat meat offered to idols hinged on a doctrinal disagreement. One group argued that, since there is only one God, it means nothing to eat meat from an animal offered to idols. The other group insisted Christians could have nothing to do with idolatry. This dispute led to hostility and judging within the Corinthian fellowship.

Paul first shows that such disputes must be approached in love (8:1-3). Love opens us up to God and others. People who approach disputes on the basis of their superior knowledge discover that the claim to "know" creates pride ("puffs up"). None of us "knows" enough, so we must be humble in holding and arguing our doctrinal opinions.

Yet after teaching the Corinthians to approach their differences in love, Paul does show who was right (1 Corinthians 10). He points out that idolatry is associated with many evils and should be avoided. It is not right to knowingly participate in anything associated with evil in one's culture.

Insight: Love and humility are to mark our honest disagreements with fellow believers who love the Lord and trust his word.

Women in church: 1 Corinthians 11. The message of equality of the sexes in the sight of God was misunderstood in Corinth. In Judaism women were separated from men in the synagogue service and were not to speak there. When some Christian women abandoned their veil when coming to church, their rejection of this cultural symbol of their womanhood was intended to demonstrate their new status as participating members of Christ's church. But Paul opposed them. He taught that a woman should not deny her gender. Wearing the veil in that culture displayed the divine order in which the source of life is historically traced from God to Adam to Eve. Women and men are equal but interdependent: each needs the other. In essence, Paul argues that women do not need to dress or act like men to affirm their equality in the church.

2 Corinthians

This is the most intimate and personal of Paul's New Testament letters. Some in Corinth responded to his earlier letter, but others opposed and even slandered the apostle who had founded their congregation. In this letter Paul not only expresses his love but also explains principles which govern his approach to ministry. These ministry principles help each of us as we seek to influence others for Jesus Christ.

Outline of 2 Corinthians

Communicating comfort: 1:3-11. Paul has known suffering and troubles and in them has experienced Jesus' comfort. He explains that such troubles are permitted by God so when others are in trouble we can share the comfort of God with them.

Insight: If you have suffered a deep loss, ask God to lead you to others who have had the same experience. Your suffering will uniquely equip you to minister to them.

Transparency: 2 Corinthians 3. God calls us to be real with others and to take off our masks. While it is true that others will see our faults, they will also see Christ. Paul explains. Moses put a veil on his face when he left the presence of God because the visible radiance generated by contact with the Lord later faded away. Paul says that, in contrast, we are constantly being transformed by the Holy Spirit, who is always with us. Our transformation is "into [Jesus'] likeness" and "with ever-increasing glory, which comes from the Lord, who is the Spirit" (3:18, NIV).

Insight: The reality of Jesus is revealed to others who see the change Christ makes in our lives over time. If we hide our real selves from others, they will not be able to witness our transformation.

New Testament giving: 2 Corinthians 8–9. The Old Testament principle of the tithe (ten percent) is not repeated in the New Testament. Instead, Paul calls on us to see all we possess as God's and to give generously by comparing what we have with the needs of others (8:13-15). There is no compulsion to

This dungeon at St. Peter Gallicantu is typical of prisons in which Paul and the disciples were often jailed.

give (8:8), nor is any set amount established (8:12). But we are encouraged to remember that "the person who plants a little will have a small harvest. But the person who plants a lot will have a big harvest" and that "God can give you more blessings than you need. Then you will always have enough of everything. You will have enough to give to every good work" (9:6,8). Surely, giving is one of the Christian graces.

Thessalonica

This Greek city was the largest business center in Europe in Paul's time. It had its own seaport and lay on a major highway, the Via Egnatia. It was a strategic city for Paul's missionary team to reach.

At the end of the first century B.C., Thessalonica was the most populous city in Macedonia. It was made a "free city" by the Romans, giving it freedom from taxation and the right to mint coins. It also had the right of self-government. In Acts 17:6-8 Luke calls the magistrates there "politarchs." Critics called this an error in the Bible, because the term does not appear in any other literature. However, inscriptions have now been found which show Luke, not the critics, was accurate!

The city had a large middle class made up of merchants, traders and workmen. Paul's stress on earning one's own way (1 Thessalonians 4:10-12; 2 Thessalonians 3:6-12) indicates the church there may have been made up of this class rather than the wealthy aristocracy.

Many Jewish people had settled in the city, and Paul went first to the synagogue there. But Jewish opposition to his message was intense. We do not know how long Paul was in Thessalonica, but he did work there as a tentmaker (1 Thessalonians 2:9). He also received two money gifts from the church in Philippi (Philippians 4:16). We also know that the church in Thessalonica became a strong one and very quickly acted to spread the Gospel throughout the surrounding province.

Outline of 1 Thessalonians

	Salutation	1:1
I.	Praise for progress	1:2–3:13
II.	Instructions	4:1–5:24
	A. Christian living	4:1-12
	B. Christ's return	4:13-18
	C. Watchful waiting	5:1-11
	D. Mutual love	5:12-15
	E. Avoiding evil	5:16-24
	Conclusion	5:25-28

Outline of 2 Thessalonians

	Salutation	1:1-2
I.	Praise for progress	1:3-12
II.	Confusion clarified	2:1-17
III.	Present priorities	3:1-15
	Final greetings	3:16-18

33 Truth for life—Paul's letters

Romans; Ephesians; Colossians; Philemon

Paul's letters to churches are both doctrinal and practical. The apostle communicates basic truths and then shows how these truths strengthen believers to live productive and godly Christian lives.

MASTERY KEYS to Paul's letters of truth for life:

- What is the theme of each of these letters?
- List three things Romans contributes to our understanding of righteousness.
- What about Ephesus makes it an appropriate background for the Ephesian letter?
- How did Christianity deal with slavery?

Rome, capital of the empire

Rome was the largest and most exciting city on earth. Spreading over seven low hills east of the Tiber River, the 800-year-old city was 12 miles across when Paul's letter arrived about A.D. 58. Rome had a population of about one million, and over half its inhabitants were slaves. (See map, page 181.)

Rome was a city of stark contrasts. Its population was generally very rich or very poor. The poor lived in tiny rooms in narrow, high apartment houses in the center city. One writer speaks of a man whose room was 200 steps up. This crowded district was often ravaged by terrible fires.

During the time of the Roman Empire, most citizens were either very rich or very poor. Rich people lived in villas such as this. Poor people lived in tiny apartments.

This is the famous Aqueduct of Caesar, one of the brick waterways through which water was brought into Rome.

Yet Rome was also a city of beauty and culture. The rich lived in great villas, boasting gardens and swimming pools. Emperors generally tried to make the city beautiful, with marble and gold covering temples and public buildings. The city boasted libraries and even publishing houses where slave copyists produced books that could be purchased for as little as $1.50.

Rome was a city with sewers. Water was carried to it by fourteen aqueducts. These stone waterways ran for 1300 miles and carried 300,000,000 gallons of water to Rome each day!

In Paul's time sports events often pitted men against wild animals, and gladiators fought to the death in the Circus Maximus. Later in Rome's coliseum many Christians were tormented and killed for the amusement of the population.

About 20,000 Jews lived in Rome in Paul's time. They experienced periodic persecution, and several times all Jews were expelled from the capital. Under persecution, the Jews, and later Christians, dug long tunnels and rooms in the soft rock under the

city. There are approximately 600 miles of these catacombs under Rome where early Christians met to worship and, at times, were even forced to live and to bury their dead.

The book of Romans

Paul's letter to the Romans does not deal with the brutalizing life in the capital of the empire. Instead, Paul focuses on the new life God has provided in Jesus Christ, organizing his teaching around the theme of righteousness. No human being is righteous in God's sight; all have sinned. But Romans tells us that God the Judge declares believers in Christ righteous in his sight. That is, he acquits us of the charge of sin. But in Romans Paul goes on to explain that God does more than this. God unites us to Jesus and gives us his Holy Spirit so that we can actually live a righteous, holy life.

We can outline Romans by its treatment of righteousness. Romans 1-3 shows that human beings are not righteous but are sinners. Romans 4-5 shows that God accepts faith in his Son in place of righteousness. Romans 6-

8 explains how God enables believers to live a righteous life. Romans 9-11 shows that this understanding of the Gospel is in harmony with the Old Testament, and Romans 12-16 shows how God's people are to live together as a righteous community.

Insight: "Righteousness" or being "made right" in the Bible refers to the way God establishes a proper relationship between himself and his creation. Righteousness is primarily God's activity, and most often means *God's* righteousness.

Outline of Romans

Nero

Nero was emperor when Paul penned his letter to the Romans. A decade later Nero would order Paul's death. Nero's speech writer was the younger brother of Gallio, the proconsul who protected Paul in Corinth (Acts 18). Nero appointed Festus, who later sent Paul on to Rome, as governor of Judea.

As emperor, Nero proved bloodthirsty and cruel. He murdered his mother, ordered one wife to commit suicide, and kicked another, who was pregnant, in the stomach, causing her death. When Rome burned in July of A.D. 64, rumors spread that Nero had caused the fire. The Roman historian Tacitus reports that Nero found a scapegoat. His *Annals* say Nero blamed "a race of men detested for their evil practices, and commonly called Chrestiani. The name was derived from Chrestus, who, in the reign of Tiberius, suffered under Pontius Pilate." Tacitus tells how Nero incited the population against the Christians, and says "they were put to death with exquisite cruelty, and to their sufferings Nero added mockery and derision. . . . At length the brutality of these measures filled every breast with pity. Humanity relented in favor of the Christians."

Observing the law: Romans 3:9-20. The

This Roman Coliseum was the arena in which early Christians were forced to fight wild animals or professional Roman fighters called gladiators. *Many Christians were martyred in this way.*

law is intended to show everyone that he or she is guilty. It is not a way of salvation.

Insight: In Romans 1–3 "law" means God's revealed standards of right and wrong.

God's justice: Romans 3:21-26. When Jesus became a sacrifice for sin, his death became the basis on which God could forgive believers of the past as well as present.

Insight: God is just and must punish sin. But God is also love, and so he bore that punishment himself through Christ.

Fully persuaded: Romans 4. Old Testament saints also trusted God completely, and that faith was counted to them as righteousness. Faith has been the key to salvation in every era.

United with him: Romans 6:1-14. In many states a woman who marries is considered to own her husband's possessions, even if he had them before the wedding. Faith so perfectly unites us to Jesus that his death and resurrection are considered ours. The doctrine of our union with Jesus is a basic tenet of Christian faith.

Fully met in us: Romans 8:1-11. We cannot keep God's law by trying. But as we rely on God's Holy Spirit, our lives will reflect the holiness law requires.

Insight: Augustine said: "Love God, and do as you please." The person who loves and responds to God will do what is good.

Accept one another: Romans 14. "Accept" means "welcome with open arms." Paul insists that we accept, rather than judge, each other concerning differences in opinions. An opinion may be a personal belief that something the Bible does not clearly say is sin is still wrong for Christians. Each person is free to have his own opinions about such matters. And we are not to criticize or condemn each other for differences in opinion.

Ephesus

Ephesus was the largest Asian city. It was an active port, but it was most famous for its magnificent Temple of Diana (or Artemis). This temple was one of the Seven Wonders of the ancient world. It featured 100 columns 55 feet tall outside the main structure. The temple building itself was 164 feet wide and 342 feet long. Each year over half a million people came to Ephesus for a month-long festival to Diana. Much of the economy of Ephesus depended on its place as a religious center. Its hotels, restaurants and curio shops, where silver replicas of the original shrine of Diana could be purchased, were all supported by the thousands of visitors who poured into Ephesus by sea and land.

But the temple had another function as well. The treasury of the temple held vast wealth. By the first century that treasury functioned as a modern bank. Kings had even financed wars with loans from the temple treasury, and so Ephesus was the financial, as well as the religious, center of Asia. Paul's letter explains the glory of God's true temple, the body of Christ, which contrasts so dramatically with the temple in Ephesus.

The book of Ephesians

The theme of Ephesians is the church. But Paul does not deal with any stone edifice like the Temple of Diana. Paul views the church as living persons, linked in unique ways to Jesus and to one another. Paul uses several different images to help the Ephesians understand how much greater the glorious spiritual structure of God is than their city's famed temple.

Outline of Ephesians

Salutation	1:1-2
I. The church is people	1:3–2:22
II. The church is family	3:1–4:16
III. The church incarnates Christ	4:17–6:20
Final Greetings	6:21-24

Enabled: Ephesians 1:15-23. The power of God that raised Jesus from the dead is at work in us because Jesus, the living head of his church, has all power.

Good works: Ephesians 2:1-10. Those who are spiritually dead can do nothing to please God. Thus, no good works can earn salvation. But Christians, who have been given life and "created in Christ Jesus," are intended by God "to do good works."

God's family: Ephesians 3:14-21. We take our name "family" from the fact that God is our Father. This family image was so important in the early church that believers commonly addressed each other as brother and sister.

Imitators of God: Ephesians 5:1-2. Jesus was the expression of God when he walked our earth. We Christians are to "live a life of love, just as Christ loved us." In this way our lives are also to display the nature and character of our God.

Insight: God's people are to be a living incarnation of Jesus in today's world.

As Christ loved the church: Ephesians 5:22-33. Husbands are to love their wives as Jesus loved the church and put the church's needs before his own. The Bible's teaching on "headship" does not support male domination but, in context, shows that husbands are to take the lead in caring for their wives, as Jesus cares for his church (see Ephesians 5:21).

The armor of God: Ephesians 6:10-20. The word for armor is *panoply.* This was the battle gear of the most heavily armed Roman foot soldiers. The symbol of the armor is Paul's way of summing up his teaching in Ephesians. The Christian community will be safe from Satan if we wear: (1) The belt of truth. Paul calls for openness and honesty for maintaining Christian unity, Ephesians 4:25. (2) The breastplate of righteousness. We are to be pure in our relationships, Ephesians 5:3. (3) The feet fitted with the Gospel of peace. We are to maintain unity so we can respond together to Christ, our head. (4) The shield of faith. We keep on trusting Christ to

work in us, Ephesians 3:20. (5) The helmet of salvation. We will not doubt or fear if we recall all God has done for us, Ephesians 1:1-11. (6) The sword of the Spirit. Only this is defined, as the word of God, because this is the only subject on which Paul has not taught in Ephesians.

Colosse

The city of Colosse lay inland but at the junction of major highways. It had a mixed population, which included a large Jewish colony. In this cosmopolitan city a variety of philosophies and religions flourished, and Christian truths were apparently reinterpreted.

Paul wrote the Colossian letter about A.D. 62. From the use of key words and phrases found in gnostic teaching, and used in this letter, many believe Colossians was written to combat a heresy called *gnosticism.* The Greek word *gnosis* means "knowledge." The gnostics claimed to have a special knowledge, and through that knowledge to know the secrets of salvation.

Gnosticism was linked with astrology, and gnostics associated angelic powers with heavenly bodies. By seeking a link with these angelic powers, the individual might be lifted to the upper realms (see Colossians 2:18, 21-23). In modern times "astral projection" and the Rosincrucean movement reflect ancient gnostic beliefs.

Most importantly, the gnostics were strict dualists. They believed that the material and spiritual worlds were completely separate. The material was only evil, and the spiritual was only good. So God, who was spiritual and good, must be totally isolated from this world. God could not have been the creator, for this would imply contact with the material. It followed also that Jesus could not have been both human and divine. If he were one of the angel intermediaries between the universe and God, he must be of a lower order to have any contact with the world.

To the gnostic, spirituality was inner and immaterial. The body was physical, and thus evil. Some gnostics determined to deny their physical nature and became ascetics. Others reasoned that since the body was evil anyway, it could do whatever it wanted and not affect the divine spark within. These gnostics indulged every sinful passion.

Colossians strikes directly against this false system of beliefs. Jesus is God. Jesus himself created the world (1:16-17). Jesus entered the world as a true human being, and God "reconciled you by Christ's physical body through death" (1:22, NIV). The Christian will find no release in the practices of the gnostic (2:16-23) but will find fulfillment by living a godly daily life (3:1-17).

There *is* a gap between the material and spiritual universe. But Jesus bridged that gap for us. Jesus lived his life on earth in union with the Father, doing the Father's will. And Jesus calls on us to daily live godly lives. As we do God's will in the real world, we will experience the fullness of the spiritual life to which God has called us in his Son.

Outline of Colossians

All God's fullness: Colossians 1:19. Jesus is the full and total expression of God. So, to know Jesus better is to know God better.

Fullness in him: Colossians 2:9. The source of spiritual vitality is already ours, Jesus himself. Deepening our relationship with Jesus is the key to the Christian's spiritual life.

Restraining sensual indulgence: Colossians 2:23. A person may control one sin, such as immorality, but his sinful nature will find another way of expression, such as pride. Such human approaches to religion may look good, but they cannot control sin.

Bear with: Colossians 3:13. The Greek word means to "put up with." Each of us is on a journey toward spiritual maturity. But none of us has arrived. So, in each of us, there is much with which others must "put up."

Philemon

About half the people in the empire were slaves. In Roman times a person might become a slave by birth or by capture in war, or parents might sell a child into slavery. Unwanted children were often abandoned at birth, and many of the empire's brothels had prostitutes who had been picked up as infants by their owners. Yet many slaves in Roman times were better fed and housed than freemen.

Slaves at times were freed by their masters. Or a slave might earn enough money to purchase his own freedom.

The New Testament urges slaves to serve their masters wholeheartedly, as if they served Christ himself (see Ephesians 6:5-9; Colossians 3:22–4:1; 1 Peter 2:18-21). But Christian masters were exhorted to be fair to all slaves and to treat Christian slaves as brothers.

Philemon is a personal letter. In it Paul begs a convert of his to welcome back a runaway slave as a brother. This brief, one-chapter letter gives us insight into the Christian dynamic that can ultimately rid the world of slavery, by affirming that master and slave are human together and, if believers, are brothers and sisters in Christ.

The Pastoral Letters

1, 2 Timothy, Titus

As the first missionaries grew older, younger members of their teams were given added responsibilities. These three New Testament letters, called the pastorals, were written by Paul to guide Timothy and Titus, two of the next generation of church leaders.

MASTERY KEYS to the pastoral letters:

- What themes are repeated in these letters, and what do they tell us of the challenges faced by the maturing church?
- What were Timothy and Titus like as persons?
- What leadership positions were there in the early church, and how did leaders lead?

Church leadership

Local offices. As churches were founded in various cities, two local leadership positions emerged. Churches had elders and deacons. Elders (*presbuteros*), who at times are called bishops (*episkopos*), are responsible for the spiritual direction of the whole church and its members. Deacons (*diakonos*) are responsible for specific practical tasks, such as the distribution of food to the needy. The term deacon means "minister" or "servant."

Itinerant teachers. In addition to these local leaders, the church had apostles and teachers. These seem to have been persons who traveled from church to church, teaching and helping local congregations solve problems. Timothy and Titus were such itinerant leaders, sent by Paul to visit churches that had serious problems.

The term "apostle" means "one sent out" and usually refers to the twelve. But Paul and Barnabas are called apostles because they were "sent out" in a special sense.

The New Testament also mentions prophets. However, there is no mention of Christian prophets in the later epistles. Many believe that as the Scriptures neared comple-tion, this office was no longer needed in the church.

How leaders led. Leaders were called to guide the spiritual growth of churches and individuals. The pastoral letters make it clear that leaders used two powerful tools in their ministry. First, leaders knew and taught God's word. Second, leaders provided an example of godliness by living the truths they taught. God, the Holy Spirit, worked through such leaders to bring the church to maturity.

These are the steps and temple of Apollo in the city of Corinth.

The three pastoral letters teach us much about the kind of persons God wants as leaders in his church. These letters warn about false teachers and tell us how to recognize them. The pastorals also help leaders understand how best to build others up in the faith. And these three letters give us special insights into the kind of teaching that uniquely expresses and builds Christian faith.

Meet Timothy

Timothy is mentioned often in Acts. Paul apparently recruited Timothy on his first missionary journey about A.D. 47-48. Timothy's father was a Greek, but his mother Eunice was a Jewish Christian. Timothy may have been a teenager when he joined the missionary team. As Timothy matured, Paul trusted him with many special missions. He traveled to Thessalonica to see how the church there was doing, and he was also sent to Corinth.

Paul, who had no children of his own, spoke of Timothy as "a dear son" or "a true son to me" (1 Timothy 1:2). Yet Paul seems to have been concerned about Timothy's shyness and urged him to be more bold. Timothy was probably in his thirties when Paul wrote telling him not to let people look down on him because of his youth (1 Timothy 4:12).

Meet Titus

Titus was a Greek Christian and an able leader. He proved more effective in a mission to Corinth than Timothy had been (2 Corinthians 7:6-15). Paul sent Titus to Crete before writing his letter. This was a difficult mission, for there were "many people who refuse to obey" there (Titus 1:10). Paul was also close to Titus, whom he called "a true son to me in the faith we share."

The book of 1 Timothy

A major emphasis in 1 Timothy is its description of elders. As persons, elders are to be above reproach, temperate, self-controlled, respectable and upright, hospitable, not heavy drinkers, not competitive but gentle, not quarrelsome or quick tempered, not materialistic, respected by nonbelievers, lovers of good. Their life-style is to exhibit godliness, faith, temperance, love, endurance, dedication to good, integrity, seriousness, response to authority, trustworthiness, humility, consideration, peaceableness.

These themes, found repeatedly in 1 Timothy, challenge us not only to select godly leaders but to become the kind of persons whom God can use to lead his church.

Insight: God places greater emphasis on a leader's character than on his talents or education. We should maintain God's priorities when we select elders for our congregations.

Outline of 1 Timothy

Greeting		1:1-2
I.	The goal of sound teaching	1:3-20
II.	Instructions for worship	2:1-15
III.	Instructions concerning elders	3:1-16
IV.	Instructions on godliness	4:1-16
V.	Instruction on ministries	5:1–6:2
VI.	Concluding exhortations	6:3-20

The goal of ministry: 1 Timothy 1:2-11. Paul urges Timothy to stop those who teach false doctrine. Why? Because God's truth produces "love, which comes from a good conscience and a sincere faith."

Because you are young: 1 Timothy 4:11-13. Older persons were thought to have learned wisdom by their years of experience. Timothy was probably in his thirties but seemed young to be a leader. Paul wrote, "set an example for the believers in speech, in life, in love, in faith and in purity." Leaders earn respect by their lives, not their years.

The widow's role: 1 Timothy 5. Widows over 60 with no family were supported by the church. In return they ministered to younger women with families. But age was not the only qualification. Widows who ministered were to have lived godly lives themselves and be known for their good deeds. We must live godly lives if we are to teach godliness.

Love of money: 1 Timothy 6:10. It is not *having* money but *loving* money that is associated with doing evil. Being wealthy isn't wrong in itself. The poor, as well as the rich, can love money.

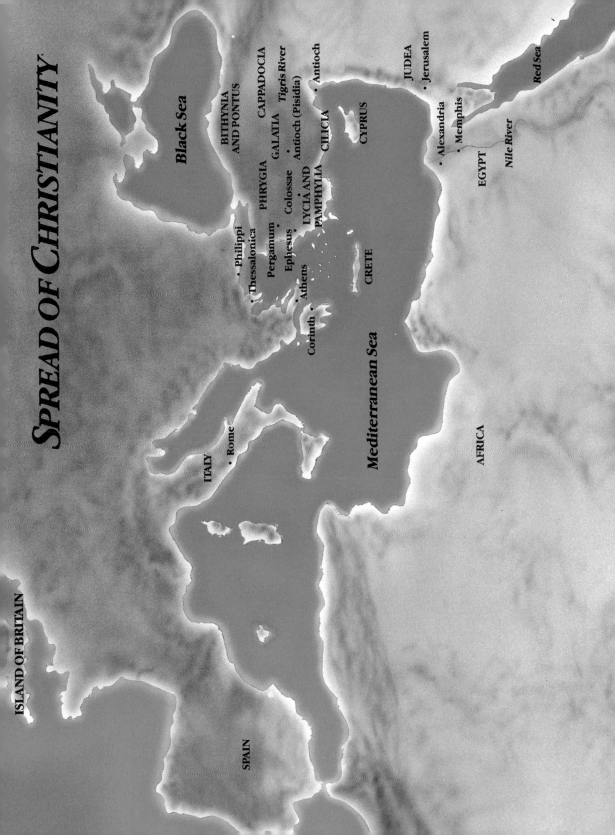

SPREAD OF CHRISTIANITY

ISLAND OF BRITAIN

SPAIN

ITALY
· Rome

Black Sea

BITHYNIA
AND PONTUS

CAPPADOCIA

PHRYGIA   GALATIA   Tigris River

Pergamum   Antioch (Pisidia)

· Philippi   Ephesus   Colossae

· Thessalonica   LYCIA AND   Antioch
    PAMPHYLIA   CILICIA

· Athens   CYPRUS

Corinth ·

CRETE

Mediterranean Sea

AFRICA

JUDEA

· Jerusalem

· Alexandria

· Memphis

EGYPT

Nile River

Red Sea

The book of 2 Timothy

This is the final letter which Paul wrote in A.D. 67, just before his execution in Rome. In it Paul encourages Timothy to be willing to suffer with him for the Gospel.

Paul looks ahead in this letter and sees difficult times. Already official persecution has begun in the Roman empire. Soon there will be an increase of evil men and imposters who "will go from bad to worse" (3:13) within the church.

Paul's advice to Timothy in view of the coming trials rings true for us as well. We are not to be ashamed to testify about our Lord (1:8). We are to hold to the doctrines of the apostles (1:13). We are to be strong in the grace of God (2:1) and endure for the sake of God's people (2:10). We are to work hard to understand and "use the true teaching in the right way" (2:15). And we are to flee youthful passions and pursue righteousness, faith, love and peace in fellowship with God's people (2:22). As long as God's people retain these commitments, we will not be led astray by false teachers or surrender our faith under persecution.

Outline of 2 Timothy

Family influence: 2 Timothy 1:3-7. Timothy came to believe as a child, influenced by his grandmother Lois and his mother Eunice. When we have a sincere faith, we influence those who are closest to us.

A trustworthy saying: 2 Timothy 2:11-13. Early Christians expressed their faith in brief sayings. "If we died with him, we will also live with him" is one of those sayings. Others are found in 1 Timothy 1:17 and 3:16.

Gently teach: 2 Timothy 2:24-26. The way

The city of Thessalonica today. It was to this ancient city that Paul wrote the New Testament letters of Thessalonians.

to win others is not by confrontation or hostile argument but by gently sharing God's truth. A loving attitude wins a hearing for the Gospel. We must remember that change depends on the work of God within a person's heart, not on his ability to debate.

God-breathed or "given by God": 2 Timothy 3:16. The Greek word describes winds filling the sails of a vessel at sea. God carried the writers of Scripture along as a wind carries a sailing ship, so that what we have is his own word.

The book of Titus

Crete. This large island, about 160 miles long and up to 35 miles wide, lay southeast of the Greek mainland. It was once the center of a great Minoan civilization. That civilization was destroyed when a volcano in the nearby Santorini Islands erupted about the time Moses led the children of Israel out of Egypt.

After that, Crete declined. Two centuries before Christ it was little but a recruiting ground for mercenary soldiers. In the first century there were a number of Jews who lived there.

The Mediterranean peoples had little respect for Cretans. Paul quoted the Greek poet Epimenedes, who wrote about 600 B.C., when he described these people as "liars, evil beasts, lazy gluttons" (Titus 1:5). Yet the Gospel Titus ministered there had the power to transform Cretans into a people "eager to do good works" (Titus 3:5).

On Crete in A.D. 67, Titus faced a church drawn from this society acknowledged to be made up of "liars . . . evil animals and lazy people who do nothing but eat" (Titus 1:12). The church was also marred by false teachers and persons with rebellious attitudes. In this letter Paul shows Titus how to teach even such people effectively, so that they might become a people who are "careful to use their lives for doing what is good" (3:8).

What kind of teaching can change the hearts of resistant people? In Titus 2 the apostle uses several different Greek words and phrases to describe effective teaching.

First, teach "what is in accord with sound doctrine"—a life of respect, self-control, faith, love and endurance (2:1-3, NIV). Second, train how to love spouses and children, to be busy, kind, and responsive (2:4-5, NIV). Third, encourage by setting an example of doing good and showing integrity so others have nothing bad to say about the teacher (2:6-8, NIV). Fourth, point to the grace of God, which itself "teaches us to say 'No' to ungodliness and worldly passions" and to live "godly lives in this present age" (2:11-14, NIV). Fifth, encourage and rebuke with all authority (2:15).

Insight: We should not think of teaching merely as saying words. Titus helps us see teaching as a process that calls for the personal involvement of teachers with learners, so that the teacher can set an example, reprove and encourage, as well as communicate information.

Outline of Titus

Hope for life forever: Titus 1:2. In the Bible "hope" does not mean to be uncertain but to look forward with confidence. The Christian is confident that God has given us eternal life and that the Lord is with us at all times.

All things are pure: Titus 1:15. The pure person is not quick to see evil in others or to make the off-color remarks the ungodly find so funny.

Insight: Seeing good is an indication of being good. But even a person who looks for good in others should recognize evil.

35 Letters of encouragement

Hebrews; 1, 2, 3 John; Jude

Others besides Paul wrote letters which have become part of our New Testament. These letters are called the "general epistles," in part, because they are not directed to any specific church but to Christians in general. James and 1, 2 Peter are also included among the general epistles (see chapter 29).

MASTERY KEYS to the letters of encouragement:

- Which New Testament letters are considered general letters?
- What is the theme or emphasis of each of the general letters?
- According to Hebrews how are the Old and New Testaments linked?
- How is Jesus superior to Old Testament law?

The book of Hebrews

Most scholars believe this letter was written to Jewish believers. Jews knew God had spoken to Moses, and they had many questions about how the message of Jesus related to the Old Testament revelation. The unknown author of this book shows that Jesus both fulfills and is superior to that which the Old Testament described. But the author shows that revelation was a "shadow," a pic-

How Jesus Keeps God's Promises

The picture		The promise	How Jesus keeps the promise	Verses in Hebrews
LAW		God will make his people good.	Jesus puts God's law in our hearts, not just on stone tablets.	8:7-13
SACRIFICE		God accepts the death of a sacrifice. This is in payment for sin, and God gives forgiveness.	Jesus' one sacrifice on the cross paid for all our sins. Now we can be forgiven forever.	9:23–10:18
HIGH PRIEST		God will listen when the priest offers sacrifices and prays for a person.	Jesus is our high priest who is alive today. He loves us and always prays for us.	4:14–5:10 7:1–8:6

ture thrown on a screen. Christ is the reality, the one who throughout all time cast the shadows, which, in turn, revealed him. And so the author sets out to reassure Jewish believers. Christ is far better than the old law to which some continue to cling.

Insight: The writing style of Hebrews is a more elegant and literary style than most of the rest of the New Testament. The author uses 168 words found nowhere else in the New Testament. There are many theories as to the authorship of the book. Scholars who once thought Paul was the probable author now rather believe it is perhaps Apollos, Barnabas, Luke or even Priscilla.

Outline of Hebrews

Exact representation: Hebrew 1:3. The phrase does not mean that Jesus is a copy of God. The Greek words teach that Jesus is a perfect manifestation of God because he is God. Just as coins are genuine when stamped by the mint, so Jesus is genuine because he perfectly is God the Father (2:4-14)!

Not angels he helps: Hebrews 2:14-18. To redeem human beings God had to become flesh and blood. The author reminds us that angels fell, too, but the Bible does not indicate that God formed a plan to redeem the fallen angels.

Insight: How greatly God must love us to stoop so low in order to lift us up.

Rest: Hebrews 3:7-13. In every generation those who trust in God are invited to experience inner rest. Only unbelief, expressed in refusal to obey God's word, can keep us from experiencing peace. So Hebrews warns us, "Today, if you hear his voice, do not harden your hearts." Only by being obedient to God can we find rest and peace.

Made perfect: Hebrews 5:9. The words "made perfect" do not imply Jesus was ever less than God. "Perfect" here is not a moral term, but instead indicates being equipped or qualified for a task. To become the source of our salvation, Jesus had to remain obedient as a human being to God the Father, despite what he suffered. Jesus lived such a life and was qualified by it to save you and me.

In this section, the writer urges those who seem about to turn back to Judaism to go on instead to Christian maturity. He raises a question for those who hesitate: What would they do, crucify "the Son of God all over again"? This would be public disgrace because it would imply his one sacrifice was not enough to save.

So these words are written to Jews who are true believers to show them how foolish their hesitation is. As the writer goes on, "we are confident of better things in your case." The writer of Hebrews wants his readers to set aside doubts so they can concentrate on living productive lives.

An end to argument: Hebrews 6:13-20. God's commitment to those who believe and obey is complete. We not only have God's word but his formal covenant promises. His word serves as an anchor for the soul.

Melchizedek: Hebrews 7. Old Testament priests were taken only from Aaron's family. But each generation died and was replaced. The writer looks back to an early king-priest once met by Abraham, to whom the patriarch gave tithes. He says that Jesus is like this priest in that (a) he is superior to Aaron, who was figuratively present when his ancestor Abraham offered the tithe, and in that (b) like Melchizedek, whose death is not mentioned, Jesus will conquer death. This second point, in which the writer argues from the silence of Scripture, uses a typical rabbinic method of interpreting the Bible to show the Jewish readers the superiority of Jesus' priesthood.

The New Covenant: Hebrews 8. The "old covenant" was the Law of Moses. It was God's standards recorded on stone tablets.

The "new covenant" was made by Christ at Calvary. It is different from the old in that God now writes his laws in the minds and on the hearts of believers, and he forgives our sins. Jesus alone has power to change us from within.

The blood of calves and goats: Hebrews 9. Old Testament sacrifices purified persons and objects outwardly, making them ceremonially "clean" so people could approach God. But Jesus entered heaven with his own blood so that "once for all" he might "do away with sin by the sacrifice of himself."

By faith: Hebrews 11. Faith has changed the lives of thousands. In this "faith hall of fame" the writer emphasizes what faith has enabled God's saints to do.

Disciplines those he loves: Hebrews 12. Hardships in life should not be viewed as punishment, but as discipline. What is the difference? A person who punishes us is angry and intent on making us pay for past failures. A person who disciplines us loves us and wants to help us do right in the future. God's discipline flows from love and is intended "for our good, that we may share in his [God's] holiness." But the passage notes that whether or not we profit from discipline depends on how we respond to it.

Shake the earth: Hebrews 12:25-29. This phrase is a technical theological term that pictures violent changes to be accomplished by God at history's end (see Haggai 2:6-8). In the future, the earth itself will be destroyed. How wonderful that the eternal kingdom which Christians receive will exist forever. What a reason to be thankful and to worship God!

Obey your leaders and be under their authority: Hebrews 13:17. In Greek the injunction means "be responsive to those God gives to guide you, and remain open to their persuasion." We do respond to our leaders, but we obey God.

Letters of the apostle John

John outlived all the other apostles. He wrote his letters during the last quarter of the first century, when the Emperor Domitian launched official persecution of Christians.

John himself settled in Ephesus, where he lived the last 35 years of his life, except when traveling to nearby cities in Asia Minor.

The younger John had been nicknamed a "son of thunder" by Jesus (Luke 9:51-55). In addition to a fiery character, John had ambition which is suggested by his mother's request that John and his brother be given great power in Jesus' coming kingdom (Matthew 20:20-27).

John's three letters show how greatly the Gospel had reshaped his character. John's warm letters are about the inner life of believers, and about our love relationship with both God and other believers. "Fellowship," which means participation or sharing, is vital to John. In his letters, this word pictures intimate and close relationships, in which we share ourselves with the Lord and with others.

In all his writings John uses key words and images. He speaks of "truth," by which John means a harmony of one's life with reality. To John "light" is God's own understanding and revelation of reality. John also speaks much of "love." To John love can only be understood or measured by the commitment to others which God demonstrated in sending Jesus to die for our sins. "Love," then, is not a feeling but a commitment. Love for God is expressed by obedience to his word. And love for others is expressed in practical ways, too, in helping those in need and welcoming them into caring, sharing relationships.

Outline of 1 John

Invitation to share joy		1:1-4
I.	By walking in light	1:5–2:29
II.	By walking in love	3–4:19
III.	By walking with faith	5:1-21

Without sin: 1 John 1:8. Walking in the light is not sinlessness, for no one is without sin. This phrase means being honest about our failures and coming immediately to confess sins to God so they can be forgiven.

Insight: The Christian's only "unforgivable sin" is the sin we refuse to confess.

Confess: 1 John 1:9. The word means "to acknowledge," not as some think to "feel sorry about." The call to confession reminds us that we need to be totally honest with God and ourselves about our sins. When we continue to confess, God not only forgives, but he keeps on cleansing us and making us pure. Accepting forgiveness is the first, vital step toward change.

The world: 1 John 2:15. The Greek word *kosmos* in the New Testament often means the "world system" or the moral order of unsaved society. This system is marked by cravings and lust (strong desires) and by a pride based on having possessions or abilities. This whole approach to life is opposed to God and his values. In Romans 12:2 Paul writes, do not "be like the people of this world" but, instead, "be changed within by a new way of thinking" (i.e., "outlook"). The Christian's values and attitudes are to be dramatically different from those of the non-Christian.

Antichrists or enemies of Christ: 1 John 2:18-26. This is John's name for persons who are enemies of Christianity. There are many now who are enemies of God. How do we recognize such persons? They deny the deity of the Son of God. All who deny the full deity of Jesus are false teachers, and any such religion is also false.

No one born of God will go on sinning: 1 John 3:9-10. Anyone may slip and fall. But because God has given Christians new life, believers will not make a lifelong habit of sin. John teaches that the believer "is not able to go on sinning, because he has become a child of God."

What love is: 1 John 3:16-20. The standard by which love is measured is Jesus, who laid down his life for us. By this measure, "anyone who has material possessions and sees his brother in need" will respond with real concern and offer to help.

Acknowledging Jesus as the Son of God: 1 John 4:15. Acknowledging Jesus means more than saying words. It means committing ourselves to obey Christ and to confess our faith in him.

The Isle of Patmos was where the Apostle John lived out his last years in exile.

The one who is in you: 1 John 4:4. We are not to fear evil spiritual forces that may be against us. God is for us, and he is greater than all.

Assurance in coming to God: 1 John 5:13-15. We know that God hears and will answer our prayers. Asking for and agreeing to what God wants for us suggests that our fellowship with God is such that his Spirit helps our prayer life. We can know God's will and have a sense of peace in praying if we live close to the Lord.

The book of Jude

Jude is another short letter in our New Testament which has only a single chapter. Jude is thought to be the brother of the James who led the Jerusalem church and, thus, the half-brother of Jesus. This conviction was held by writers in the early church and is supported by Matthew 13:55 and Mark 6:3.

Jude writes in dark times when false teachers have infiltrated the church. While Jude had hoped to write a letter about salvation, he felt a need instead "to encourage you to fight hard for the faith" (vs 3).

In this short letter Jude describes false teachers in terms found also in 2 Peter and in the pastorals. These people introduce wrong teachings and refuse to accept the Master, Jesus, (2 Peter 2:11). They brag (2 Peter 2:10; Jude 1-6), hate authority (2 Peter 2:10; Jude 8), follow the evil things their sinful selves want (2 Peter 2:10; Jude 4-19) and are motivated by money (2 Peter 2:15; Jude 12). Their ministry is characterized by appeal to the "lustful desires of the human nature" and by promises of the "freedom" to be depraved (2 Peter 2:17-18; Jude 16).

Outline of Jude

	Greeting	1-2
I.	False teachers described	3-7
II.	False teachers' behavior	8-10
III.	False teachers' motives	11-16
IV.	Resisting false teachers	17-23
	Praise to God	24-27

Build yourself up: Jude 20. The way to resist false teachers is to concentrate on truth, godliness and prayer. Jude expresses his confidence that we can resist in his closing doxology of praise: "To him who is able to keep you from falling and to present you before his glorious presence without fault and with great joy—to the only God our Savior . . ." (vss 24-25, NIV).

36 Revealing things to come
Revelation

Revelation is the last book in the New Testament. It is the only prophetic book, containing a vision which God gave to the Apostle John, the last living apostle. Its language makes it difficult to understand and has led to different approaches to interpretation.

MASTERY KEYS to the book of Revelation:

- What are characteristics of the two major approaches to understanding Revelation?
- What makes symbolic language so difficult to interpret?
- What is gained from reading Revelation?

The book of Revelation

Revelation is the last New Testament book to be written. John had been exiled to Patmos, a barren island about 37 miles from the coast of Asia Minor (see map). There John had a vision in which an angel revealed "what must soon happen" (1:1). The book begins with messages to seven contempo-

Aegean Sea

- Pergamum
  - Thyatira
- Sardis
  - Philadelphia
- Smyrna
- Laodicea
- Ephesus
- Miletus

Patmos

THE SEVEN CHURCHES OF ASIA

rary churches, and then in powerful prophetic language it sets out to unveil the future. It was probably written just before John was released on the death of the Roman emperor Domitian in A.D. 96.

The book of Revelation is a type of literature known as apocalyptic. "Apocalypse," a Greek word, means an "uncovering" or a "disclosure." Apocalyptic literature uses symbols and visions and is often related to God's judgment. There are several apocalyptic sections in the Old Testament (Ezekiel 38–39; Daniel 2,7,8). This type of literature usually predicts the future and is reassuring to God's oppressed people.

Interpreting Revelation

The powerful images and language of Revelation have fascinated Christians for centuries, but the book has been difficult to understand. There have been four main ways of interpreting Revelation.

(1) The preterits ("the past") see most of the predictions in the book as already having been fulfilled in the years immediately following John's time.

(2) On the other hand, the futurists think that almost nothing after the fourth chapter has yet been fulfilled. They see Revelation predicting the events shortly before the second coming of Christ.

(3) The continuous historical approach views the book as picturing a series of events from Pentecost to the end of time. The Roman Catholic church is pictured as the evil force in the book. This approach was popular among leaders of the Protestant Reformation.

(4) The philosophy of history (sometimes called poetic) school thinks that Revelation is not referring to specific events at all. Rather it shows principles of God's dealing with the church in history. For a detailed discussion of these four viewpoints see Ray Summers, *Worthy Is the Lamb* (Broadman, 1951).

Message of Revelation

There are several powerful lessons to be learned from Revelation regardless of the system of interpretation followed.

(1) Jesus is always with his people and hears their cries and prayers.

(2) All worship is due to the Father and Jesus the Son.

(3) The importance of the faithfulness and perseverance of God's people is emphasized.

(4) Satan and the forces of evil are doomed.

(5) The final triumph of the church is certain.

(6) God's justice is sure.

Symbolic language

Symbols are words or images that stand for something other than themselves. For instance, a dove is used in the Bible as a symbol for the Holy Spirit. Often the Bible identifies its symbols, stating specifically what a particular symbol means. Other symbols are interpreted by looking at what they are associated with in other biblical passages.

The book of Revelation explains some of its own symbols. Included are seven lampstands, standing for seven churches in Asia (1:20); seven lamps of fire, standing for the Spirit of God (4:5); bowls of incense, standing for the prayers of the saints (5:8); a giant dragon, standing for Satan (12:9), etc. Other symbols which may be understood from Old Testament references include an iron rod (2:27), standing for punishment of evildoers in Psalm 2:9; the key of David (3:7), standing for the Messiah's authority in Isaiah 22:22; the rainbow (10:1), standing for God's mercy in Genesis 9:8-17.

Many other symbols are used in this book, and many are understood differently by different interpreters.

Prophetic language

Even where symbols are not used, it is hard to understand many images in prophetic language. There is a simple reason for this. The prophets could only use words and ideas of their own time to describe what they saw. Imagine that a person who lived 500 years ago saw a modern city with its airports, freeways, electric lights and signs. How could a person possibly describe to people of his own time what he saw?

Much prophecy is like this. After an event foretold in the Bible has happened, we say, "Oh, that's what this means!" Many believe we will say the same thing when what John describes takes place. But until then much about his vision will remain a mystery.

Outline of Revelation

John's vision
Revelation 1

John is known as the disciple whom Jesus loved. At the Last Supper John was leaning close to the Lord, not just to hear, but also to be near him. Now the aged John sees a vision of Jesus in all his glory with blazing eyes and a voice "like the noise of flooding water." John says, "when I saw him, I fell down at his feet like a dead man." The loving Jesus of the Gospels is also the glorious and powerful Jesus of Revelation.

The seven churches

Most view these churches (see map, page 209) as typical of modern churches, as well as historical. Each is described and then exhorted. The churches and what each represents are as follows:

- EPHESUS, hardworking, but has lost its love for God it had at the beginning; needs to love again (2:1-7).
- SMYRNA, persecuted and poor; needs to remain faithful (2:8-11).
- PERGAMUM, remains true to God but tolerates immorality; needs to repent of evil ways (2:12-17).
- THYATIRA, active but tolerates immorality; needs to hold to the truth (2:18-19).
- SARDIS, spiritually dead; needs to wake up and obey (3:1-6).
- PHILADELPHIA, weak but patiently enduring; needs to hold on (3:7-13).
- LAODICEA, spiritually poor; needs to be earnest and change their hearts under God's discipline (3:14-21).

Insight: Each church may represent individuals as well as churches. Apply what Christ says to these churches to yourself.

A vision of hell
Revelation 20

The book of Revelation speaks of a resurrection of all the dead after the resurrection

The book of Revelation describes how the earth will someday be totally destroyed.

of believers. At that time the dead are "judged by what they had done" (Revelation 20:12). Those whose deeds are judged to be evil and those whose names are not found in the book of life are thrown into a place called "the lake of fire." Revelation 19:20 describes it as "the fiery lake of burning sulfur" and 20:10 calls it a place of torment.

While this may be symbolic language, it is clear that there is a real hell. In fact, Jesus often warned his listeners about hell (Matthew 5:22, 29, 30; 7:19; 23:15; 25:30, 41; Mark 9:43,45; Luke 12:47-48; 16:19-31). The message of Scripture is that each human being faces an endless, self-conscious existence after death, and that some human beings will spend eternity in a terrible place of punishment.

Some have wondered how a loving God could condemn people to such a place. The Bible's answer is that he does not. Jesus even taught that hell was prepared "for the devil and his helpers" (Matthew 25:41). In fact, Jesus died on the cross so that no one need be condemned to hell. Each person makes his own choice. In Christ's death God has done all he could to deliver human beings from eternal judgment.

Insight: The only person who can condemn you is you by refusing to respond to the Good News of God's love and refusing to obey Jesus as Savior and Lord.

A vision of heaven
Revelation 21—22

The Bible tells us that this universe will be destroyed, to be replaced by a fresh new universe of beauty and holiness (see 2 Peter 3:10-13). Revelation describes the new heaven and earth with its capital, the Holy City or New Jerusalem, over 1350 miles long, wide and high!

But what is most important is that in the renewal we will see God's face, and there will be no need of a sun, for the Lord will be the light present with us forever. In the beautiful words of Revelation, "God's home is with men. He will live with them, and they will be his people. God himself will be with them and will be their God. He will wipe away every tear from their eyes. There will be no more death, sadness, crying or pain. All the old ways are gone" (Revelation 21:3-4).

Insight: Paul says it so well. "We have sufferings now. But the sufferings we have now are nothing compared to the great glory that will be given us" (Romans 8:18).

Come, Lord Jesus
Revelation 22:17

The Bible ends with a vision of what God has planned for those who love him. In view of that vision, we can only look forward with delight and rejoice in Jesus' promise."Yes, I am coming soon" (Revelation 22:20).

INDEX

Table of Charts

Old Testament

New Testament

Table of Maps

Old Testament

New Testament

INDEX

Note: In this Index, page numbers following the boldface bullet [•] in an entry indicate photographs or illustrations.